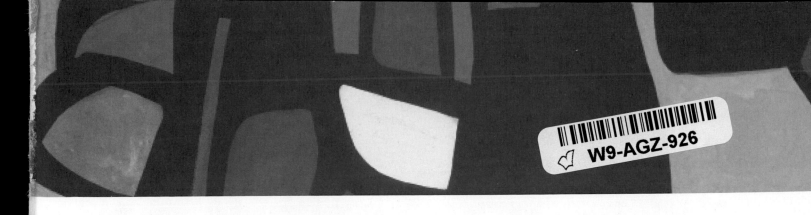

PERSONAL
MANAGEMENT
WORKBOOK

Compiled by
John R. Schermerhorn Jr. and
Robert L. Holbrook, Jr.
Ohio University

To my sons John Christian and Charles Porter

While you played	It's later now.	Think	Home,
I wrote.	Don't worry.	of all the fun	now and forever,
But always,	Time	we have.	will always be
I was listening	means love shared,	Here, there, everywhere,	wherever
and loving	by you	doing things	I can be
you.	and me.	together.	with you.
1984	1986	1989	1992

Time	Hurry home	Songs riding winds.	On the mountain,
has its ways,	when you can.	Mimi,	by the Irish lake,
doesn't it?	Come laughing, sons.	Uncle George,	find beauty and
Not enough,	Tell us	Uncle Nelson.	peace.
not enough,	your	Whispers and choirs.	Fairies dance
I often say.	wonderful stories.	Silence speaks.	there.
1996	1999	2002	2004

PUBLISHER   Susan Elbe
ASSOCIATE PUBLISHER   Judith R. Joseph
SENIOR ACQUISITIONS EDITOR   Jayme Heffler
PROJECT EDITOR   Cindy Rhoads
MARKETING MANAGER   Heather King
SENIOR DESIGNER   Harry Nolan
SENIOR PHOTO EDITOR   Sara Wight
COVER AND INTERIOR DESIGN   Harry Nolan
ILLUSTRATION COORDINATOR   Sandra Rigby

COVER AND CHAPTER OPENER ART   Judith Rothschild
Cummington '41
1946
gouache on board
6 13/16 x 6 3/4 inches
Courtesy of The Judith Rothschild Foundation

This book was set in 10/12 Garamond Book by Progressive Information Technologies and printed and bound by R.R. Donnelley and Sons. The cover was printed by Lehigh Press.

This book is printed on acid-free paper.

The paper in this book was manufactured by a mill whose forest management programs include sustained yield harvesting of its timberlands. Sustained yield harvesting principles ensure that the number of trees cut each year does not exceed the amount of new growth.

To order books or for customer service please, call 1-800-CALL WILEY (225-5945).

ISBN 10: 0-471-76348-9
ISBN 13: 978-0-471-76348-2

Printed in the United States of America
10 9 8 7 6 5 4 3 2 1

Memorandum

TO: Students

FROM: John R. Schermerhorn, Jr. and Robert L. (Lenie) Holbrook, Jr.

SUBJECT: Your *Personal Management Workbook*

Welcome to the *Personal Management Workbook* that we have prepared to accompany the Personal Management Update of *Management, 8th edition.*

Today's work environments are quite different from ones your parents and grandparents experienced when beginning their careers. Increasing globalization, technological advances, and the rapid pace of change force today's organizations to be flexible in order to survive. Likewise, you must be flexible in order to succeed in your own career.

The knowledge and skills you possess are insufficient to bring you lasting career success. You must not only upgrade your personal capabilities and understandings throughout your academic program, but also build a commitment to continuous learning that will hold throughout your future work experiences. The first step in meeting this challenge is to develop a personal action plan. That is where the *Personal Management Workbook* can help.

The workbook involves you in an integrated set of activities with one common goal - your personal and professional development. By following the workbook you will gain insights that can help guide the completion of your academic program and smooth your career transition to the business world. The individual activities are developed from text Personal Management features, self-assessments and experiential exercises, as well as cases for critical thinking, integrating cases, and active learning projects.

The workbook puts course resources at your fingertips when you need them. If you follow the workbook you will find yourself applying management concepts right now, as you study the text and participate in course activities, and as you think seriously about your career readiness. As an added bonus, the materials needed to help you formalize the results into an electronic student portfolio are also included.

We have been using the activities and projects of the *Personal Management Workbook* in our courses as we work with undergraduates just like you. Their feedback helped us refine the elements and make them as meaningful as possible. We hope you will use and benefit from them.

While we want you to succeed, in your course and in your career, you must realize that this will not happen without substantial effort on your part. The habits you develop in college ultimately will follow you into the world of business. Why not make a commitment today to use the *Personal Management Workbook* as a learning resource? If you take the time to apply yourself throughout the management course, we are confident that you will be satisfied with the outcomes that follow.

PERSONAL MANAGEMENT FEATURES

PERSONAL MANAGEMENT ACTIVITIES

SELF-ASSESSMENTS

EXPERIENTIAL EXERCISES

STUDENT PORTFOLIO BUILDER

CASES FOR CRITICAL THINKING

INTEGRATING CASES

ACTIVE LEARNING PROJECTS

MASTER LIST OF FEATURES, ACTIVITIES, ASSESSMENTS, AND EXERCISES

Chapter Topic	PM Feature	PM Activity	Assessment	Exercise
1: New Workplace	1: Self-Awareness	1: Strengths/Weaknesses	1: A 21st-Century Manager 2: Emotional Intelligence	None
2: Management	2: Learning Style	2: Continuous Improvement	3: Learning Tendencies 4: Managerial Assumptions	None
3: Ethics/Social Responsibility	3: Personal Character	3: Integrity	5: Terminal Values Survey 6: Instrumental Values Survey	6: Ethical Dilemmas
4: Environment/Culture	4: Diversity Maturity	4: Competitive Advantage	7: Diversity Awareness	7: What You Value in Work
5: Global Dimensions	5: Cultural Awareness	5: Global	8: Global Readiness Index 9: Time Orientation	None
6: Entrepreneurship	6: Risk-Taking	6: Creativity	10: Entrepreneurship Orientation	8: Organizational Culture
7: Decision Making	7: Self-Confidence	7: Career Information	11: Your Intuitive Ability 12: Assertiveness	None
8: Planning/Controlling	8: Time Management	8: Timeline	13: Time Management Profile	9: Beating Time Wasters
9: Strategic Management	9: Critical Thinking	9: SWOT	14: Facts and Inferences	10: Personal Career Planning
10: Organizing	10: Empowerment	10: Structures	15: Empowering Others	16: Leading...Participation
11: Design/Work Processes	11: Tolerance for Ambiguity	11: Organization Design	16: Turbulence Tolerance Test 17: Organizational Design	None
12: Human Resource Management	12: Professionalism	12: Orientation	18: Are You Cosmopolitan 19: Performance Appraisal	None
13: Leading	13: Networking	13: Six Degrees	20: T-P Leadership 21: T-T Leadership Style 22: Least-Preferred Coworker	None
14: Motivation	14: Initiative	14: Motivation	23: Student Engagement Survey 24: Job Design Choices	23: The Best Job Design
15: Behavior/Performance	15: Problem Solving Style	15: Big Five Plus	25: Cognitive Style 26: Internal/External Control	None
16: Teams	16: Team Contributions	16: Team Ready	27: Team Leader Skills	26: Lost At Sea 27: Work Team Dynamics
17: Communication/Interpersonal Skills	17: Communication; Interpersonal Skills	17: Think/Write	12: Assertiveness 28: Conflict Management Styles	None
18: Change	18: Strength and Energy	18: Life Stress	29: Stress Self-Test 30: Work-Life Balance	None

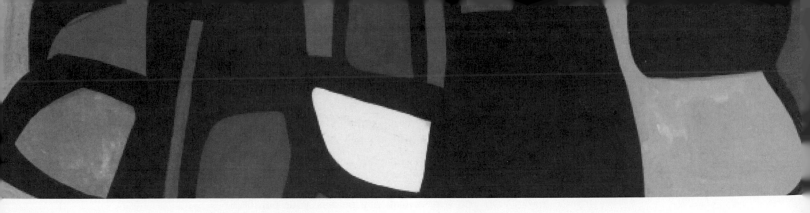

PERSONAL

MANAGEMENT

FEATURES

SELF-AWARENESS is one of those concepts that is easy to talk about but very hard to master. What do you really know about yourself? How often do you take a critical look at your attitudes, behaviors, skills, and accomplishments? Do you ever realistically assess your personal strengths and weaknesses—both as you see them and as others do? A high degree of self-awareness is essential for personal adaptibility, to be able to grow and develop in changing times. This figure, called the Johari Window, offers a way of comparing what we know about ourselves with what others know about us.[59] Our "open" areas are often small, while the "blind spot," "the unknown," and the "hidden" areas can be quite large. Think about the personal implications of the Johari Window. Are you willing to probe the unknown, uncover your blind spots, and discover talents and weaknesses that may be hidden? As your self-awareness expands, you will find many insights for personal growth and development.

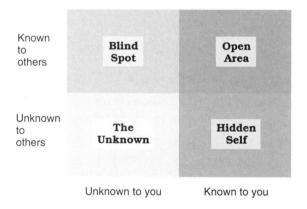

Known to others — Blind Spot — Open Area

Unknown to others — The Unknown — Hidden Self

Unknown to you — Known to you

Get to know yourself better ▶
Complete Self-Assessments #1 — **21st–Century Manager,** and #2 — **Emotional Intelligence,** from the Management Learning Workbook.

Now is a very good time for you to examine your LEARNING STYLE. Every person a manager deals with is unique; most problem situations are complex; and things are always changing. Success in management only comes to those who thrive on learning. Some people learn by watching; they observe others and model what they see. Others learn by doing; they act and experiment, learning as they go. There is no one best way to learn about managing— there is only the need to learn . . . all the time, from others, from formal training, and from real experiences. An organization development manager at PepsiCo once said: "I believe strongly in the notion that enhancing managers' knowledge of their strengths and particularly their weaknesses is integral to ensuring long-term, sustainable performance improvement and executive success."[24] The problem is that many of us never dig deep enough to both get this depth of personal understanding and use it to set learning goals. You can start here by keeping a personal strengths and weaknesses scorecard.

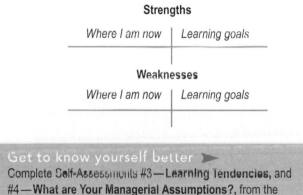

Strengths

Where I am now	Learning goals

Weaknesses

Where I am now	Learning goals

Get to know yourself better ➤

Complete Self-Assessments #3—**Learning Tendencies**, and #4—**What are Your Managerial Assumptions?**, from the Management Learning Workbook.

PERSONAL CHARACTER is a foundation for all that we do. It establishes our integrity and provides an ethical anchor for our behavior in the workplace and in life overall. Persons of high integrity can always be confident in the self-respect it provides, even in the most difficult of situations. Those who lack it are destined to perpetual insecurity, acting inconsistently and suffering not only in self-esteem but also in the esteem of others. How strong is your personal character? How well prepared are you to deal with the inevitable ethical dilemmas and challenges in work and in life? Can you give specific examples showing how your behavior lives up to these Six Pillars of Character identified by the Josephson Institute of Ethics.[36]

- *Trustworthiness*—Honesty, integrity, reliability in keeping promises, loyalty
- *Respect*—Civility, courtesy and decency, dignity, tolerance, and acceptance
- *Responsibility*—Sense of accountability, pursuit of excellence, self-restraint
- *Fairness*—Commitment to process, impartiality, equity
- *Caring*—Concern for others, benevolence, altruism
- *Citizenship*—Knowing the law, being informed, volunteering

Get to know yourself better ▶
Complete Self-Assessments #5—**Terminal Values Survey,** and #6—**Instrumental Values Survey;** and Exercises #6—**Confronting Ethical Dilemmas** from the Management Learning Workbook.

DIVERSITY MATURITY is essential if you are to work well in today's organizations. It is a cornerstone for personal inclusivity. Consultant Roosevelt Thomas uses the following questions when testing diversity maturity among people in the workplace. Answer the questions. Be honest; admit where you still have work left to do. Use your answers to help set future goals to ensure that your actions, not just your words, consistently display positive diversity values.

- Do you accept responsibility for improving your performance?
- Do you understand diversity concepts?
- Do you make decisions about others based on their abilities?
- Do you understand that diversity issues are complex?
- Are you able to cope with tensions in addressing diversity?
- Are you willing to challenge the way things are?
- Are you willing to learn continuously?

Get to know yourself better ▶
Complete Self-Assessment #7 — **Diversity Awareness,** and **Exercise #7 — What Do You Value in Work?,** from the Management Learning Workbook.

The complications of world events are ever-present reminders that CULTURAL AWARENESS is one of the great challenges of the 21st century. Consultant Richard Lewis warns of "cultural spectacles" that limit our vision, causing us to see and interpret things with the biases of our own culture.[59] You must learn to take off the spectacles and broaden your cultural horizons. The college campus is a great place to start. Its rich community of international students can take you around the world every day. Do you know for example that in Asian cultures Confucian values like the following are very influential?[60]

- *Harmony*—works well in a group, doesn't disrupt group order, puts group before self-interests.
- *Hierarchy*—accepts authority and hierarchical nature of society, doesn't challenge superiors.
- *Benevolence*—acts kind and understanding toward others, paternalistic, willing to teach and help subordinates.
- *Loyalty*—loyal to organization and supervisor, dedicated to job, grateful for job and support of superior.
- *Learning*—eager for new knowledge, works hard to learn new job skills, strives for high performance.

Get to know yourself better ➤
Complete Self-Assessments #8—**Global Readiness Index,** and #9—**Time Orientation,** from the Management Learning Workbook.

Not everyone is comfortable with RISK TAKING. The uncertainty of risky situations is unsettling, and the anxieties are threatening for some of us. But risks, small and large, are a part of everyday living. In school and around campus there are many opportunities to explore your openness to risk and entrepreneurial tendencies. What will it take for you to start your own business or propose a new venture to your employer? Two former managers of Footlocker stores took the risk, and it paid off handsomely.[10] After noticing that customers kept asking for sports caps unavailable in stores, Glenn Campbell and Scott Molander decided to start a store of their own—Hat World. "People thought we were crazy," Campbell says. But Hat World took off, selling over 6000 caps in two months. The entrepreneurs opened four more stores within a year. At last check, Campbell and Molander's risk turned into a firm with annual sales of $150+ million. Could this story be yours some day?

Get to know yourself better ▶

Complete Self-Assessment #10—**Entrepreneurship Orientation,** and Exercise #8—**Which Organization Culture Fits You?,** from the Management Learning Workbook.

Managers must have the SELF-CONFIDENCE to not only make decisions but also to implement them. Too many of us find all sorts of excuses for doing everything but that— we have difficulty deciding and we have difficulty acting. Opportunities to improve and develop your self-confidence abound, especially through involvement in the many student organizations on your campus. Carole Clay Winters was the first member of her family to go to college. On the encouragement of an economics professor, she joined Students in Free Enterprise (SIFE) and ended up on a team teaching business concepts to elementary school children in the local community.[27] Her team was chosen to participate in a national competition. They didn't win, but Carole did. "I felt my life had changed," she said. "I realized that if I could answer all the questions being posed by some of the country's most powerful executives, I had what I needed to become an executive myself." Carole went on to become manager in the Washington, D.C., office of KPMG. What about you? Do you have the self-confidence to make decisions relating to your career goals and future success? Are you taking full advantage of opportunities, on campus and off, to experience the responsibilities of leadership and gain confidence in your decision-making capabilities?

Get to know yourself better ▶
Complete Self-Assessments #11—**Your Intuitive Ability,** and #12—**Assertiveness,** from the Management Learning Workbook.

Time is one of our most precious resources, and TIME MANAGEMENT is an essential skill in today's high-pressure and fast-paced world of work. Some 77 percent of managers in one survey said the new digital age has increased the number of decisions they have to make; 43 percent complained there was less time available to make them. Others say that 20 percent of their telephone time is wasted.[12] Of course, you have to be careful in defining "waste." It isn't a waste of time to occasionally relax, take a breather from work, and find humor and pleasure in social interaction. Such breaks help us gather energies to do well in our work. But it is a waste to let friends dominate your time so that you don't work on a term paper until it is too late to write a really good one, or delay a decision to apply for an internship until the deadline is passed. Perhaps you are one of those who plans to do so many things in a day that you never get to the most important ones. Perhaps you don't plan, let events take you where they may, and on many days don't accomplish much at all. Learning to manage your time better will serve you very well in the future, both at work and in your personal life.

Get to know yourself better ➤
Complete Self-Assessments #13— **Time Management Profile**, and Exercise #9— **Beating the Time Wasters**, from the Management Learning Workbook.

CRITICAL THINKING is essential for executive leadership success. It is an analytical skill that involves the ability to gather and interpret information for decision making in a problem context. A good way to develop this skill is through case studies and problem-solving projects in your courses. But beware! One of the risks of our information-rich environment is over-reliance on what we hear or read—especially when it comes from the Web. A lot of what circulates on the Web is anecdotal, superficial, irrelevant, and even just plain inaccurate. You must be disciplined, cautious, and discerning in interpreting the credibility and usefulness of any information that you retrieve. Once you understand this and are willing to invest the time for critical thinking, the Web offers a world of opportunities. Consider your personal career strategy: How well prepared are you to succeed in the *future* job market, not just the present one. At the website of the *U.S. Bureau of Labor Statistics* you can find the latest data on unemployment, productivity, and the economies of states, regions, and major metropolitan areas. The site also offers an up-to-date *Career Guide to Industries.* Take a look and practice information gathering for critical thinking about your career.

Get to know yourself better ➤
Complete Self-Assessments #14—**Facts and Inferences,** and Exercise #10—**Personal Career Planning,** from the Management Learning Workbook.

It takes a lot of trust to be comfortable with **EMPOWERMENT**. But if you aren't willing and able to empower others, you'll not only compromise your own performance but also add to the stress of daily work. Empowerment involves allowing and helping others to do things, even things that you might be very good at doing yourself. The beauty of organizations is synergy — bringing together the contributions of many people to achieve something that is much greater than what any individual can accomplish alone. Empowerment gives synergy a chance. But many people, perhaps even you, suffer from control anxiety. They don't empower others because they fear losing control over a task or situation. In groups, they want or try to do everything by themselves; they are afraid to trust other team members with important tasks. Being "unwilling to let go," they try to do too much, with the risk of missed deadlines and even poor performance; they deny others opportunities to contribute, losing the benefits of their talents and often alienating them in the process. Does this description apply to you? Now is a good time to think seriously about your personal style: Are you someone who empowers others, or do you suffer from control anxiety and an unwillingness to delegate?

Get to know yourself better ➤
Complete Assessments #15 — **Empowering Others,** and Exercise #16 — **Leading Through Participation** from the Management Learning Workbook.

It is easy to make decisions when you have perfect information. But in the new world of work, you will often face unstructured problems and have to make decisions with incomplete information under uncertain conditions. Depending on your TOLERANCE FOR AMBIGUITY, you may be comfortable or uncomfortable dealing with these new realities. It takes personal flexibility and lots of confidence to cope well with unpredictability. Some people have a hard time dealing with the unfamiliar. They prefer to work with directions that minimize ambiguity and provide clear decision-making rules; they like the structure of mechanistic organizations with bureaucratic features. Other people are willing and able to perform in less-structured settings that give them lots of flexibility in responding to changing situations; they like the freedom of organic organizations designed for adaptation. You must find a good fit between your personal preferences and the nature of the organizations in which you choose to work. To achieve this fit, you have to both know yourself and be able to read organizational cultures and structures. And whatever your tolerance for ambiguity may be, the best time to explore these issues of person–organization fit is now, before you take your first or next job.

Get to know yourself better ➤
Complete Self-Assessments #16—**Turbulence Tolerance Test,** *and #17*—**Organizational Design Preferences,** from the Management Learning Workbook.

PROFESSIONALISM! What does this term mean? If you are in human resource management, the code of ethics of the Society for Human Resource Management offers a framework for consideration.[18] SHRM defines "Professional Responsibility" as:

- adding value to your organization
- contributing to its ethical success
- serving as a leadership role model for ethical conduct
- accepting personal responsibility for one's decisions and actions
- promoting fairness and justice in the workplace
- being truthful in communications
- protecting the rights of individuals
- striving to meet high standards of competence
- strengthening one's competencies continually

Although valuable for human resource professionals, these guidelines are a good starting point for anyone who wants to meet high standards of professionalism at work. What about you? How well do you score? Would you add anything to make this list more meaningful to your career?

Get to know yourself better ➤
Complete Self-Assessments #18—**Are You Cosmopolitan?** and #19—**Performance Appraisal Assumptions**, from the Management Learning Workbook.

Leadership is an interpersonal process. You either lead well or poorly in large part due to your ability to relate well to other people. Furthermore, in today's high-performance work settings, with their emphasis on horizontal structures, cross-functional teams, and projects, leading requires skillful NETWORKING. Within teams, across functions and in day-to-day work encounters, the best leaders get things done because they build and maintain positive working relationships with others. In the social context of organizations, there is very little you can do by yourself; the vast majority of work gets done because people in your networks help you out. For some of us, networking is as natural as walking down the street. For others, it is a big challenge in the intimidating realm of interpersonal relationships. But even if you fall into this last category, the fact remains: To be a successful leader you need networking skills. Don't underestimate the challenge; be prepared for leadership. Do you have confidence in these networking skills?

- *Network identification*—knowing and finding the right people to work with.
- *Network building*—engaging others and relating to them in positive ways.
- *Network maintenance*—actively nurturing and supporting others in their work.

Get to know yourself better ➤
Complete Self-Assessments #20—**T-P Leadership Questionnaire,** #21-**T-T Leadership,** and #22—**Least Preferred CoWorker Scale,** from the Management Learning Workbook.

It is very difficult to say that someone completely lacks INITIATIVE. Each of us has to display a certain amount of initiative just to survive each day. But the initiative of people at work varies greatly, just as it does among students. The issue for you becomes: Do you have the self-initiative to work hard and apply your talents to achieve high performance in school, in a job, on an assigned task? Don't hide from the answer. The way you work now in school or in a job is a good predictor of the future. Part of the key to initiative lies in a good person–job fit, finding the right job in the right career field. The rest, however, is all up to you. Only you can decide that you want to work really hard. Look at the following criteria for someone high in self-initiative. Consider how you behave as a student or in a job. Can you honestly say that each statement accurately describes you?

- Willing to look for problems, and fix them.
- Willing to do more than required, to work beyond expectations.
- Willing to help others when they are stuck or overwhelmed.
- Willing to try and do things better; not being comfortable with the status quo.
- Willing to think ahead; to craft ideas and make plans for the future.

Get to know yourself better ➤
Complete Self-Assessments #23 — **Student Engagement Survey,** and #24 — **Job Design Choices,** and Experiential Exercise #23 – **Best Job Design,** from the Management Learning Workbook.

Your **PROBLEM-SOLVING STYLE** is likely to differ from those of people you study and work with. It is important to understand your style and learn about problems that can occur as styles clash when you work with others. Which of the four master problem-solving styles shown here best describes you?[18]

- *Sensation-Thinker:* STs take a realistic approach to problem solving, preferring "facts," clear goals, and certainty.

- *Intuitive-Thinker:* NTs are comfortable with abstraction and unstructured situations, tending to be idealistic and to avoid details.

- *Intuitive-Feeler:* NFs are insightful, like to deal with broad issues, and value flexibility and human relationships.

- *Sensation-Feeler:* SFs emphasize analysis using facts, while being open communicators and respectful of feelings and values.

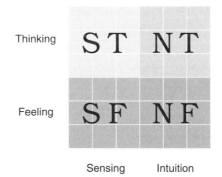

Thinking   ST   NT

Feeling   SF   NF

Sensing   Intuition

Get to know yourself better ➤
Complete Self-Assessments #25—**Cognitive Style,** and #26—**Internal-External Control**, from the Management Learning Workbook.

No one can deny that teams are indispensable in today's organizations. And importantly, you cannot deny that a large part of your career success will depend on your skills at working in and leading teams. The question of the day is: Are you ready for truly valuable **TEAM CONTRIBUTIONS?** Consider this list of critical skills that you must have in order to contribute significantly to the success of work teams:

- Good at encouraging and motivating others.
- Good at accepting suggestions.
- Good at listening to different points of view.
- Good at communicating information and ideas.
- Good at persuasion.
- Good at conflict resolution and negotiating.
- Good at building consensus.
- Good at fulfilling commitments.

Ask yourself the tough questions. In your classes and/or at work, are you making these contributions to the teams in which you are asked to participate? Push the question even further. Ask others who know and work with you to assess your performance and contributions as a group member. What suggestions do they have for how you could improve your team contributions?

Get to know yourself better ➤
Complete Self-Assessments #27—**Team Leader Skills**, and Exercises #26—**Lost at Sea**, and #27 **Work Team Dynamics**, from the Management Learning Workbook

COMMUNICATION and INTERPERSONAL SKILLS top the lists of characteristics looked for in employment candidates by corporate recruiters today. Yet there are some worrisome statistics out there. An amazing 81 percent of college professors in one survey rated high school graduates as "fair" or "poor" in writing clearly; 78 percent rated students the same in spelling and use of grammar. In an American Management Association survey, managers rated their bosses only slightly above average (3.51 on a 5-point scale) on these important dimensions of communication—transforming ideas into words, credibility, listening and asking questions, written and oral presentations.[8] There is no doubt that we are in very challenging times when it comes to finding internships and full-time jobs in a streamlined economy. Strong communication and interpersonal skills could differentiate you from others wanting the same job. What about it? Can you convince a recruiter that you have the skills you need to run effective meetings, write informative reports, use e-mail correctly, deliver persuasive presentations, conduct job interviews, work well with others on a team, keep conflicts constructive and negotiations positive, network with peers and mentors, and otherwise communicate enthusiasm to the people with whom you work?

Write good reports
Run meetings
Use e-mail well
Work well in teams
Your communication & interpersonal skills
Network with peers & mentors
Give persuasive presentations
Negotiate deals
Conduct job interviews

It may strike you as odd to talk here about personal STRENGTH AND ENERGY, but the fact is that it isn't easy to work today. One national survey of American workers, for example, found 54 percent feeling overworked, 55 percent overwhelmed by their workloads, 56 percent not having enough time to complete their work, 59 percent not having enough time for reflection, and 45 percent having to do too many things at once.[27] At a minimum this reminds us that work in the 21st century can be very stressful. And just as to play tennis or some other sport, we have to get and stay in shape for work. This means building strength and energy to best handle the inevitable strains and anxieties of organizational changes, job pressures, and the potential conflicts between work demands and personal affairs.

- Is it hard to relax after a day in class?
- Does it take effort to concentrate in your spare time?
- Do you lay awake thinking and worrying about events of the day?
- Are you so tired that you are unable to join friends or family in a leisure activities?

Any "yes" answer indicates the need to do a better job of building and sustaining your capacities to handle heavy workloads. And if you think things are tough as a student, get ready. The real challenges lie ahead!

Get to know yourself better ▶
Complete Self-Assessments #29—**Stress Self-Test,** and #30—**Work-Life Balance,** from the Management Learning Workbook.

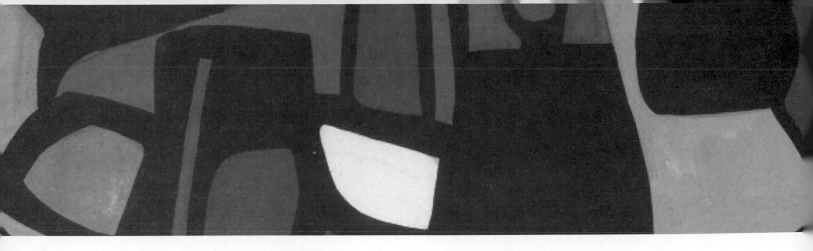

PERSONAL MANAGEMENT ACTIVITIES

The recommended assessments, activities, and projects associated with the Management 8e Update Edition are designed to help you gain a better sense of your skills/abilities, career goals, and how well the two match up. With proper attention to the assignments, by the time you finish this course, you should have a clear idea of where you are going and what it takes to get there.

If you have not done so already, take a moment to read the Personal Management feature for Chapter 1. The Johari Window defines four areas of self-awareness. The key to effective relationships and complete information about you is to expand the size of the open area. You do this by reducing the hidden and blind areas. To reduce the blind area, we must be open to information the others provide about us. How carefully do you listen when others provide feedback about your abilities? To reduce the hidden area, you must be willing to reveal information about yourself to others. How comfortable are you when it comes to sharing things about yourself?

To begin the process of discovery, select two individuals that know you through difference experiences or contexts. For example, your first choice might be a roommate or friend. A second choice might be your employer or a professor. Approach each person at a convenient time. Your request for information will catch them off guard, so be sure to do it at a time when they are not distracted by other tasks and can provide a thoughtful response. Explain that you are working on assignment about self-awareness and need feedback about your abilities. Ask each person to identify one strength and weakness you possess. Make sure they provide both. Ask for clarification if you need it, but do not be defensive. You are simply gathering information.

Putting It All Together. Reflect on your experience. How difficult was the assignment? Was it easier to receive feedback related to your strengths than your weaknesses? What did you observe when your acquaintances provided feedback? Did they seem comfortable in their roles? Write a brief summary of the strengths and weaknesses identified by your acquaintances. Consider the circumstances that allowed each acquaintance to develop this knowledge about you. Were there any surprises in what you discovered? How does what you learned relate to the key personal characteristics for managerial success identified in Chapter 1?

The activity associated with Chapter 1 had you seek feedback from acquaintances about your strengths and weaknesses. Review the Personal Management feature for Chapter 2. Spend some time developing a comprehensive list of strengths and weaknesses. Do not worry about whether the list is complete; you can add to it later. Examine a variety of situations, including academic experiences, past/present jobs, social experiences (e.g., friendship groups, sports and other performance-based groups), and organizations in which you participate. Think about times when you experienced success. What was your role (i.e., what did you contribute that led to success)? Carefully consider failures – individual and group. What held you back? What limitations kept you from being as successful as you wanted?

Personal development is about transformation – moving from your present state to a higher level of performance. It involves continuous improvement – small, incremental steps to get better – not an "all at once" transformation. When you grasp this, you will be able to establish useful goals and increase the likelihood of reaching them.

Putting It All Together. Take a look at your list of strengths and weaknesses. Focus specifically on areas where you need improvement. What type of work situations cause you to struggle? Are there certain types of tasks where you rarely succeed? Why? Is it because you lack a skill or special knowledge? Now step back and consider whether these weaknesses are likely to hinder career progress. What can you do to overcome these limitations? Develop an action plan for dealing with weaknesses that must be eliminated in order to be successful in your career. Action steps might involve taking a college course, finding a mentor to guide you in the process of acquiring new skills, or simply resolving to keep trying in situations until you succeed. Be specific about what it will take to improve. You may to review Manager's Notepad 14.1 for guidelines on setting reasonable goals.

PERSONAL MANAGEMENT – CAREER FOCUS
CHAPTER 3 ACTIVITY: INTEGRITY

Chapter 3 defines an ethical dilemma as "a situation that requires a choice regarding a possible course of action that . . . may be considered unethical." Some examples include offering a bribe to a government official in order to gain access to a foreign market or burying chemical waste on company property to avoid an expensive disposal fee. How would you respond if you became aware of such actions? What would you do if your boss directed you to take these actions (remember the Harvard Business Review survey)? It is easy to resolve ethical dilemmas when reading abstract cases in a classroom. It is another thing when making ethical choices puts your job at risk.

One of the best ways to avoid ethical dilemmas is to join organizations that have good reputations and well-defined codes of ethics. Inevitably, most of us face ethical dilemmas at some point in our careers as evidenced by a survey reported in Chapter 3. It may be something as simple as the temptation to "fudge" amounts on a travel expense report or as serious as a boss sexually harassing a co-worker. One way to handle ethical situations is to pre-determine your responses. The best way to do this is by defining your ethical standards.

Putting It All Together. Develop your own personal ethical code. A good starting point is to clarify your own values. Assessments 5 and 6 will help you do this. You may find it helpful to begin with a professional code of conduct. Does your major/profession have a governing body (e.g., medicine is governed by the American Medical Association, law by the American Bar Association)? Most professional organizations have a code of conduct/ethics. Ask one of your major professors if you are not sure where to begin. Review the Personal Management feature for Chapter 3. The Six Pillars of Character can serve as a guide for determining your own personal code. Now complete Exercise 6. Did your personal code help you determine what to do? If not, is there any way to strengthen this code so that it becomes clear how to go about handling situations like those in the exercise?

For Chapter 2, the Personal Management activity had you focus on personal weaknesses. You developed an action plan to overcome them. If you did not complete this activity, do so now. Chapter 4 discusses the role of organizational environment and culture. You are introduced to the term competitive advantage. Competitive advantage exists when "a core competency clearly sets an organization apart from its competitors and gives it an advantage in the marketplace." Just like organizations, individuals can have core competencies – special strengths. What about you? Is there something that you do really well? Maybe you have an eye for detail and organization. Perhaps you are exceptionally creative. It could be that you are artistically gifted, in music or photography. Alternatively, you may have strong interpersonal skills.

Putting It All Together. Take another look at your list of strengths and weaknesses. Look carefully at those things you identified as strengths. What one or two things do you have a knack for doing that no one else seems to be able to do better? What do others constantly approach you to do because they know you can do it better than they can? If you cannot come up with anything, then take another look at your strengths. Is there something in this list that you particularly enjoy doing and can develop/refine to set yourself apart from others? A may just be a matter of application and experience. Once you determine your core competency, the next step is to determine where it will give you a competitive advantage. What types of jobs utilize this skill? Where (i.e., in what organizations, settings) would you be required to do this? Think about the career path you are on. How likely is it that your core competency will give you a competitive advantage? If the answer is "not likely," then you may want to consider alternate jobs/career fields.

How comfortable are you when it comes to interacting with individuals from different cultures? Take a moment to consider the Personal Management feature associated with Chapter 5. Most colleges and universities have an international student population. How proactive have you been when it comes to meeting and getting to know students from other cultures? Are you comfortable working with students from other geographic regions? Or do you tend to maintain an ethnocentric attitude? An honest assessment here may reveal how prepared you are to work in a global economy.

Do you have what it takes to be a part of a multinational company? Test yourself. If you have not done so already, complete Assessment 8. What about your comfort level doing business in other cultures? Try Assessment 9.

Putting It All Together. Most organizations today have some global dimension even if it is simply a website accessible anywhere in the world. Expanding markets in China and throughout Asia are compelling businesses to gain an international presence. To what extent are you willing to be involved with a multinational company? Spend some time researching organizations that have the jobs you are interested in. Visit their websites. Do they have locations in other countries? Are they looking for employees with language skills and/or international experience? What are the chances you might be asked to visit a foreign country as part of a business assignment? As you define your short-range career goals, it is wise to consider the global dimension. Are you willing to relocate to other geographic regions? Other countries? To what extent do you want to be involved with a multinational organization? If these are career features that interest you, how prepared are you to take advantage of international opportunities? Think about these issues as you develop a statement about your preferred work setting/organization.

Take a moment to review the Personal Management feature for Chapter 6. Entrepreneurs are described as risk takers. Risk comes into play when someone pursues an opportunity that others fail to capitalize upon. One reason entrepreneurs succeed is because they apply creative solutions to these opportunities. Entrepreneurs like Earl Graves, Anita Roddick, and Fred Smith saw markets where others did not. Post-it Notes® arose from another project failure at 3M.

Complete Assessment 10 (if you have not done so already). How did you score in terms of your entrepreneurial orientation? We may not all have what it takes to be an entrepreneur, but we can be creative (at times). When do you get your best ideas? Is there a particular time of day when you are most likely to be creative? What stimulates your thinking? Do you work better alone or when you are able to bounce ideas off others? Are you more effective when you have time to process thoughts and reflect on what you encounter? Think back to how Jeff Taylor got his idea for Monster.com (Chapter 1).

Which of the following situations have you found to be stimulating?

Σ • In the shower

Σ • Just after you go to bed

Σ • First thing in the morning

Σ • After watching a quiz show

Σ • Listening to soft music (e.g., jazz)

What do these situations have in common? They are times when we are generally relaxed. It is easier to generate good ideas when we are relaxed. Csikzentmihalyi (1990) refers to this as "flow." Complete Exercises 15 and 29. Try them at different times of the day and in different places. Try working through the problems/puzzles with someone else.

Putting It All Together. Write a brief summary statement describing situations when you are most likely to be creative. To what extent will your job/career path require creativity? How likely is it that your job arrangements will be effective for stimulating creativity? If the answer is "not likely," then what steps will you need to take to ensure creative time is present?

Reference: M. Csikzentmihalyi (1990). Flow: The psychology of optimal experience. New York: Harper & Row.

Begin by reviewing the Personal Management feature for this chapter if you have not done so already. Just how much confidence do you have in the career path you have chosen? To what extent did family and friends, as opposed to personal interests and abilities, determine your choice? Are you taking the right courses and developing the necessary skills to succeed? How do you know? Upon what are you basing your answers to the questions posed here?

As you think about what it takes for success, determine how well you are doing at this point in your academic preparation. Maybe you started work on a major only to discover that you are not as interested as you once were. Maybe you are having difficulty completing required work that others seem to be doing with ease. Be careful not to escalate your commitment. You may be tempted to think "I have spent too much time (taking courses) and money to change majors now." Review Manager's Notepad 7.3. The primary reasons for continuing your current path are that you enjoy and have the aptitude for what you are doing. Ability is also important, but that will come in time as long as you have the willingness (motivation) to learn.

Putting It All Together. Spend time researching your career path. Seek out individuals that are already in the field. [Note: If you are unable to identify professionals, talk to an academic advisor whose expertise most closely matches your interests.] Find out how long it took them to get where they are. Ask them where they started, what jobs they held prior to their current position, and how long it took to advance from one position to the next. Ask questions to determine what entry-level jobs will be available when you graduate. Finally, find out what expectations prospective employers will have with respect to knowledge, skills, and experience.

PERSONAL MANAGEMENT—CAREER FOCUS
CHAPTER 8 ACTIVITY: TIMELINE

In the previous activity, you spent time thinking about and collecting information related to your career path. Chapter 8 describes the importance of planning—setting objectives and determining how to accomplish them. Take a moment to think about your future. What would you like to be doing 10 years after you graduate? Be specific. You may want to identify personal, as well as professional, goals. Write them down. What will it take to reach these goals? Use the information you collected for the Student Activity for Chapter 7. Identify intermediate steps to reach your ultimate objective(s).

Review the Personal Management feature for Chapter 8. Effective time management is a critical element for achieving short-term goals. When the timeframe associated with goals is longer (i.e., 3–5 years or longer), it is easier to be distracted and not manage time—progress toward goals—effectively. Exercise 9 (Beating the Time Wasters) addresses the importance of prioritizing events. Low-priority events, while generally easy to complete and satisfying when accomplished, can get in the way of reaching truly important goals. Take a second look at the events you identified as intermediate steps. Are all of these important for helping you reach your ultimate personal and professional goals? Will any of them interfere with your ability to stay focused on your 10-year outcomes? Revise your list as necessary.

Putting It All Together. Develop a visual timeline that covers where you are now through 10 years after graduation. Mark key events on your timeline that represent points where you expect to reach intermediate and/or long-range goals. Be realistic. Now develop a brief narrative describing each goal.

PERSONAL MANAGEMENT – CAREER FOCUS
CHAPTER 9 ACTIVITY: SWOT

Begin this activity by reviewing the Personal Management feature for Chapter 9. In Chapter 7, you were introduced to intuitive thinking–responding imaginatively to a problem based on a quick and broad evaluation of the situation and alternative courses of action. Take a look at your score for Assessment 11 (complete the assessment now if you have not done so). Are you an intuitive thinker? Anticipating and planning for the future require some intuitive ability.

As directed in the Personal Management feature, consult the U.S. Bureau of Labor Statistics website. Draw on the research you completed for the Personal Management Activity associated with Chapter 7. What trends do you see developing, particularly in your career field?

Putting It All Together. Conduct a personal SWOT analysis. Begin by making a list of your strengths and weaknesses. Use the information you developed for the Student Activity associated with Chapter 1 and revise as necessary. This list should be relatively short. In other words, the strengths you identify should represent core competencies–things you do exceptionally well that give you an advantage over your competitors. Weaknesses, on the other hand, would be limitations that would put you at a disadvantage in relation to your competition.

Continue your analysis by looking at the external environment. Start with a broad perspective. What things are happening in the global economy? Are there new markets emerging? How does your career field look? What opportunities exist (or will exist)? Is technology influencing this? Now consider the negative side. Are there changes that have the potential to shrink the job market? What about customer pressure to reduce prices? Is the product or service associated with your career field considered a necessity or a luxury item? Does demand fluctuate with changes in the economy? What about technology? Are changes occurring so rapidly that your education and training might not be keeping pace?

Finish the analysis by putting the two components together. Do your strengths put you in a position to take advantage of the opportunities you see developing? In other words, are your skills, abilities, and experiences going to be in high demand? If not, are there one or two areas (possibly identified as weaknesses) where you need to concentrate in the next few years? Take a close look at your weaknesses. Are there items that may limit your potential to succeed? For example, if one of your opportunities is the growth of jobs associated with emerging international markets and you list cultural awareness or comfort with new environments as a weakness, you may not be in a position to take advantage. Seeing this now will give you a chance to develop an action plan to be better prepared.

In the activity for Chapter 7, you began to gather data related to your career field. Using this information or by investigating the leading companies in your career field, identify prevailing structural characteristics. For example, are these organizations typically flat or steep? Flat organizations have wider spans of control and employees have to display more initiative because there is less direction. In steep organizations, there will generally be more control mechanisms, which gives employees less discretion about how to do things. Do organizations in your field delegate work to and empower employees? If so, you must be prepared to take more responsibility and be accountable for producing results.

Putting It All Together. Develop a general description of organizations in your career field. You may have to make some initial choices to focus your efforts. For example, a marketing major might work in a variety of industries and organizations. Begin by identifying whether businesses in your career field are product- or service-based organizations. Now, describe the general structure (e.g., functional, divisional). Do employees work through formal or informal structural arrangements? Once you identify general features, move on to more specific organizational characteristics, such as command structure, span of control, and decision making.

Chapter 10 introduced you to organizational structure. The activity associated with that chapter had you re-search the structures of organizations most likely to have the jobs you would be interested in upon graduating. Now let's consider design. Take a look at Figure 11.2. The graphic introduces two extreme forms of organiza-tional design and the features associated with each. Keep in mind that design is a continuum. In other words, organizations may display various combinations of mechanistic and organic features. Be careful not to over-generalize design to specific categories of business. While traditional manufacturing organizations tend to be highly mechanistic, so do service-based organizations such as hospitals and banks. Innovative organizations are more likely to adopt organic designs, but even creative-based businesses can be mechanistic. A publish-ing house like John Wiley & Sons would be a good example. Some organizations may be mechanistic while embedding organic features within the overall structure. A good example would be the "skunkworks" at Apple Computer.

Complete Assessments 16 and 17 if you have not done so already. Assessment 16 may be difficult to grasp. Consider the Personal Management feature for Chapter 11. Now think about turbulence (or ambiguity) in a different context. Think back on the different class experiences you have. Do you prefer classes where the professor spells out the requirements in detail or leaves it up to you to decide how to do things? Do you prefer the structure of multiple-choice questions or the looseness of essay-type questions (where you might not know exactly what and how much to write)? Do you prefer individual or group-based assignments?

Putting It All Together. Write a summary description of your organizational design preference (you may al-ready have this if you completed the Self-Discovery Project). Take the results of Assessment 17 and your own class-based experiences into account. Take the research you did for the Personal Management Activity in Chapter 10 to the next level. In that activity, you identified features of organizations in your career field. Does your description indicate organic or mechanistic designs? In all likelihood, there may be some variation in de-sign across organizations, so focus on the general pattern. How well does your design preference match up with the typical organizational design in your career field? Identify steps you must take to ensure a better per-son–organization fit.

One of the lessons of Chapter 1 is that the new economy is changing the way people approach their careers. Your grandparents and, to lesser degree, your parents could focus on finding a job with a good company and making a career of it. This option rarely presents itself in today's economy. Therefore, you have to be flexible. Review the Personal Management Feature for Chapter 12. Employees today are more loyal to their professions than they are to organizations.

How do you define yourself? Complete Assessment 18 (if you have not done so already). What does your score indicate about your orientation? Most students think in terms of their career, which is probably defined by a major. If that is the case for you, it means you have more of a professional orientation. Will this change? Do you want it to change?

Putting It All Together. Chapter 12 discusses the importance of career development. One step in the planning process is identifying career goals. In previous activities, you developed a list of strengths and weaknesses. You refined your strengths to determine which ones give you a competitive advantage. Those activities helped you address the "who am I?" question. The personal SWOT analysis you performed in the Chapter 9 activity focused your thinking on matching strengths with opportunities. This activity got you started on addressing the "where do I want to go?" and "how do I get there" questions. Let's refine the "go" question a bit more.

Chapter 9 talked about the importance of strategy. Organizational strategies tend to be comprehensive (extensive) plans. You should have a strategy for your career, but it should be more concise. This is your career objective. Develop a career objective. Remember, this should be short and generally written as a phrase. Now take a close look. Does it convey the elements of your job/career that are really important to you? Is it specific? Statements such as "a job in a growing company with opportunity to advance," while professional sounding are not meaningful. What kind of job do you want? (Think about the research you did for the Chapter 7 activity.) What kind of organization? (Again, think about the work you completed for the Chapters 10 and 11 activities). Do phrases such as "opportunity to advance" add value to your objective (in words, isn't this understood)? As a last check on your objective, try giving it to a of couple friends. Ask them if they understand what you want to do.

Several years ago, three college friends developed a game based on the "small world phenomenon." The game requires players to link actors and actresses to Kevin Bacon by identifying common movies. The idea has more than entertainment value. In 1967, Stanley Milgram reported on an experiment that gave rise to this principle. The basic premise is that everyone in the world can be reached by a short chain of social acquaintances.

Networks, our connections with others, are important business tools. They can help you find a job, generate clients, and raise capital. Moreover, researcher Mark Granovetter (1973) argues that weak ties (i.e., connections with acquaintances and colleagues) are more important for personal advancement than strong ties (i.e., connections with family and friends).

Review the Personal Management feature for Chapter 13. Just how effective are you at networking? How well developed is your social and professional network?

Putting It All Together. Take a moment to make a list of professionals you know. Note their jobs/career field and organization. Start with family members/relatives. Expand the list to family friends. Be sure to include contacts developed through your own work and academic experience.

Is your list extensive enough to produce the contacts you need to get your career moving? If not, begin to think about opportunities to expand your network. Are you a member of any professional/service organizations at your college? Do these organizations host speakers and/or hold social events that include alumni or other professionals? Make it a practice to attend these events. Take advantage of the opportunity by introducing yourself to outsiders. Be prepared to talk about your career interests and seek advice from these people.

References:

Stanley Milgram (1967). The small world problem. Psychology Today, 5 (May), 60-67.
Mark Granovetter (1973). The strength of weak ties. The American Journal of Sociology, 78 (6),

What does it take to motivate you? If you answer without thinking, you will likely say "money." Think about what you read in Chapter 14. Extrinsic rewards, which include pay, are administered by others and typically are not effective motivators. Intrinsic rewards, self-administered, tend to be better for motivating. Why do so many people believe money is a motivator? Consider the Two-Factor Theory. The theory identifies job-related factors that influence satisfaction and dissatisfaction. Is satisfaction (or dissatisfaction) comparable to motivation (or lack of motivation)? No. Salary (money) is classified as a hygiene factor, determining our level of dissatisfaction. According to Frederick Herzberg, money will only keep us from having negative feelings about our jobs/employer.

Still, money is important. Money enables us to fulfill a variety of needs. It can contribute to motivation to the extent that it helps satisfy active needs, such as physiological, safety, or esteem. Money establishes a sense of equity or confirms the instrumentality aspect of expectancy. It affirms our worth to the organization. Clearly money is important, but do not be distracted by it as you think about what motivates you.

Complete Assessment 24. A score above 4.0 indicates a desire for growth-need satisfaction at work. Review your responses to Exercise 7 and Exercise 23 (complete these now if you have not previously done so). What do your responses say about what it takes to motivate you? How well does your current job satisfy these characteristics? This may not matter because most of us are employed temporarily during college simply to meet our financial obligations. With career employment it is different. Take a moment to consider the Personal Management feature for Chapter 14. Initiative is a measure of an individual characteristic, but the amount of initiative you display at work is also a function of the job.

Putting It All Together. Write a brief summary statement of job features that appeal most to you (i.e., describe what you are looking for in a job). Do jobs associated with your career field match your interests and provide features that will motivate you? If the answer is "yes," then you should have no trouble staying motivated and maintaining initiative. If the answer is "no," then you have to consider whether you have enough self-initiative to sustain your career early on and reach levels that will offer what you seek. Otherwise, you may want to consider alternate jobs/career fields.

Chapter 15 focuses on work arrangements and the relationship to personal satisfaction and job performance. The importance of the work environment is reinforced by the steel worker's comments in the section on quality of work life. As you complete this activity, keep in mind that there will generally be some degree of flexibility in the way a job is designed. Be sure to consider a range of jobs and organizations.

In a variety of assessments and activities throughout the term, you have had the opportunity to examine various aspects of your personality and work style. In addition, several of the activities emphasized the role of person–job and person–organization fit. While other factors such as pay, supervision, and policies influence satisfaction, the job itself and the degree of fit are two very important contributors. Since there is a strong relationship between satisfaction and other key organizational outcomes, absenteeism and turnover in particular, you want to maximize the chances that you will be in the majority of American workers that indicate some degree of satisfaction with their jobs.

Putting It All Together. Review Figure 15.2 and the descriptions of the Big Five personality traits. You may wish to consider the other personality dimensions included in the figure. Rate yourself on each of the Big Five factors. Now review the organizational descriptions you developed in the activities associated with Chapter 10 and Chapter 11. How well does your personality mesh with these organizational characteristics? Do potential jobs offer features that will be compatible with your personality/personal work style? To what extent is a match or mismatch likely to influence your attitudes about working? Work attitudes are important because they ultimately contribute to your willingness to perform (i.e., effort).

The Personal Management Activity in Chapter 15 introduced you to work arrangements that influence worker satisfaction and productivity. Chapter 16 deals with a specific type of arrangement—teams—that is a prominent feature of the new workplace. There is a simple explanation for this trend. Teamwork produces synergistic effects. Your text identifies a number of additional positive benefits that result from the use of teams. Review the Personal Management Feature associated with Chapter 16. How successful have you been as a team player? Does the answer suggest anything about your career readiness?

Putting It All Together. Try to recall a variety of team-based experiences from your past. You may want to draw on extracurricular activities (e.g., sports, band). Think about social experiences, such as friendship groups, fraternities, or sororities. Now consider work teams. Most likely, these will be related to your academic pursuits, but may include jobs. Categorize these experiences as positive or negative. What are the factors that differentiate them? In other words, what things were present or absent that made these experiences either positive or negative?

How are your writing skills? Consider the assignments you completed this quarter. Did you communicate effectively? What kind of reaction do you think your writing created? Take a moment to review the Personal Management Feature for Chapter 17. Why do you think such a high percentage of students have trouble writing? The Personal Management Activity for Chapter 4 talked about creating a competitive advantage. Are your communication skills a strength or a weakness? One way to make sure they work in your favor is to practice and learn from your mistakes.

Imagine getting on an elevator and discovering that the only other individual riding with you is the Human Resource Director for a prestigious company. You seize the moment and ask about entry-level positions. The HR Director indicates they are hiring and asks about your career plans. You have three minutes to make a positive impression. What will you say? Would you be able to communicate this information clearly and concisely?

Putting It All Together. Take a moment now to write a brief summary (3–5 sentences) of your goals for the next ten years. Use a narrative format, that is, write it out using complete sentences. Think of this as a speech you will be delivering to an audience of strangers. Trade your summary with another class member. Have them read and evaluate it while you do the same for them. Revise it based on the feedback you receive. Choose a different class member. Do not let them see your revised summary. Simply read it to them. Did this person understand your goals? Using the feedback provided, revise your statement. Your "elevator speech" will come in handy during those networking opportunities (refer back to Chapter 13).

Congratulations! You reached the end of the course. Hopefully, you know considerably more about management, yourself, and your career goals. If you invested the effort to produce a comprehensive career development plan, you may think accomplishing it will be a daunting task. You are not alone. Many 20-something college students are overwhelmed by the transition from student, dependent on others, to graduate, independent and out on their own. In fact, the phenomenon is so well–documented it is now referred to as the "quarterlife crisis" (Robbins & Wilner, 2001). As Robbins and Wilner (2001) note, the steps of your life have been clearly marked to this point. Now you must strike out and face a number of choices on your own. Your development plan can help guide you through those career decisions you will inevitably face. If it does not, revise it! Just as you would in decision making, you should evaluate the results of your plan and take corrective action as necessary.

Putting It All Together. Review your score on Assessment 29 (complete it if you have not already done so). Type A personalities are more likely to experience stress. What mechanisms do you have to combat stress in your life? Take a moment to reflect on and make note of your coping mechanisms. Social activities and exercise routines are valuable, but do not overlook the importance of healthy social relationships both inside and outside the workplace.

Reference: A. Robbins, & A. Wilner (2001). Quarterlife crisis: The unique challenges of life in your twenties. New York: Penguin Putnam.

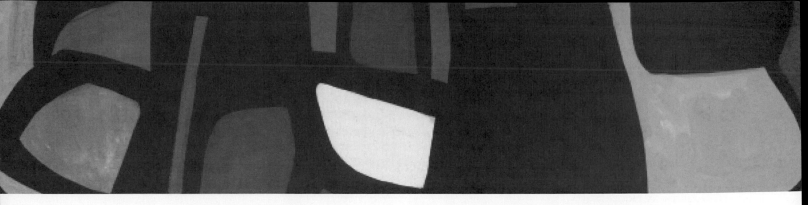

SELF-ASSESSMENTS

PERSONAL MANAGEMENT – CAREER FOCUS
SELF-ASSESSMENT SCORESHEET

Complete the following self-assessments. Record your score. Include a brief interpretation.

Your Managerial Assumptions (Assessment #4)

X Score: ☐   Y Score: ☐

Interpretation:

Global Readiness Index (Assessment #8)

Global Mindset: ☐   Global Knowledge: ☐
Global Work Skills: ☐

Interpretation:

Entrepreneurship Orientation (Assessment #10): ☐

Interpretation:

Your Intuitive Ability (Assessment #11): ☐

Interpretation:

Time Management Profile (Assessment #13): ☐

Interpretation:

Turbulence Tolerance Test (Assessment #16): ☐

Interpretation:

Organizational Design Preference (Assessment #17): ☐

Interpretation:

T-P Leadership Questionnaire (Assessment #20)

T Score: ☐   P Score: ☐

Interpretation:

Conflict Management Styles (Assessment #28)

Competing: ☐   Collaborating: ☐   Compromising: ☐   Avoiding: ☐
Accommodating: ☐

Interpretation:

Stress Self-Test (Assessment #29): ☐

Interpretation:

- -

ASSESSMENT 1

A 21st-Century Manager?

Instructions

Rate yourself on the following personal characteristics. Use this scale.

S = Strong, I am very confident with this one.
G = Good, but I still have room to grow.
W = Weak, I really need work on this one.
U = Unsure, I just don't know.

1. *Resistance to stress:* The ability to get work done even under stressful conditions.

2. *Tolerance for uncertainty:* The ability to get work done even under ambiguous and uncertain conditions.

3. *Social objectivity:* The ability to act free of racial, ethnic, gender, and other prejudices or biases.

4. *Inner work standards:* The ability to personally set and work to high performance standards.

5. *Stamina:* The ability to sustain long work hours.

6. *Adaptability:* The ability to be flexible and adapt to changes.

7. *Self-confidence:* The ability to be consistently decisive and display one's personal presence.

8. *Self-objectivity:* The ability to evaluate personal strengths and weaknesses and to understand one's motives and skills relative to a job.

9. *Introspection:* The ability to learn from experience, awareness, and self-study.

10. *Entrepreneurism:* The ability to address problems and take advantage of opportunities for constructive change.

Scoring

Give yourself 1 point for each S, and 1/2 point for each G. Do not give yourself points for W and U responses. Total your points and enter the result here [PMF = ___].

Interpretation

This assessment offers a self-described *profile of your management foundations (PMF).*

Are you a perfect 10, or is your PMF score something less than that? There shouldn't be too many 10s around. Ask someone who knows you to assess you on this instrument. You may be surprised at the differences between your PMF score as you described it and your PMF score as described by someone else. Most of us, realistically speaking, must work hard to grow and develop continually in these and related management foundations. This list is a good starting point as you consider where and how to further pursue the development of your managerial skills and competencies. The items on the list are recommended by the American Assembly of Collegiate Schools of Business (AACSB) as the skills and personal characteristics that should be nurtured in college and university students of business administration. Their success— and yours—as 21st-century managers may well rest on (1) an initial awareness of the importance of these basic management foundations and (2) a willingness to strive continually to strengthen them throughout the work career.

Source: See *Outcome Measurement Project,* Phase I and Phase II Reports (St. Louis: American Assembly of Collegiate Schools of Business, 1986 and 1987).

ASSESSMENT 2

Emotional Intelligence

Instructions

Rate yourself on how well you are able to display the abilities for each item listed below. As you score each item, try to think of actual situations in which you have been called upon to use the ability. Use the following scale.

1	2	3	4	5	6	7
Low Ability		Neutral		High Ability		

1 2 3 4 5 6 7 **1.** Identify changes in physiological arousal.

1 2 3 4 5 6 7 **2.** Relax when under pressure in situations.

1 2 3 4 5 6 7 **3.** Act productively when angry.

1 2 3 4 5 6 7 **4.** Act productively in situations that arouse anxiety.

1 2 3 4 5 6 7 **5.** Calm yourself quickly when angry.

1 2 3 4 5 6 7 **6.** Associate different physical cues with different emotions.

1 2 3 4 5 6 7 **7.** Use internal "talk" to affect your emotional states.

1 2 3 4 5 6 7 **8.** Communicate your feelings effectively.

1 2 3 4 5 6 7 **9.** Reflect on negative feelings without being distressed.

1 2 3 4 5 6 7 **10.** Stay calm when you are the target of anger from others.

1 2 3 4 5 6 7 **11.** Know when you are thinking negatively.

1 2 3 4 5 6 7 **12.** Know when your "self-talk" is instructional.

1 2 3 4 5 6 7 **13.** Know when you are becoming angry.

1 2 3 4 5 6 7 **14.** Know how you interpret events you encounter.

1 2 3 4 5 6 7 **15.** Know what senses you are currently using.

1 2 3 4 5 6 7 **16.** Accurately communicate what you experience.

1 2 3 4 5 6 7 **17.** Identify what information influences your interpretations.

1 2 3 4 5 6 7 **18.** Identify when you experience mood shifts.

1 2 3 4 5 6 7 **19.** Know when you become defensive.

1 2 3 4 5 6 7 **20.** Know the impact your behavior has on others.

1 2 3 4 5 6 7 **21.** Know when you communicate incongruently.

1 2 3 4 5 6 7 **22.** "Gear up" at will.

1 2 3 4 5 6 7 **23.** Regroup quickly after a setback.

1 2 3 4 5 6 7 **24.** Complete long-term tasks in designated time frames.

1 2 3 4 5 6 7 **25.** Produce high energy when doing uninteresting work.

1 2 3 4 5 6 7 **26.** Stop or change ineffective habits.

1 2 3 4 5 6 7 **27.** Develop new and more productive patterns of behavior.

1 2 3 4 5 6 7 **28.** Follow words with actions.

1 2 3 4 5 6 7 **29.** Work out conflicts.

1 2 3 4 5 6 7 **30.** Develop consensus with others.

1 2 3 4 5 6 7 **31.** Mediate conflict between others.

1 2 3 4 5 6 7 **32.** Exhibit effective interpersonal communication skills.

1 2 3 4 5 6 7 **33.** Articulate the thoughts of a group.

1 2 3 4 5 6 7 **34.** Influence others, directly or indirectly.

1 2 3 4 5 6 7 **35.** Build trust with others.

1 2 3 4 5 6 7 **36.** Build support teams.

1 2 3 4 5 6 7 **37.** Make others feel good.

1 2 3 4 5 6 7 **38.** Provide advice and support to others, as needed.

1 2 3 4 5 6 7 **39.** Accurately reflect people's feelings back to them.

1 2 3 4 5 6 7 **40.** Recognize when others are distressed.

1 2 3 4 5 6 7 **41.** Help others manage their emotions.

1 2 3 4 5 6 7 **42.** Show empathy to others.

1 2 3 4 5 6 7 **43.** Engage in intimate conversations with others.

1 2 3 4 5 6 7 **44.** Help a group to manage emotions.

1 2 3 4 5 6 7 **45.** Detect incongruence between others' emotions or feelings and their behaviors.

Scoring

This instrument measures six dimensions of your emotional intelligence. Find your scores as follows.

Self-awareness—Add scores for items 1, 6, 11, 12, 13, 14, 15, 16, 17, 18, 19, 20, 21
Managing emotions—Add scores for items 1, 2, 3, 4, 5, 7, 9, 10, 13, 27
Self-motivation—Add scores for items 7, 22, 23, 25, 26, 27, 28
Relating well—Add scores for items 8, 10, 16, 19, 20, 29, 30, 31, 32, 33, 34, 35, 36, 37, 38, 39, 42, 43, 44, 45
Emotional mentoring—Add scores for items 8, 10, 16, 18, 34, 35, 37, 38, 39, 40, 41, 44, 45

Interpretation

The prior scoring indicates your self-perceived abilities in these dimensions of emotional intelligence. To further examine your tendencies, go back for each dimension and sum the number of responses you had that were 4 and lower (suggesting lower ability), and sum the number of responses you had that were 5 or better (suggesting higher ability). This gives you an indication by dimension of where you may have room to grow and develop your emotional intelligence abilities.

Source: Scale from Hendrie Weisinger, *Emotional Intelligence at Work* (San Francisco: Jossey-Bass, 1998), pp. 214–15. Used by permission.

ASSESSMENT 3

Learning Tendencies

Instructions

In each of the following pairs, distribute 10 points between the two statements to best describe how you like to learn. For example:

__3__ (a) I like to read.
__7__ (b) I like to listen to lectures.

1. _____ (a) I like to learn through working with other people and being engaged in concrete experiences.

_____ (b) I like to learn through logical analysis and systematic attempts to understand a situation.

2. _____ (a) I like to learn by observing things, viewing them from different perspectives, and finding meaning in situations.

_____ (b) I like to learn by taking risks, getting things done, and influencing events through actions taken.

Scoring

Place "dots" on the following graph to record the above scores: "Doing" = 2b. "Watching" = 1b. "Feeling" = 1a. "Thinking" = 2a. Connect the dots to plot your learning tendencies.

Interpretation

This activity provides a first impression of your learning tendencies or style. Four possible learning styles are identified on the graph—convergers, accommodators, divergers, and assimilators. Consider the following descriptions for their accuracy in describing you. For a truly good reading on your learning tendencies, ask several others to com-

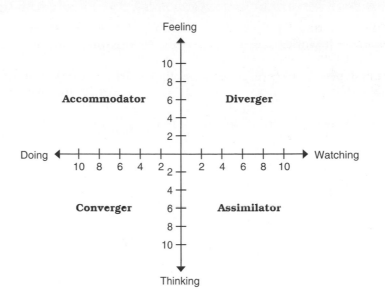

plete the Step 1 questions for you, and then assess how their results compare with your own perceptions.

Convergers—combined tendencies toward abstract conceptualization (thinking) and active experimentation (doing). They like to learn in practical situations. They prefer to deal with technical issues and solve problems through systematic investigation of alternatives. Good at experimentation, finding new ways of doing things, making decisions.

Accommodators—combine concrete experience (feeling) with active experimentation (doing). They like to learn from hands-on experience. They prefer "gut" responses to problems rather than systematic analysis of alternatives. Good at influencing others, committing to goals, seeking opportunities.

Divergers—combine concrete experience (feeling) with reflective observation (watching). They like to learn from observation. They prefer to participate in brainstorming and imaginative information gathering. Good at listening, imagining, and being sensitive to feelings.

Assimilators—combine abstract conceptualization (thinking) with reflective observation (watching). They like to learn through information. They prefer ideas and concepts to people and value logical reasoning. Good at organizing information, building models, and analyzing data.

Source: Developed from David A. Kolb, "Learning Style Inventory" (Boston, MA: McBer & Company, 1985); see also his article "On Management and the Learning Process," in David A. Kolb, Irwin M. Rubin, and James M. McIntyre, eds., *Organizational Psychology: A Book of Readings*, 2nd ed. (Englewood Cliffs, NJ: Prentice-Hall, 1974), pp. 27–42.

ASSESSMENT 4

What Are Your Managerial Assumptions?

Instructions

Read the following statements. Use the space in the margins to write "Yes" if you agree with the statement, or "No" if you disagree with it.

Force yourself to take a "yes" or "no" position. Do this for every statement.

1. Are good pay and a secure job enough to satisfy most workers?

2. Should a manager help and coach subordinates in their work?

3. Do most people like real responsibility in their jobs?

4. Are most people afraid to learn new things in their jobs?

5. Should managers let subordinates control the quality of their work?

6. Do most people dislike work?

7. Are most people creative?

8. Should a manager closely supervise and direct the work of subordinates?

9. Do most people tend to resist change?

10. Do most people work only as hard as they have to?

11. Should workers be allowed to set their own job goals?

12. Are most people happiest off the job?

13. Do most workers really care about the organization they work for?

14. Should a manager help subordinates advance and grow in their jobs?

Scoring

Count the number of "yes" responses to items 1, 4, 6, 8, 9, 10, 12; write that number here as [X = ___]. Count the number of "yes" responses to items 2, 3, 5, 7, 11, 13, 14; write that score here [Y = ___].

Interpretation

This assessment sheds insight into your orientation toward Douglas McGregor's Theory X (your "X" score) and Theory Y (your "Y" score) assumptions. You should review the discussion of McGregor's thinking in Chapter 2 and consider further the ways in which you are likely to behave toward other people at work. Think, in particular, about the types of "self-fulfilling prophecies" you are likely to create.

ASSESSMENT 5

Terminal Values Survey

Instructions

Rate each of the following values in terms of its importance to you. Think about each value *in terms of its importance as a guiding principle in your life.* As you work, consider each value in relation to all the other values listed in the survey.

Terminal Values

1. A comfortable life	1	2	3	4	5	6	7
	Of lesser importance				Of greater importance		

2. An exciting life	1	2	3	4	5	6	7
	Of lesser importance				Of greater importance		

3. A sense of accomplishment	1	2	3	4	5	6	7
	Of lesser importance				Of greater importance		

4. A world at peace

1	2	3	4	5	6	7
Of lesser importance				Of greater importance		

5. A world of beauty

1	2	3	4	5	6	7
Of lesser importance				Of greater importance		

6. Equality

1	2	3	4	5	6	7
Of lesser importance				Of greater importance		

7. Family security

1	2	3	4	5	6	7
Of lesser importance				Of greater importance		

8. Freedom

1	2	3	4	5	6	7
Of lesser importance				Of greater importance		

9. Happiness

1	2	3	4	5	6	7
Of lesser importance				Of greater importance		

10. Inner harmony

1	2	3	4	5	6	7
Of lesser importance				Of greater importance		

11. Mature love

1	2	3	4	5	6	7
Of lesser importance				Of greater importance		

12. National security

1	2	3	4	5	6	7
Of lesser importance				Of greater importance		

13. Pleasure

1	2	3	4	5	6	7
Of lesser importance				Of greater importance		

14. Salvation

1	2	3	4	5	6	7
Of lesser importance				Of greater importance		

15. Self-respect

1	2	3	4	5	6	7
Of lesser importance				Of greater importance		

16. Social recognition

1	2	3	4	5	6	7
Of lesser importance				Of greater importance		

17. True friendship

1	2	3	4	5	6	7
Of lesser importance				Of greater importance		

18. Wisdom

1	2	3	4	5	6	7
Of lesser importance				Of greater importance		

Scoring

To score this instrument, you must multiply your score for each item times a "weight"—e.g., (#3 × 5) = your new question 3 score.

1. Calculate your Personal Values Score as: (#1 × 5) + (#2 × 4) + (#3 × 4) + (#7) + (#8) + (#9 × 4) + (#10 × 5) + (#11 × 4) + (#13 × 5) + (#14 × 3) + (#15 × 5) + (#16 × 3) + (#17 × 4) + (#18 × 5)

2. Calculate your Social Values Score as: (#4 × 5) + (#5 × 3) + (#6 × 5) + (#12 × 5)

3. Calculate your Terminal Values Score as: Personal Values – Social Values

Interpretation

Terminal values reflect a person's preferences concerning the "ends" to be achieved. They are the goals individuals would like to achieve in their lifetimes.

Different value items receive different weights in this scale. (Example: "A comfortable life" receives a weight of "5" while "Freedom" receives a weight of "1.") Your score on Personal Values has your Social Values score subtracted from it to determine your Terminal Values score.

Source: Adapted from James Weber, "Management Value Orientations: A Typology and Assessment," *International Journal of Value Based Management*, vol. 3, no. 2 (1990), pp. 37–54.

ASSESSMENT 6

Instrumental Values Survey

Instructions

Rate each of the following values in terms of its importance to you. Think about each value *in terms of its importance as a guiding principle in your life.* As you work, consider each value in relation to all the other values listed in the survey.

Instrumental Values

1. Ambitious

1	2	3	4	5	6	7
Of lesser importance				Of greater importance		

2. Broadminded

1	2	3	4	5	6	7
Of lesser importance				Of greater importance		

3. Capable

1	2	3	4	5	6	7
Of lesser importance				Of greater importance		

4. Cheerful

	1	2	3	4	5	6	7
	Of lesser importance				Of greater importance		

5. Clean

	1	2	3	4	5	6	7
	Of lesser importance				Of greater importance		

6. Courageous

	1	2	3	4	5	6	7
	Of lesser importance				Of greater importance		

7. Forgiving

	1	2	3	4	5	6	7
	Of lesser importance				Of greater importance		

8. Helpful

	1	2	3	4	5	6	7
	Of lesser importance				Of greater importance		

9. Honest

	1	2	3	4	5	6	7
	Of lesser importance				Of greater importance		

10. Imaginative

	1	2	3	4	5	6	7
	Of lesser importance				Of greater importance		

11. Independent

	1	2	3	4	5	6	7
	Of lesser importance				Of greater importance		

12. Intellectual

	1	2	3	4	5	6	7
	Of lesser importance				Of greater importance		

13. Logical

	1	2	3	4	5	6	7
	Of lesser importance				Of greater importance		

14. Loving

	1	2	3	4	5	6	7
	Of lesser importance				Of greater importance		

15. Obedient

	1	2	3	4	5	6	7
	Of lesser importance				Of greater importance		

16. Polite

	1	2	3	4	5	6	7
	Of lesser importance				Of greater importance		

17. Responsible

	1	2	3	4	5	6	7
	Of lesser importance				Of greater importance		

18. Self-controlled

	1	2	3	4	5	6	7
	Of lesser importance				Of greater importance		

Scoring

To score this instrument, you must multiply your score for each item times a "weight"—e.g., (#3 × 5) = your new question 3 score.

1. Calculate your Competence Values Score as: (#1 × 5) + (#2 × 2) + (#3 × 5) + (#10 × 5) + (#11 × 5) + (#12 × 5) + (#13 × 5) + (#17 × 4)

2. Calculate your Moral Values Score as: (#4 × 4) + (#5 × 3) + (#6 × 2) + (#7 × 5) + (#8 × 5) + (#9 × 2) + (#14 × 5) + (#15) + (#16 × 3)

3. Calculate your Instrumental Values Score as: Competence Values− Moral Values

Interpretation

Instrumental Values are defined as the "means" for achieving desired ends. They represent how you might go about achieving your important end states, depending on the relative importance you attach to the instrumental values.

Different value items receive different weights in this scale. (Example: "Ambitious" receives a weight of "5" while "Obedient" receives a weight of "1.") Your score on Competence Values has your Moral Values score subtracted from it to determine your Instrumental Values score.

Source: Adapted from James Weber, "Management Value Orientations: A Typology and Assessment," *International Journal of Value Based Management,* vol. 3, no. 2 (1990), pp. 37–54.

- - - - - - - - - ╠ **ASSESSMENT 7** ╣ - - - - - - - - - - - - - - - -

Diversity Awareness

Instructions

Complete the following questionnaire.

Diversity Awareness Checklist

Consider where you work or go to school as the setting for the following questions. Indicate "O" for often, "S" for sometimes, and "N" for never in response to each of the following questions as they pertain to the setting.

___ **1.** How often have you heard jokes or remarks about other people that you consider offensive?

___ **2.** How often do you hear men "talk down" to women in an attempt to keep them in an inferior status?

___ **3.** How often have you felt personal discomfort as the object of sexual harassment?

___ **4.** How often do you work or study with African Americans or Hispanics?

___ **5.** How often have you felt disadvantaged because members of ethnic groups other than yours were given special treatment?

___ **6.** How often have you seen a woman put in an uncomfortable situation because of unwelcome advances by a man?

___ **7.** How often does it seem that African Americans, Hispanics, Caucasians, women, men, and members of other minority demographic groups seem to "stick together" during work breaks or other leisure situations?

___ **8.** How often do you feel uncomfortable about something you did and/or said to someone of the opposite sex or a member of an ethnic or racial group other than yours?

___ **9.** How often do you feel efforts are made in this setting to raise the level of cross-cultural understanding among people who work and/or study together?

___ **10.** How often do you step in to communicate concerns to others when you feel actions and/or words are used to the disadvantage of minorities?

Scoring

There are no correct answers for the Diversity Awareness Checklist.

Interpretation

In the diversity checklist, the key issue is the extent to which you are "sensitive" to diversity issues in the workplace or university. Are you comfortable with your responses? How do you think others in your class responded? Why not share your responses with others and examine different viewpoints on this important issue?

Source: Items for the WV Cultural Awareness Quiz selected from a longer version by James P. Morgan, Jr., and published by University Associates, 1987. Used by permission.

ASSESSMENT 8

Global Readiness Index

Instructions

Rate yourself on each of the following items to establish a baseline measurement of your readiness to participate in the global work environment.

Rating Scale

1 = Very Poor
2 = Poor
3 = Acceptable
4 = Good
5 = Very Good

___ **1.** I understand my own culture in terms of its expectations, values, and influence on communication and relationships.

___ **2.** When someone presents me with a different point of view, I try to understand it rather than attack it.

___ **3.** I am comfortable dealing with situations where the available information is incomplete and the outcomes unpredictable.

___ **4.** I am open to new situations and am always looking for new information and learning opportunities.

___ **5.** I have a good understanding of the attitudes and perceptions toward my culture as they are held by people from other cultures.

___ **6.** I am always gathering information about other countries and cultures and trying to learn from them.

___ **7.** I am well informed regarding the major differences in government, political, and economic systems around the world.

___ **8.** I work hard to increase my understanding of people from other cultures.

___ **9.** I am able to adjust my communication style to work effectively with people from different cultures.

___ **10.** I can recognize when cultural differences are influencing working relationships and adjust my attitudes and behavior accordingly.

Scoring

The goal is to score as close to a perfect "5" as possible on each of the three dimensions of global readiness. Develop your scores as follows.

Items (1 + 2 + 3 + 4)/4
= ___ Global Mindset Score
Items (5 + 6 + 7)/3
= ___ Global Knowledge Score
Items (8 + 9 + 10)/3
= ___ Global Work Skills Score

Interpretation

To be successful in the 21st-century work environment, you must be comfortable with the global economy and the cultural diversity that it holds. This requires a *global mindset* that is receptive to and respectful of cultural differences, *global knowledge* that includes the continuing quest to know and learn more about other nations and cultures, and *global work skills* that allow you to work effectively across cultures.

_____

Source: Developed from "Is Your Company Really Global?," *Business Week* (December 1, 1997).

ASSESSMENT 9

Time Orientation

Instructions

This instrument examines your tendencies to favor "monochronic" or "polychronic" time orientations. Rate your tendencies for each item below using the following scale.

Rating Scale:

1 = Almost never   2 = Seldom
3 = Sometimes   4 = Usually
            5 = Almost always

___ **1.** I like to do one thing at a time.

___ **2.** I have a strong tendency to build lifetime relationships.

___ **3.** I concentrate on the job at hand.

___ **4.** I base the level of promptness on the particular relationship.

___ **5.** I take time commitments (deadlines, schedules) seriously.

___ **6.** I borrow and lend things often and easily.

___ **7.** I am committed to the job.

___ **8.** Intimacy with family and friends is more important than respecting their privacy.

___ **9.** I adhere closely to plans.

___ **10.** I put obligations to family and friends before work concerns.

___ **11.** I am concerned about not disturbing others (follow rules of privacy).

___ **12.** I change plans often and easily.

___ **13.** I emphasize promptness in meetings.

___ **14.** I am committed to people and human relationships.

___ **15.** I show great respect for private property (seldom borrow or lend).

___ **16.** I am highly distractible and frequently interrupt what I am doing.

___ **17.** I am comfortable with short-term relationships.

___ **18.** I like to do many things at once.

Scoring

To obtain your *monochronic time orientation* score, sum results for items 1, 3, 5, 7, 9, 11, 13, 15, 17. To obtain your *polychronic time orientation* score, sum results for items 2, 4, 6, 8, 10, 12, 14, 16, 18.

Interpretation

A person high in monochronic time orientation approaches time in a linear fashion with things dealt with one at a time in an orderly fashion. Time is viewed as a precious commodity, not to be wasted; this person values punctuality and promptness.

A person high in polychronic time orientation tends to do a number of things at once, intertwining them together in a dynamic process that considers changing circumstances. Commitments are viewed as objectives, but capable of adjustment when necessary.

Cultural differences in orientations toward time can be observed. Tendencies toward monochronic time orientation are common to North America and northern European cultures. Tendencies toward polychronic time orientation are common in cultures of the Middle East, Asia, and Latin America.

Source: Adapted from J. Ned Seelye and Alan Seelye-James. *Culture Clash* (Lincolnwood, IL: NTC Business Books, 1996).

ASSESSMENT 10

Entrepreneurship Orientation

Instructions

Answer the following questions.

1. What portion of your college expenses did you earn (or are you earning)?
(a) 50 percent or more
(b) less than 50 percent
(c) none

2. In college, your academic performance was/is
(a) above average.
(b) average.
(c) below average.

3. What is your basic reason for considering opening a business?
(a) I want to make money.
(b) I want to control my own destiny.
(c) I hate the frustration of working for someone else.

4. Which phrase best describes your attitude toward work?
(a) I can keep going as long as I need to; I don't mind working for something I want.
(b) I can work hard for a while, but when I've had enough, I quit.

(c) Hard work really doesn't get you anywhere.

5. How would you rate your organizing skills?
(a) superorganized
(b) above average
(c) average
(d) I do well to find half the things I look for.

6. You are primarily a(n)
(a) optimist.
(b) pessimist.
(c) neither.

7. You are faced with a challenging problem. As you work, you realize you are stuck. You will most likely
(a) give up.
(b) ask for help.
(c) keep plugging; you'll figure it out.

8. You are playing a game with a group of friends. You are most interested in
(a) winning.
(b) playing well.
(c) making sure that everyone has a good time.
(d) cheating as much as possible.

9. How would you describe your feelings toward failure?
(a) Fear of failure paralyzes me.
(b) Failure can be a good learning experience.
(c) Knowing that I might fail motivates me to work even harder.
(d) "Damn the torpedoes! Full speed ahead."

10. Which phrase best describes you?
(a) I need constant encouragement to get anything done.
(b) If someone gets me started, I can keep going.
(c) I am energetic and hardworking—a self-starter.

11. Which bet would you most likely accept?
(a) A wager on a dog race
(b) A wager on a racquetball game in which you play an opponent
(c) Neither. I never make wagers.

12. At the Kentucky Derby, you would bet on
(a) the 100-to-1 long shot.
(b) the odds-on favorite.
(c) the 3-to-1 shot.
(d) none of the above.

Scoring

Give yourself 10 points for each of the following answers: 1a, 2a, 3c, 4a, 5a, 6a, 7c, 8a, 9c, 10c, 11b, 12c; total the scores and enter the results here [I = ___]. Give yourself 8 points for each of the following answers:

3b, 8b, 9b; total the scores and enter the results here [II = ___]. Give yourself 6 points for each of the following answers; 2b, 5b; total the scores and enter the results here [III = ___]. Give yourself 5 points for this answer: 1b; enter the result here [IV = ___]. Give yourself 4 points for this answer: 5c; enter the result here [V = ___]. Give yourself 2 points for each of the following answers: 2c, 3a, 4b, 6c, 9d, 10b, 11a, 12b; total the scores and enter the results here [VI = ___]. Any other scores are worth 0 points. Total your summary scores for I + II + III + IV + V + VI and enter the result here [EP = ___].

Interpretation

This assessment offers an impression of your *entrepreneurial profile,* or EP. It compares your characteristics with those of typical entrepreneurs. Your instructor can provide further information on each question as well as some additional insights into the backgrounds of entrepreneurs. You may locate your EP score on the following grid.

100 + = Entrepreneur extraordinaire
80–99 = Entrepreneur
60–79 = Potential entrepreneur
 0–59 = Entrepreneur in the rough

Source: Instrument adapted from Norman M. Scarborough and Thomas W. Zimmerer, *Effective Small Business Management,* 3rd ed. (Columbus: Merrill, 1991), pp. 26–27. Used by permission.

ASSESSMENT 11

Your Intuitive Ability

Instructions

Complete this survey as quickly as you can. Be honest with yourself. For each question, select the response that most appeals to you.

1. When working on a project, do you prefer to
(a) be told what the problem is but be left free to decide how to solve it?
(b) get very clear instructions about how to go about solving the problem before you start?

2. When working on a project, do you prefer to work with colleagues who are
(a) realistic?
(b) imaginative?

3. Do you most admire people who are
(a) creative?
(b) careful?

4. Do the friends you choose tend to be
(a) serious and hard working?
(b) exciting and often emotional?

5. When you ask a colleague for advice on a problem you have, do you
(a) seldom or never get upset if he or she questions your basic assumptions?
(b) often get upset if he or she questions your basic assumptions?

6. When you start your day, do you
(a) seldom make or follow a specific plan?
(b) usually first make a plan to follow?

7. When working with numbers do you find that you
(a) seldom or never make factual errors?
(b) often make factual errors?

8. Do you find that you
(a) seldom daydream during the day and really don't enjoy doing so when you do it?
(b) frequently daydream during the day and enjoy doing so?

9. When working on a problem, do you
(a) prefer to follow the instructions or rules when they are given to you?
(b) often enjoy circumventing the instructions or rules when they are given to you?

10. When you are trying to put something together, do you prefer to have
(a) step-by-step written instructions on how to assemble the item?
(b) a picture of how the item is supposed to look once assembled?

11. Do you find that the person who irritates you *the most* is the one who appears to be
(a) disorganized?
(b) organized?

12. When an unexpected crisis comes up that you have to deal with, do you
(a) feel anxious about the situation?
(b) feel excited by the challenge of the situation?

Scoring

Total the number of "a" responses circled for questions 1, 3, 5, 6, 11; enter the score here [A = ___]. Total the number of "b" responses for questions 2, 4, 7, 8, 9, 10, 12; enter the score here [B = ___]. Add your "a" and "b" scores and enter the sum here [A + B = ___]. This is your *intuitive score.* The highest possible intuitive score is 12; the lowest is 0.

Interpretation

In his book *Intuition in Organizations* (Newbury Park, CA: Sage, 1989), pp. 10–11, Weston H. Agor states, "Traditional analytical techniques . . . are not as useful as they once were for guiding major decisions. . . . If you hope to be better prepared for tomorrow, then it only seems logical to pay some attention to the use and development of intuitive skills for decision making." Agor developed the preceding survey to help people assess their tendencies to use intuition in decision making. Your score offers a general impression of your strength in this area. It may also suggest a need to further develop your skill and comfort with more intuitive decision approaches.

Source: AIM Survey (El Paso, TX: ENFP Enterprises, 1989). Copyright ©1989 by Weston H. Agor. Used by permission.

ASSESSMENT 12

Assertiveness

Instructions

This instrument measures tendencies toward aggressive, passive, and assertive behaviors in work situations. For each statement below, decide which of the following answers best fits you.

1 = Never true
2 = Sometimes true
3 = Often true
4 = Always true

___ **1.** I respond with more modesty than I really feel when my work is complimented.

___ **2.** If people are rude, I will be rude right back.

3. Other people find me interesting.

4. I find it difficult to speak up in a group of strangers.

5. I don't mind using sarcasm if it helps me make a point.

6. I ask for a raise when I feel I really deserve it.

7. If others interrupt me when I am talking, I suffer in silence.

8. If people criticize my work, I find a way to make them back down.

9. I can express pride in my accomplishments without being boastful.

10. People take advantage of me.

11. I tell people what they want to hear if it helps me get what I want.

12. I find it easy to ask for help.

13. I lend things to others even when I don't really want to.

14. I win arguments by dominating the discussion.

15. I can express my true feelings to someone I really care for.

16. When I feel angry with other people, I bottle it up rather than express it.

17. When I criticize someone else's work, they get mad.

18. I feel confident in my ability to stand up for my rights.

Scoring

Obtain your scores as follows:

Aggressiveness tendency score—Add items 2, 5, 8, 11, 14, and 17
Passive tendency score—Add items 1, 4, 7, 10, 13, and 16
Assertiveness tendency score—Add items 3, 6, 9, 12, 15, and 18

Interpretation

The maximum score in any single area is 24. The minimum score is 6. Try to find someone who knows you well. Have this person complete the instrument also as it relates to you. Compare his or her impression of you with your own score. What is this telling you about your behavior tendencies in social situations?

_____

Source: From Douglas T. Hall, Donald D. Bowen, Roy J. Lewicki, and Francine S. Hall, *Experiences in Management and Organizational Behavior,* 2nd ed. (New York: Wiley, 1985). Used by permission.

ASSESSMENT 13

Time Management Profile

Instructions

Complete the following questionnaire by indicating "Y" (yes) or "N" (no) for each item. Force yourself to respond yes or no. Be frank and allow your responses to create an accurate picture of how you tend to respond to these kinds of situations.

1. When confronted with several items of similar urgency and importance, I tend to do the easiest one first.

2. I do the most important things during that part of the day when I know I perform best.

3. Most of the time I don't do things someone else can do; I delegate this type of work to others.

4. Even though meetings without a clear and useful purpose upset me, I put up with them.

___ **5.** I skim documents before reading them and don't complete any that offer a low return on my time investment.

___ **6.** I don't worry much if I don't accomplish at least one significant task each day.

___ **7.** I save the most trivial tasks for that time of day when my creative energy is lowest.

___ **8.** My workspace is neat and organized.

___ **9.** My office door is always "open"; I never work in complete privacy.

___ **10.** I schedule my time completely from start to finish every workday.

___ **11.** I don't like "to do" lists, preferring to respond to daily events as they occur.

___ **12.** I "block" a certain amount of time each day or week that is dedicated to high-priority activities.

Scoring

Count the number of "Y" responses to items 2, 3, 5, 7, 8, 12. [Enter that score here ___.] Count the number of "N" responses to items 1, 4, 6, 9, 10, 11. [Enter that score here ___.] Add together the two scores.

Interpretation

The higher the total score, the closer your behavior matches recommended time management guidelines. Reread those items where your response did not match the desired one. Why don't they match? Do you have reasons why your behavior in this instance should be different from the recommended time management guideline? Think about what you can do (and how easily it can be done) to adjust your behavior to be more consistent with these guidelines. For further reading, see Alan Lakein, *How to Control Your Time and Your Life* (New York: David McKay, no date), and William Oncken, *Managing Management Time* (Englewood Cliffs, NJ: Prentice Hall, 1984).

Source: Suggested by a discussion in Robert E. Quinn, Sue R. Faerman, Michael P. Thompson, and Michael R. McGrath, *Becoming a Master Manager: A Contemporary Framework* (New York: Wiley, 1990), pp. 75–76.

ASSESSMENT 14

Facts and Inferences

Preparation

Read the following report:

Often, when we listen or speak, we don't distinguish between statements of fact and those of inference. Yet there are great differences between the two. We create barriers to clear thinking when we treat inferences (guesses, opinions) as if they are facts. You may wish at this point to test your ability to distinguish facts from inferences by taking the accompanying fact-inference test based on those by Haney (1973).

Instructions

Carefully read the following report and the observations based on it. Indicate whether you think the observations are true, false, or doubtful on the basis of the information presented in the report. Write T if the observation is definitely true, F if the observation is definitely false, and ? if the observation may be either true or false. Judge each observation in order. Do not reread the observations after you have indicated your judgment, and do not change any of your answers.

A well-liked college instructor had just completed making up the final examinations and had turned off the lights in the office. Just then a tall, broad figure with dark glasses appeared and demanded the examination. The professor opened the drawer. Everything in the drawer was picked up, and the individual ran down the corridor. The president was notified immediately.

___ 1. The thief was tall, broad, and wore dark glasses.

___ 2. The professor turned off the lights.

___ 3. A tall figure demanded the examination.

___ 4. The examination was picked up by someone.

___ 5. The examination was picked up by the professor.

___ 6. A tall, broad figure appeared after the professor turned off the lights in the office.

___ 7. The man who opened the drawer was the professor.

___ 8. The professor ran down the corridor.

___ 9. The drawer was never actually opened.

___ 10. Three persons are referred to in this report.

When told to do so by your instructor, join a small work group. Now, help the group complete the same task by making a consensus decision on each item. Be sure to keep a separate record of the group's responses and your original individual responses.

Scoring

Your instructor will read the correct answers. Score both your individual and group responses.

Interpretation

To begin, ask yourself if there was a difference between your answers and those of the group for each item. If so, why? Why do you think people, individually or in groups, may answer these questions incorrectly? Good planning depends on good decision making by the people doing the planning. Being able to distinguish "facts" and understand one's "inferences" are important steps toward improving the planning process. Involving others to help do the same can frequently assist in this process.

_____

Source: Joseph A. Devito, *Messages: Building Interpersonal Communication Skills,* 3rd ed. (New York: HarperCollins, 1996), referencing William Haney, *Communicational Behavior: Text and Cases,* 3rd ed. (Homewood, IL: Irwin, 1973). Reprinted by permission.

ASSESSMENT 15

Empowering Others

Instructions

Think of times when you have been in charge of a group—this could be a full-time or part-time work situation, a student work group, or whatever. Complete the following questionnaire by recording how you feel about each statement according to this scale:

1 = Strongly disagree   2 = Disagree   3 = Neutral   4 = Agree   5 = Strongly agree

When in charge of a group, I find that:

___ 1. Most of the time other people are too inexperienced to do things, so I prefer to do them myself.

___ 2. It often takes more time to explain things to others than to just do them myself.

___ 3. Mistakes made by others are costly, so I don't assign much work to them.

____ **4.** Some things simply should not be delegated to others.

____ **5.** I often get quicker action by doing a job myself.

____ **6.** Many people are good only at very specific tasks and so can't be assigned additional responsibilities.

____ **7.** Many people are too busy to take on additional work.

____ **8.** Most people just aren't ready to handle additional responsibilities.

____ **9.** In my position, I should be entitled to make my own decisions.

Scoring

Total your responses: enter the score here [____].

Interpretation

This instrument gives an impression of your *willingness to delegate*. Possible scores range from 9 to 45. The higher your score, the more willing you appear to be to delegate to others. Willingness to delegate is an important managerial characteristic: It is essential if you—as a manager—are to "empower" others and give them opportunities to assume responsibility and exercise self-control in their work. With the growing importance of empowerment in the new workplace, your willingness to delegate is worth thinking about seriously. Be prepared to share your results and participate in general class discussion.

Source: Questionnaire adapted from L. Steinmetz and R. Todd, *First Line Management*, 4th ed. (Homewood, IL: BPI/Irwin, 1986), pp. 64–67. Used by permission.

ASSESSMENT 16

Turbulence Tolerance Test

Instructions

The following statements were made by a 37-year-old manager in a large, successful corporation. How would you like to have a job with these characteristics? Using the following scale, choose your response to the left of each statement.

0 = This feature would be very unpleasant for me.
1 = This feature would be somewhat unpleasant for me.
2 = I'd have no reaction to this feature one way or another.
3 = This would be enjoyable and acceptable most of the time.
4 = I would enjoy this very much; it's completely acceptable.

____ **1.** I regularly spend 30 to 40 percent of my time in meetings.

____ **2.** Eighteen months ago my job did not exist, and I have been essentially inventing it as I go along.

____ **3.** The responsibilities I either assume or am assigned consistently exceed the authority I have for discharging them.

____ **4.** At any given moment in my job, I have on the average about a dozen phone calls to be returned.

____ **5.** There seems to be very little relation in my job between the quality of my performance and my actual pay and fringe benefits.

____ **6.** About 2 weeks a year of formal management training is needed in my job just to stay current.

____ **7.** Because we have very effective equal employment opportunity (EEO) in my company and because it is thoroughly multinational, my job consistently brings me into close working contact at a professional level with people of many races, ethnic groups and nationalities, and of both sexes.

___ **8.** There is no objective way to measure my effectiveness.

___ **9.** I report to three different bosses for different aspects of my job, and each has an equal say in my performance appraisal.

___ **10.** On average about a third of my time is spent dealing with unexpected emergencies that force all scheduled work to be postponed.

___ **11.** When I have to have a meeting of the people who report to me, it takes my secretary most of a day to find a time when we are all available, and even then, I have yet to have a meeting where everyone is present for the entire meeting.

___ **12.** The college degree I earned in preparation for this type of work is now obsolete, and I probably should go back for another degree.

___ **13.** My job requires that I absorb 100–200 pages of technical materials per week.

___ **14.** I am out of town overnight at least 1 night per week.

___ **15.** My department is so interdependent with several other departments in the company that all distinctions about which departments are responsible for which tasks are quite arbitrary.

___ **16.** In about a year I will probably get a promotion to a job in another division that has most of these same characteristics.

___ **17.** During the period of my employment here, either the entire company or the division I worked in has been reorganized every year or so.

___ **18.** While there are several possible promotions I can see ahead of me, I have no real career path in an objective sense.

___ **19.** While there are several possible promotions I can see ahead of me, I think I have no realistic chance of getting to the top levels of the company.

___ **20.** While I have many ideas about how to make things work better, I have no direct influence on either the business policies or the personnel policies that govern my division.

___ **21.** My company has recently put in an "assessment center" where I and all other managers will be required to go through an extensive battery of psychological tests to assess our potential.

___ **22.** My company is a defendant in an antitrust suit, and if the case comes to trial, I will probably have to testify about some decisions that were made a few years ago.

___ **23.** Advanced computer and other electronic office technology is continually being introduced into my division, necessitating constant learning on my part.

___ **24.** The computer terminal and screen I have in my office can be monitored in my bosses' offices without my knowledge.

Scoring

Add up all of your scores and then divide the total by 24. This is your "Turbulence Tolerance Test" (TTT) score.

Interpretation

This instrument gives an impression of your tolerance for managing in turbulent times—something likely to characterize the world of work well into the new century. In general, the higher your TTT score, the more comfortable you seem to be with turbulence and change—a positive sign.

For comparison purposes, the average TTT scores for some 500 MBA students and young managers was 1.5–1.6. The test's author suggests TTT scores may be interpreted much like a grade point average in which 4.0 is a perfect "A". On this basis, a 1.5 is below a "C"! How did you do?

Source: Peter B. Vail, *Managing as a Performance Art: New Ideas for a World of Chaotic Change* (San Francisco: Jossey-Bass, 1989), pp. 8–9. Used by permission.

Organizational Design Preference

Instructions

In the margin near each item, write the number from the following scale that shows the extent to which the statement accurately describes your views.

5 = strongly agree
4 = agree somewhat
3 = undecided
2 = disagree somewhat
1 = strongly disagree

I prefer to work in an organization where

1. goals are defined by those in higher levels.

2. work methods and procedures are specified.

3. top management makes important decisions.

4. my loyalty counts as much as my ability to do the job.

5. clear lines of authority and responsibility are established.

6. top management is decisive and firm.

7. my career is pretty well planned out for me.

8. I can specialize.

9. my length of service is almost as important as my level of performance.

10. management is able to provide the information I need to do my job well.

11. a chain of command is well established.

12. rules and procedures are adhered to equally by everyone.

13. people accept the authority of a leader's position.

14. people are loyal to their boss.

15. people do as they have been instructed.

16. people clear things with their boss before going over his or her head.

Scoring

Total your scores for all questions. Enter the score here [___].

Interpretation

This assessment measures your preference for working in an organization designed along "organic" or "mechanistic" lines (see Chapter 11). The higher your score (above 64), the more comfortable you are with a mechanistic design; the lower your score (below 48), the more comfortable you are with an organic design. Scores between 48 and 64 can go either way. This organizational design preference represents an important issue in the new workplace. Indications are that today's organizations are taking on more and more organic characteristics. Presumably, those of us who work in them will need to be comfortable with such designs.

Source: John F. Veiga and John N. Yanouzas. *The Dynamics of Organization Theory: Gaining a Macro Perspective* (St. Paul, MN: West, 1979), pp. 158–60. Used by permission.

Are You Cosmopolitan?

Instructions

Answer the following questions.

1. You believe it is the right of the professional to make his or her own decisions about what is to be done on the job.
Strongly disagree 1 2 3 4 5 Strongly agree

2. You believe a professional should stay in an individual staff role regardless of the income sacrifice.
Strongly disagree 1 2 3 4 5 Strongly agree

3. You have no interest in moving up to a top administrative post.
Strongly disagree 1 2 3 4 5 Strongly agree

4. You believe that professionals are better evaluated by professional colleagues than by management.
Strongly disagree 1 2 3 4 5 Strongly agree

5. Your friends tend to be members of your profession.
Strongly disagree 1 2 3 4 5 Strongly agree

6. You would rather be known or get credit for your work outside rather than inside the company.
Strongly disagree 1 2 3 4 5 Strongly agree

7. You would feel better making a contribution to society than to your organization.
Strongly disagree 1 2 3 4 5 Strongly agree

8. Managers have no right to place time and cost schedules on professional contributors.
Strongly disagree 1 2 3 4 5 Strongly agree

Scoring

Add your score for each item to get a total score between 8 and 40.

Interpretation

A "cosmopolitan" identifies with the career profession, and a "local" identifies with the employing organization. A score of 30–40 suggests a "cosmopolitan" work orientation, 10–20 a "local" orientation, and 20–30 a "mixed" orientation.

Source: Developed from Joseph A. Raelin, *The Clash of Cultures, Managers and Professionals,* (Boston: Harvard Business School Press, 1986).

Performance Appraisal Assumptions

Instructions

In each of the following pairs of statements, check off the statement that best reflects your assumptions about performance evaluation.

Performance evaluation is

1. (a) a formal process that is done annually.
(b) an informal process done continuously.

2. (a) a process that is planned for subordinates.
(b) a process that is planned with subordinates.

3. (a) a required organizational procedure.
(b) a process done regardless of requirements.

4. (a) a time to evaluate subordinates' performance.

(b) a time for subordinates to evaluate their manager.

5. (a) a time to clarify standards.
(b) a time to clarify the subordinate's career needs.

6. (a) a time to confront poor performance.
(b) a time to express appreciation.

7. (a) an opportunity to clarify issues and provide direction and control.
(b) an opportunity to increase enthusiasm and commitment.

8. (a) only as good as the organization's forms.
(b) only as good as the manager's coaching skills.

Scoring

There is no formal scoring for this assessment, but there may be a pattern to your responses. Check them again.

Interpretation

In general, the "a" responses represent a more traditional approach to performance appraisal that emphasizes its *evaluation* function. This role largely puts the supervisor in the role of documenting a subordinate's performance for control and administrative purposes. The "b" responses represent a more progressive approach that includes a strong emphasis on the *counseling* or *development* role. Here, the supervisor is concerned with helping the subordinate do better and with learning from the subordinate what he or she needs to be able to do better. There is more of an element of reciprocity in this role. It is quite consistent with new directions and values emerging in today's organizations.

Source: Developed in part from Robert E. Quinn, Sue R. Faerman, Michael P. Thompson, and Michael R. McGrath, *Becoming a Master Manager: A Contemporary Framework* (New York: Wiley, 1990), p. 187. Used by permission.

ASSESSMENT 20

"T-P" Leadership Questionnaire

Instructions

The following items describe aspects of leadership behavior. Respond to each item according to the way you would most likely act if you were the leader of a work group. Circle whether you would most likely behave in the described way: always (A), frequently (F), occasionally (O), seldom (S), or never (N).

A F O S N **1.** I would most likely act as the spokesperson of the group.

A F O S N **2.** I would encourage overtime work.

A F O S N **3.** I would allow members complete freedom in their work.

A F O S N **4.** I would encourage the use of uniform procedures.

A F O S N **5.** I would permit the members to use their own judgment in solving problems.

A F O S N **6.** I would stress being ahead of competing groups.

A F O S N **7.** I would speak as a representative of the group.

A F O S N **8.** I would push members for greater effort.

A F O S N **9.** I would try out my ideas in the group.

A F O S N **10.** I would let the members do their work the way they think best.

A F O S N **11.** I would be working hard for a promotion.

A F O S N **12.** I would tolerate postponement and uncertainty.

A F O S N **13.** I would speak for the group if there were visitors present.

A F O S N **14.** I would keep the work moving at a rapid pace.

A F O S N **15.** I would turn the members loose on a job and let them go to it.

A F O S N **16.** I would settle conflicts when they occur in the group.

A F O S N **17.** I would get swamped by details.

A F O S N **18.** I would represent the group at outside meetings.

A F O S N **19.** I would be reluctant to allow the members any freedom of action.

A F O S N **20.** I would decide what should be done and how it should be done.

A F O S N **21.** I would push for increased performance.

A F O S N **22.** I would let some members have authority which I could otherwise keep.

A F O S N **23.** Things would usually turn out as I had predicted.

A F O S N **24.** I would allow the group a high degree of initiative.

A F O S N **25.** I would assign group members to particular tasks.

A F O S N **26.** I would be willing to make changes.

A F O S N **27.** I would ask the members to work harder.

A F O S N **28.** I would trust the group members to exercise good judgment.

A F O S N **29.** I would schedule the work to be done.

A F O S N **30.** I would refuse to explain my actions.

A F O S N **31.** I would persuade others that my ideas are to their advantage.

A F O S N **32.** I would permit the group to set its own pace.

A F O S N **33.** I would urge the group to beat its previous record.

A F O S N **34.** I would act without consulting the group.

A F O S N **35.** I would ask that group members follow standard rules and regulations.

Scoring/Interpretation

Score the instrument as follows.

a. Write a "1" next to each of the following items if you scored them as S (seldom) or N (never).
8, 12, 17, 18, 19, 30, 34, 35

b. Write a "1" next to each of the following items if you scored them as A (always) or F (frequently).
1, 2, 3, 4, 5, 6, 7, 9, 10, 11, 13, 14, 15, 16, 20, 21, 22, 23, 24, 25, 26, 27, 28, 29, 31, 32, 33

c. Circle the "1" scores for the following items, and then add them up to get your TOTAL "P" SCORE = ___.
3, 5, 8, 10, 15, 18, 19, 22, 23, 26, 28, 30, 32, 34, 35

d. Circle the "1" scores for the following items, and then add them up to get your TOTAL "T" SCORE = ___.
1, 2, 4, 6, 7, 9, 11, 12, 13, 14, 16, 17, 20, 21, 23, 25, 27, 29, 31, 33

e. Record your scores on the following graph to develop an indication of your tendencies toward task-oriented leadership, people-oriented leadership, and shared leadership. Mark your T and P scores on the appropriate lines, then draw a line between these two points to determine your shared leadership score.

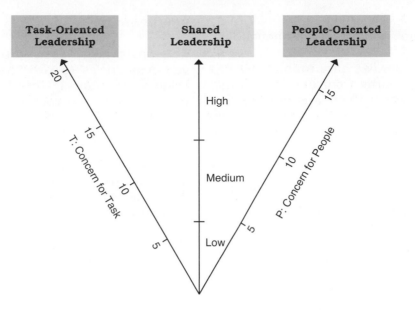

Source: Modified slightly from "T-P Leadership Questionnaire," University Associates, Inc., 1987. Used by permission.

"T-T" Leadership Style

Instructions

For each of the following 10 pairs of statements, divide five points between the two according to your beliefs or perceptions of yourself or according to which of the two statements characterizes you better. The 5 points may be divided between the a and b statements in any one of the following ways: 5 for a, 0 for b; 4 for a, 1 for b; 3 for a, 2 for b; 1 for a, 4 for b; 0 for a, 5 for b, but not equally (2-1/2) between the two. Weigh your choices between the two according to which one characterizes you or your beliefs better.

1. (a) As leader I have a primary mission of maintaining stability.
(b) As leader I have a primary mission of change.

2. (a) As leader I must cause events.
(b) As leader I must facilitate events.

3. (a) I am concerned that my followers are rewarded equitably for their work.
(b) I am concerned about what my followers want in life.

4. (a) My preference is to think long range: What might be.
(b) My preference is to think short range: What is realistic.

5. (a) As a leader I spend considerable energy in managing separate but related goals.
(b) As a leader I spend considerable energy in arousing hopes, expectations, and aspirations among my followers.

6. (a) Although not in a formal classroom sense, I believe that a significant part of my leadership is that of teacher.
(b) I believe that a significant part of my leadership is that of facilitator.

7. (a) As leader I must engage with followers on an equal level of morality.
(b) As leader I must represent a higher morality.

8. (a) I enjoy stimulating followers to want to do more.
(b) I enjoy rewarding followers for a job well done.

9. (a) Leadership should be practical.
(b) Leadership should be inspirational.

10. (a) What power I have to influence others comes primarily from my ability to get people to identify with me and my ideas.
(b) What power I have to influence others comes primarily from my status and position.

Scoring

Circle your points for items 1b, 2a, 3b, 4a, 5b, 6a, 7b, 8a, 9b, 10a and add up the total points you allocated to these items; enter the score here [T = ___]. Next, add up the total points given to the uncircled items 1a, 2b, 3a, 4b, 5a, 6b, 7a, 8b, 9a, 10b; enter the score here [T = ___].

Interpretation

This instrument gives an impression of your tendencies toward "transformational" leadership (your T score) and "transactional" leadership (your T score). You may want to refer to the discussion of these concepts in Chapter 13. Today, a lot of attention is being given to the transformational aspects of leadership—those personal qualities that inspire a sense of vision and the desire for extraordinary accomplishment in followers. The most successful leaders of the future will most likely be strong in both "T"s.

_____

Source: Questionnaire by W. Warner Burke, Ph.D. Used by permission.

- - - - - - - - - - **ASSESSMENT 22** - - - - - - - - - - - - - - - - -

Least-Preferred Coworker Scale

Instructions

Think of all the different people with whom you have ever worked—in jobs, in social clubs, in student projects, or whatever. Next think of the *one person* with whom you could work *least* well—that is, the person with whom you had the most difficulty getting a job done. This is the one person—a peer, boss, or subordinate—with whom you would least want to work. Describe this person by circling numbers at the appropriate points on each of the following pairs of bipolar adjectives. Work rapidly. There are no right or wrong answers.

Pleasant	8 7 6 5 4 3 2 1	Unpleasant
Friendly	8 7 6 5 4 3 2 1	Unfriendly
Rejecting	1 2 3 4 5 6 7 8	Accepting
Tense	1 2 3 4 5 6 7 8	Relaxed
Distant	1 2 3 4 5 6 7 8	Close
Cold	1 2 3 4 5 6 7 8	Warm
Supportive	8 7 6 5 4 3 2 1	Hostile
Boring	1 2 3 4 5 6 7 8	Interesting
Quarrelsome	1 2 3 4 5 6 7 8	Harmonious
Gloomy	1 2 3 4 5 6 7 8	Cheerful
Open	8 7 6 5 4 3 2 1	Guarded
Backbiting	1 2 3 4 5 6 7 8	Loyal
Untrustworthy	1 2 3 4 5 6 7 8	Trustworthy
Considerate	8 7 6 5 4 3 2 1	Inconsiderate
Nasty	1 2 3 4 5 6 7 8	Nice
Agreeable	8 7 6 5 4 3 2 1	Disagreeable
Insincere	1 2 3 4 5 6 7 8	Sincere
Kind	8 7 6 5 4 3 2 1	Unkind

Scoring

This is called the "least-preferred coworker scale" (LPC). Compute your LPC score by totaling all the numbers you circled; enter that score here [LPC = ___].

Interpretation

The LPC scale is used by Fred Fiedler to identify a person's dominant leadership style (see Chapter 13). Fiedler believes that this style is a relatively fixed part of one's personality and is therefore difficult to change. This leads Fiedler to his contingency views, which suggest that the key to leadership success is finding (or creating) good "matches" between style and situation. If your score is 73 or above, Fiedler considers you a "relationship-motivated" leader; if your score is 64 or below, he considers you a "task-motivated" leader. If your score is between 65 and 72, Fiedler leaves it up to you to determine which leadership style is most like yours.

Source: Fred E. Fiedler and Martin M. Chemers, *Improving Leadership Effectiveness: The Leader Match Concept,* 2nd ed. (New York: Wiley, 1984). Used by permission.

ASSESSMENT 23

Student Engagement Survey

Instructions

Use the following scale to indicate the degree to which you agree with the following statements:

1—No agreement
2—Weak agreement
3—Some agreement
4—Considerable agreement
5—Very strong agreement

1. Do you know what is expected of you in this course?

2. Do you have the resources and support you need to do your coursework correctly?

3. In this course, do you have the opportunity to do what you do best all the time?

4. In the last week, have you received recognition or praise for doing good work in this course?

5. Does your instructor seem to care about you as a person?

6. Is there someone in the course who encourages your development?

7. In this course, do your opinions seem to count?

8. Does the mission/purpose of the course make you feel your study is important?

9. Are other students in the course committed to doing quality work?

10. Do you have a best friend in the course?

11. In the last six sessions, has someone talked to you about your progress in the course?

12. In this course, have you had opportunities to learn and grow?

Scoring

Score the instrument by adding up all your responses. A score of 0–24 suggests you are "actively disengaged" from the learning experience; a score of 25–47 suggests you are "moderately engaged"; a score of 48–60 indicates you are "actively engaged."

Interpretation

This instrument suggests the degree to which you are actively "engaged" or "disengaged" from the learning opportunities of your course. It is a counterpart to a survey used by the Gallup Organization to measure the "engagement" of American workers. The Gallup results are surprising—indicating that up to 19 percent of U.S. workers are actively disengaged, with the annual lost productivity estimated at some $300 billion per year. One has to wonder: What are the costs of academic disengagement by students?

Source: This survey was developed from a set of "Gallup Engagement Questions" presented in John Thackray, "Feedback for Real," *Gallup Management Journal* (March 15, 2001), retrieved from http:// gmj.gallup.com/management_articles/employee_ engagement/article.asp?i = 238&p = 1, June 5, 2003; data reported from James K. Harter, "The Cost of Disengaged Workers," Gallup Poll (March 13, 2001).

ASSESSMENT 24

Job Design Choices

Instructions

People differ in what they like and dislike about their jobs. Listed below are 12 pairs of jobs. For each pair, indicate which job you would prefer. Assume that everything else about the jobs is the same—pay attention only to the characteristics actually listed for each pair of jobs. If you would prefer the job in Column A, indicate how much you prefer it by putting a check mark in a blank to the left of the Neutral point. If you prefer the job in Column B, check one of the blanks to the right of Neutral. Check the Neutral blank only if you find the two jobs equally attractive or unattractive. Try to use the Neutral blank sparingly.

Column A

Column B

1. A job that offers little or no challenge.

Strongly prefer A   Neutral   Strongly prefer B

A job that requires you to be completely isolated from coworkers.

2. A job that pays well.

Strongly prefer A   Neutral   Strongly prefer B

A job that allows considerable opportunity to be creative and innovative.

3. A job that often requires you to make important decisions.

Strongly prefer A   Neutral   Strongly prefer B

A job in which there are many pleasant people to work with.

4. A job with little security in a somewhat unstable organization.

Strongly prefer A   Neutral   Strongly prefer B

A job in which you have little or no opportunity to participate in decisions that affect your work.

5. A job in which greater responsibility is given to those who do the best work.

Strongly prefer A   Neutral   Strongly prefer B

A job in which greater responsibility is given to loyal employees who have the most *seniority.*

6. A job with a supervisor who sometimes is highly critical.

Strongly prefer A   Neutral   Strongly prefer B

A job that does not require you to use much of your talent.

7. A very routine job.

Strongly prefer A   Neutral   Strongly prefer B

A job in which your coworkers are not very friendly.

8. A job with a supervisor who respects you and treats you fairly.

Strongly prefer A   Neutral   Strongly prefer B

A job that provides constant opportunities for you to learn new and interesting things.

9. A job that gives you a real chance to develop yourself personally.

Strongly prefer A   Neutral   Strongly prefer B

A job with excellent vacation and fringe benefits.

10. A job in which there is a real chance you could be laid off.

Strongly prefer A   Neutral   Strongly prefer B

A job that offers very little chance to do challenging work.

11. A job that gives you little freedom and independence to do your work in the way you think best.

Strongly prefer A   Neutral   Strongly prefer B

A job with poor working conditions.

12. A job with very satisfying teamwork.

Strongly prefer A   Neutral   Strongly prefer B

A job that allows you to use your skills and abilities to the fullest extent.

Scoring/Interpretation

People differ in their need for psychological growth at work. This instrument measures the degree to which you seek growth-need satisfaction. Score your responses as follows:

For items 1, 2, 7, 8, 11, and 12 give yourself the following points for each item:

1	2	3	4	5	6	7
Strongly prefer A   Neutral   Strongly prefer B

For items 3, 4, 5, 6, 9, and 10 give yourself the following points for each item:

7	6	5	4	3	2	1
Strongly prefer A   Neutral   Strongly prefer B

Add up all of your scores and divide by 12 to find the average. If you score above 4.0, your desire for growth-need satisfaction through work tends to be high and you are likely to prefer an enriched job. If you score below 4.0, your desire for growth-need satisfaction through work tends to be low and you are likely to not be satisfied or motivated with an enriched job.

Source: Reprinted by permission from J. R. Hackman and G. R. Oldham, *The Job Diagnostic Survey: An Instrument for the Diagnosis of Jobs and the Evaluation of Job Redesign Projects, Technical Report 4* (New Haven, CT: Yale University, Department of Administrative Sciences, 1974).

Cognitive Style

Instructions

This assessment is designed to get an impression of your cognitive style, based on the work of psychologist Carl Jung. For each of the following 12 pairs, place a "1" next to the statement that best describes you. Do this for each pair even if the description you choose may not be perfect.

1. ___ (a) I prefer to learn from experience.
   ___ (b) I prefer to find meanings in facts and how they fit together.

2. ___ (a) I prefer to use my eyes, ears, and other senses to find out what is going on.
   ___ (b) I prefer to use imagination to come up with new ways to do things.

3. ___ (a) I prefer to use standard ways to deal with routine problems.
   ___ (b) I prefer to use novel ways to deal with new problems.

4. ___ (a) I prefer to learn from experience.
   ___ (b) I prefer to find meanings in facts and how they fit together.

5. ___ (a) I am patient with details but get impatient when they get complicated.
   ___ (b) I am impatient and jump to conclusions but am also creative, imaginative, and inventive.

6. ___ (a) I enjoy using skills already mastered more than learning new ones.
   ___ (b) I like learning new skills more than practicing old ones.

7. ___ (a) I prefer to decide things logically.
   ___ (b) I prefer to decide things based on feelings and values.

8. ___ (a) I like to be treated with justice and fairness.
   ___ (b) I like to be praised and to please other people.

9. ___ (a) I sometimes neglect or hurt other people's feelings without realizing it.

___ (b) I am aware of other people's feelings.

10. ___ (a) I give more attention to ideas and things than to human relationships.
    ___ (b) I can predict how others will feel.

11. ___ (a) I do not need harmony; arguments and conflicts don't bother me.
    ___ (b) I value harmony and get upset by arguments and conflicts.

12. ___ (a) I am often described as analytical, impersonal, unemotional, objective, critical, hard-nosed, rational.
    ___ (b) I am often described as sympathetic, people-oriented, unorganized, uncritical, understanding, ethical.

Scoring

Sum your scores as follows, and record them in the space provided. (Note that the Sensing and Feeling scores will be recorded as negatives.)

$(-\ \ )$ *Sensing (S Type)* $= 1a + 2a + 3a + 4a + 5a + 6a$

$(\ \ \ )$ *Intuitive (N Type)* $= 1b + 2b + 3b + 4b + 5b + 6b$

$(\ \ \ )$ *Thinking (T Type)* $= 7a + 8a + 9a + 10a + 11a + 12a$

$(-\ \ )$ *Feeling (F Type)* $= 7b + 8b + 9b + 10b + 11b + 12b$

Plot your scores on the following graph. Place an "X" at the point that indicates your suggested problem-solving style.

Interpretation

This assessment examines cognitive style through the contrast of personal tendencies toward information gathering (sensation vs. intuition) and information evaluation (feeling vs. thinking) in one's approach to problem solving. The result is a classification of four master cognitive styles, with the following characteristics. Read the descriptions and consider the implications of your suggested style, including how well you might work with persons whose styles are very different.

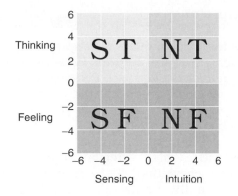

Sensation Thinkers: STs tend to emphasize the impersonal rather than the personal and take a realistic approach to problem solving. They like hard "facts," clear goals, certainty, and situations of high control.

Intuitive Thinkers: NTs are comfortable with abstraction and unstructured situations. They tend to be idealistic, prone toward intellectual and theoretical positions; they are logical and impersonal but also avoid details.

Intuitive Feelers: NFs prefer broad and global issues. They are insightful and tend to avoid details, being comfortable with intangibles; they value flexibility and human relationships.

Sensation Feelers: SFs tend to emphasize both analysis and human relations. They tend to be realistic and prefer facts; they are open communicators and sensitive to feelings and values.

Source: Developed from Donald Bowen, "Learning and Problem-Solving: You're Never Too Jung," in Donald D. Bowen, Roy J. Lewicki, Donald T. Hall, and Francine S. Hall, eds., *Experiences in Management and Organizational Behavior,* 4th ed. (New York: Wiley, 1997), pp. 7–13; and John W. Slocum, Jr., "Cognitive Style in Learning and Problem Solving," ibid., pp. 349–353.

ASSESSMENT 26

Internal/External Control

Instructions

Circle either "a" or "b" to indicate the item you most agree with in each pair of the following statements.

1. (a) Promotions are earned through hard work and persistence.
(b) Making a lot of money is largely a matter of breaks.

2. (a) Many times the reactions of teachers seem haphazard to me.
(b) In my experience I have noticed that there is usually a direct connection between how hard I study and the grades I get.

3. (a) The number of divorces indicates that more and more people are not trying to make their marriages work.
(b) Marriage is largely a gamble.

4. (a) It is silly to think that one can really change another person's basic attitudes.
(b) When I am right I can convince others.

5. (a) Getting promoted is really a matter of being a little luckier than the next guy.
(b) In our society an individual's future earning power is dependent on his or her ability.

6. (a) If one knows how to deal with people, they are really quite easily led.
(b) I have little influence over the way other people behave.

7. (a) In my case the grades I make are the results of my own efforts; luck has little or nothing to do with it.
(b) Sometimes I feel that I have little to do with the grades I get.

8. (a) People like me can change the course of world affairs if we make ourselves heard.
(b) It is only wishful thinking to believe that one can really influence what happens in society at large.

9. (a) Much of what happens to me is probably a matter of chance.
(b) I am the master of my fate.

10. (a) Getting along with people is a skill that must be practiced.
(b) It is almost impossible to figure out how to please some people.

Scoring

Give 1 point for 1b, 2a, 3a, 4b, 5b, 6a, 7a, 8a, 9b, 10a.

8–10 = high *internal* locus of control

6–7 = moderate *internal* locus of control

5 = mixed locus of control

3–4 = moderte *external* locus of control

Interpretation

This instrument offers an impression of your tendency toward *internal locus of control or external locus of control.* Persons with a high internal locus of control tend to believe they have control over their own destinies. They may be most responsive to opportunities for greater self-control in the workplace. Persons with a high external locus of control tend to believe that what happens to them is largely in the hands of external people or forces. They may be less comfortable with self-control and more responsive to external controls in the workplace.

Source: Instrument from Julian P. Rotter, "External Control and Internal Control," *Psychology Today* (June 1971), p. 42. Used by permission.

ASSESSMENT 27

Team Leader Skills

Instructions

Consider your experience in groups and work teams. Ask: "What skills do I bring to team leadership situations?" Then, complete the following inventory by rating yourself on each item using this scale.

1 = Almost Never
2 = Seldom
3 = Sometimes
4 = Usually
5 = Almost Always

1 2 3 4 5 **1.** I facilitate communications with and among team members between team meetings.

1 2 3 4 5 **2.** I provide feedback/coaching to individual team members on their performance.

1 2 3 4 5 **3.** I encourage creative and "out-of-the-box" thinking.

1 2 3 4 5 **4.** I continue to clarify stakeholder needs/expectations.

1 2 3 4 5 **5.** I keep team members' responsibilities and activities focused within the team's objectives and goals.

1 2 3 4 5 **6.** I organize and run effective and productive team meetings.

1 2 3 4 5 **7.** I demonstrate integrity and personal commitment.

1 2 3 4 5 **8.** I have excellent persuasive and influence skills.

1 2 3 4 5 **9.** I respect and leverage the team's cross-functional diversity.

1 2 3 4 5 **10.** I recognize and reward individual contributions to team performance.

1 2 3 4 5 **11.** I use the appropriate decision-making style for specific issues.

1 2 3 4 5 **12.** I facilitate and encourage border management with the team's key stakeholders.

1 2 3 4 5 **13.** I ensure that the team meets its team commitments.

1 2 3 4 5 **14.** I bring team issues and problems to the team's attention and focus on constructive problem solving.

1 2 3 4 5 **15.** I provide a clear vision and direction for the team.

Scoring

The inventory measures seven dimensions of team leadership. Add your scores for the items listed next to each dimension below to get an indication of your potential strengths and weaknesses.

1,9	Building the Team
2,10	Developing People
3,11	Team Problem Solving/Decision Making
4,12	Stakeholder Relations
5,13	Team Performance
6,14	Team Process
7,8,15	Providing Personal Leadership

Interpretation

The higher the score, the more confident you are on the particular skill and leadership capability. When considering the score, ask yourself if others would rate you the same way. Consider giving this inventory to people who have worked with you in teams and have them rate you. Compare the results to your self-assessment. Also, remember that it is doubtful that any one team leader is capable of exhibiting all the skills listed above. More and more, organizations are emphasizing "top-management teams" that blend a variety of skills, rather than depending on the vision of the single, heroic leader figure. As long as the necessary leadership skills are represented within the membership, it is more likely that the team will be healthy and achieve high performance. Of course, the more skills you bring with you to team leadership situations, the better.

Source: Developed from Lynda McDermott, Nolan Brawley, and William Waite, *World Class Teams: Working across Borders* (New York: Wiley, 1998).

ASSESSMENT 28

Conflict Management Styles

Instructions

Think of how you behave in conflict situations in which your wishes differ from those of one or more persons. In the space to the left of each of the following statements, write the number from the following scale that indicates how likely you are to respond that way in a conflict situation.

1 = very unlikely   2 = unlikely
3 = likely   4 = very likely

____ **1.** I am usually firm in pursuing my goals.

____ **2.** I try to win my position.

____ **3.** I give up some points in exchange for others.

____ **4.** I feel that differences are not always worth worrying about.

____ **5.** I try to find a position that is intermediate between the other person's and mine.

____ **6.** In approaching negotiations, I try to be considerate of the other person's wishes.

____ **7.** I try to show the logic and benefits of my positions.

___ 8. I always lean toward a direct discussion of the problem.

___ 9. I try to find a fair combination of gains and losses for both of us.

___ 10. I attempt to work through our differences immediately.

___ 11. I try to avoid creating unpleasantness for myself.

___ 12. I try to soothe the other person's feelings and preserve our relationship.

___ 13. I attempt to get all concerns and issues immediately out in the open.

___ 14. I sometimes avoid taking positions that would create controversy.

___ 15. I try not to hurt others' feelings.

Scoring

Total your scores for items 1, 2, 7; enter that score here [*Competing* = ___]. Total your scores for items 8, 10, 13; enter that score here [*Collaborating* = ___]. Total your scores for items 3, 5, 9; enter that score here [*Compromising* = ___]. Total your scores for items 4, 11, 14; enter that score here [*Avoiding* = ___]. Total your scores for items 6, 12, 15; enter that score here [*Accommodating* = ___].

Interpretation

Each of the scores above corresponds to one of the conflict management styles discussed in Chapter 16. Research indicates that each style has a role to play in management but that the best overall conflict management approach is collaboration; only it can lead to problem solving and true conflict resolution. You should consider any patterns that may be evident in your scores and think about how to best handle the conflict situations in which you become involved.

_____

Source: Adapted from Thomas-Kilmann, *Conflict Mode Instrument.* Copyright © 1974, Xicom, Inc., Tuxedo, NY 10987. Used by permission.

ASSESSMENT 29

Stress Self-Test

Instructions

Complete the following questionnaire. Circle the number that best represents your tendency to behave on each bipolar dimension.

Am casual about appointments	1 2 3 4 5 6 7 8	Am never late
Am not competitive	1 2 3 4 5 6 7 8	Am very competitive
Never feel rushed	1 2 3 4 5 6 7 8	Always feel rushed
Take things one at a time	1 2 3 4 5 6 7 8	Try to do many things at once
Do things slowly	1 2 3 4 5 6 7 8	Do things fast
Express feelings	1 2 3 4 5 6 7 8	"Sit on" feelings
Have many interests	1 2 3 4 5 6 7 8	Have few interests but work

Scoring

Total the numbers circled for all items, and multiply this by 3; enter the result here [___].

Interpretation

This scale is designed to measure your personality tendency toward Type A or Type B behaviors. As described in Chapter 18, a Type A personality is associated with high stress. Persons who are Type A tend to bring stress on themselves even in situations where others are relatively stress free. This is an important characteristic to be able to identify in yourself and in others.

Points	Personality
120+	A+
106 – 119	A
100 – 105	A–
90 – 99	B+
below 90	B

Source: Adapted from R. W. Bortner. "A Short Rating Scale as a Potential Measure of Type A Behavior," *Journal of Chronic Diseases*, vol. 22 (1966), pp. 87–91. Used by permission.

ASSESSMENT 30

Work-Life Balance

Instructions

Complete this inventory by circling the number that indicates the extent to which you agree or disagree with each of the following statements.

1. How much time do you spend on nonwork-related activities such as taking care of family, spending time with friends, participating in sports, enjoying leisure time?
Almost none/never   1 2 3 4 5   Very much/always

2. How often do family duties and nonwork responsibilities make you feel tired out?
Almost none/never   1 2 3 4 5   Very much/always

3. How often do you feel short of time for family-related and nonwork activities?
Almost none/never   1 2 3 4 5   Very much/always

4. How difficult is it for you to do everything you should as a family member and friend to others?
Almost none/never   1 2 3 4 5   Very much/always

5. I often feel that I am being run ragged, with not enough time in a day to do everything and do it well.
Completely disagree   1 2 3 4 5   Completely agree

6. I am given entirely too much work to do.
Strongly disagree   1   2   3   4   5   Strongly agree

7. How much conflict do you feel there is between the demands of your job and your family, and nonwork activities life?
Not at all/never   1   2   3   4   5   A lot/very often

8. How much does your job situation interfere with your family life?
Not at all/never   1   2   3   4   5   A lot/very often

9. How much does your family life and nonwork activities interfere with your job?
Not at all/never   1   2   3   4   5   A lot/very often
Submit Response Reset Fields

Scoring

1. Family Demand Score: Total items #1, #2, #3, #4 and divide by 4.

2. Work Demand Score: Total items #5, #6 and divide by 2.

3. Work-Family Conflict Score: Total items #7, #8, #9 and divide by 3.

Your responses to items 1–4 are totaled and divided by 4, giving you the Life Demand score. Your responses to items 5–6 are totaled and divided by 2, resulting in your Work Demand score. Responses to items 7–9 are summed and divided by 3, giving your Work-Life conflict score.

Interpretation

Compare yourself to these scores from a sample of Chinese and American workers.

	U.S.	Chinese	Your Scores
Life Demand	3.53	2.58	4
Work Demand	2.83	2.98	4
Work-Life Conflict	2.53	2.30	4.67

Are there any suprises in this comparison?

Work-life conflict is defined as "a form of interrole conflict in which the role pressures from the work and family nonwork domains are mutually noncompatible in some respect." Demands of one role make it difficult to satisfy demands of the others.

Source: Based on Nini Yang, Chao. D. Chen, Jaepil Choi, and Yimin Zou, "Sources of Work-Family Conflict: A Sino–U.S. Comparison of the Effects of Work and Family Demands," *Academy of Management Journal,* vol. 43, no. 1, pp. 113–123.

EXPERIENTIAL EXERCISES

My Best Manager

Preparation

Working alone, make a list of the *behavioral attributes* that describe the *best* manager you have ever worked for. This could be someone you worked for in a full-time or part-time job, summer job, volunteer job, student organization, or whatever. If you have trouble identifying an actual manager, make a list of behavioral attributes of the type of manager you would most like to work for in your next job.

Instructions

Form into groups as assigned by your instructor, or work with a nearby classmate.

Share your list of attributes and listen to the lists of others. Be sure to ask questions and make comments on items of special interest. Work together to create a master list that combines the unique attributes of the "best" managers experienced by members of your group. Have a spokesperson share that list with the rest of the class.

Source: Adapted from John R. Schermerhorn, Jr., James G. Hunt, and Richard N. Osborn, *Managing Organizational Behavior,* 3rd ed. (New York: Wiley, 1988), pp. 32–33. Used by permission.

What Managers Do

Preparation

Think about the questions that follow. Record your answers in the spaces provided.

1. How much of a typical manager's time would you expect to be allocated to these relationships? (total should = 100%)

___% of time working with
  subordinates
___% of time working with boss
___% of time working with peers and
  outsiders

2. How many hours per week does the average manager work? ___ hours

3. What amount of a manager's time is typically spent in the following activities? (total should = 100%)

___% in scheduled meetings
___% in unscheduled meetings
___% doing desk work
___% talking on the telephone
___% walking around the organization/
  work site

Instructions

Talk over your responses with a nearby classmate. Explore the similarities and differences in your answers. Be prepared to participate in a class discussion led by your instructor.

Defining Quality

Preparation

Write your definition of the word *quality* here. QUALITY =

Instructions

Form groups as assigned by your instructor. (1) Have each group member present a definition of the word *quality*. After everyone has presented, come up with a consensus definition of *quality*. That is, determine and write down one definition of the word with which every member can agree. (2) Next, have the group assume the position of top manager in each of the following organizations. Use the group's *quality* definition to state for each a *quality objective* that can guide the behavior of members in producing high-"quality" goods and/or services for customers or clients. Elect a spokesperson to share group results with the class as a whole.

Organizations:

a. A college of business administration

b. A community hospital

c. A retail sporting goods store

d. A fast-food franchise restaurant

e. A United States post office branch

f. A full-service bank branch

g. A student-apartment rental company

h. A used textbook store

i. A computer software firm

What Would the Classics Say?

Preparation

Consider this situation:

Six months into his new job, Bob, a laboratory worker, is performing just well enough to avoid being fired. When hired he was carefully selected and had the abilities required to do the job really well. At first Bob was enthusiastic about his new job, but now he isn't performing up to this high potential. Fran, his supervisor, is concerned and wonders what can be done to improve this situation.

Instructions

Assume the identify of one of the following persons: Frederick Taylor, Henri Fayol, Max Weber, Abraham Maslow, Chris Argyris. Assume that *as this person* you have been asked by Fran for advice on the management situation just described. Answer these questions as you think your assumed identity would respond. Be prepared to share your answers in class and to defend them based on the text's discussion of this person's views.

1. As *(your assumed identity)*, what are your basic beliefs about good management and organizational practices?

2. As *(your assumed identity)*, what do you perceive may be wrong in this situation that would account for Bob's low performance?

3. As *(your assumed identity)*, what could be done to improve Bob's future job performance?

The Great Management History Debate

Preparation

Consider the question "What is the best thing a manager can do to improve productivity in her or his work unit?"

Instructions

The instructor will assign you, individually or in a group, to one of the following positions. Complete the missing information as if you were the management theorist referred to. Be prepared to argue and defend your position before the class.

• Position A: "Mary Parker Follett offers the best insight into the question. Her advice would be to . . . " (advice to be filled in by you or the group).

• Position B: "Max Weber's ideal bureaucracy offers the best insight into the question. His advice would be to . . . " (advice to be filled in by you or the group).

• Position C: "Henri Fayol offers the best insight into the question. His advice would be to . . . " (advice to be filled in by you or the group).

• Position D: "The Hawthorne studies offer the best insight into the question. Elton Mayo's advice would be to . . . " (advice to be filled in by you or the group).

Confronting Ethical Dilemmas

Preparation

Read and indicate your response to each of the situations below.

a. Ron Jones, vice president of a large construction firm, receives in the mail a large envelope marked "personal." It contains a competitor's cost data for a project that both firms will be bidding on shortly. The data are accompanied by a note from one of Ron's subordinates saying: "This is the real thing!" Ron knows that the data could be a major advantage to his firm in preparing a bid that can win the contract. *What should he do?*

b. Kay Smith is one of your top-performing subordinates. She has shared with you her desire to apply for promotion to a new position just announced in a different division of the company. This will be tough on you since recent budget cuts mean you will be unable to replace anyone who leaves, at least for quite some time. Kay knows this and in all fairness has asked your permission before she submits an application. It is rumored that the son of a good friend of your boss is going to apply for the job. Although his credentials are less impressive than Kay's, the likelihood is that he will get the job if she doesn't apply. *What will you do?*

c. Marty Jose got caught in a bind. She was pleased to represent her firm as head of the local community development committee. In fact, her supervisor's boss once held this position and told her in a hallway conversation, "Do your best and give them every support possible." Going along with this, Marty agreed to pick up the bill (several hundred dollars) for a dinner meeting with local civic and business leaders. Shortly thereafter, her supervisor informed everyone that the entertainment budget was being eliminated in a cost-saving effort. Marty, not wanting to renege on supporting the community development committee, was able to charge the dinner bill to an advertising budget. Eventually, an internal auditor discovered the mistake and reported it to you, the personnel director. Marty is scheduled to meet with you in a few minutes. *What will you do?*

Instructions

Working alone, make the requested decisions in each of these incidents. Think carefully about your justification for the decision. Meet in a group assigned by your instructor. Share your decisions and justifications in each case with other group members. Listen to theirs. Try to reach a group consensus on what to do in each situation and why. Be prepared to share the group decisions, and any dissenting views, in general class discussion.

What Do You Value in Work?

Preparation

Rank order the nine items in terms of how important (9 = most important) they would be to you in a job.

How important is it to you to have a job that:
___ Is respected by other people?
___ Encourages continued development of knowledge and skills?
___ Provides job security?
___ Provides a feeling of accomplishment?
___ Provides the opportunity to earn a high income?
___ Is intellectually stimulating?
___ Rewards good performance with recognition?

___ Provides comfortable working conditions?

___ Permits advancement to high administrative responsibility?

Instructions

Form into groups as designated by your instructor. Within each group, the *men in the group* will meet to develop a consensus ranking of the items as they think the *women* in the Beutell and Brenner survey ranked them. The reasons for the rankings should be shared and discussed so they are clear to everyone. The *women in the group* should not participate in this ranking task. They should listen to the discussion and be prepared to comment later in class discussions. A spokesperson for the men in the group should share the group's rankings with the class.

Optional Instructions

Form into groups as designated by your instructor but with each group consisting entirely of men or women. Each group should meet and decide which of the work values members of the *opposite* sex ranked first in the Beutell and Brenner survey. Do this again for the work value ranked last. The reasons should be discussed, along with the reasons why each of the other values probably was not ranked first . . . or last. A spokesperson for each group should share group results with the rest of the class.

_____

Source: Adapted from Roy J. Lewicki, Donald D. Bowen, Douglas T. Hall, and Francine S. Hall, *Experiences in Management and Organizational Behavior,* 3rd ed. (New York: Wiley, 1988), pp.23–26. Used by permission.

- - - - - - - - - - - EXERCISE 8 -

Which Organizational Culture Fits You?

Instructions

Indicate which one of the following organizational cultures you feel most comfortable working in.

1. A culture that values talent, entrepreneurial activity, and performance over commitment; one that offers large financial rewards and individual recognition.

2. A culture that stresses loyalty, working for the good of the group, and getting to know the right people; one that believes in "generalists" and step-by-step career progress.

3. A culture that offers little job security; one that operates with a survival mentality, stresses that every individual can make a difference, and focuses attention on "turnaround" opportunities.

4. A culture that values long-term relationships; one that emphasizes systematic career development, regular training, and advancement based on gaining functional expertise.

Interpretation

These labels identify the four different cultures: 1 = "the baseball team," 2 = "the club," 3 = "the fortress," and 4 = "the academy."

Discuss results in work groups assigned by your instructor. To some extent, your future career success may depend on working for an organization in which there is a good fit between you and the prevailing corporate culture. This exercise can help you learn how to recognize various cultures, evaluate how well they can serve your needs, and recognize how they may change with time. A risk taker, for example, may be out of place in a "club" but fit right in with a "baseball team." Someone who wants to seek opportunities wherever they may occur may be out of place in an "academy" but fit right in with a "fortress."

_____

Source: Developed from Carol Hymowitz, "Which Corporate Culture Fits You?" *Wall Street Journal* (July 17, 1989), p. B1.

Beating the Time Wasters

Preparation

1. Make a list of all the things you need to do tomorrow. Prioritize each item in terms of *how important it is to create outcomes that you can really value.* Use this classification scheme:

(A) Most important, top priority

(B) Important, not top priority

(C) Least important, low priority

Look again at all activities you have classified as B. Reclassify any that are really A's or C's. Look at your list of A's. Reclassify any that are really B's or C's. Double-check to make sure you are comfortable with your list of C's.

2. Make a list of all the "time wasters" that often interfere with your ability to accomplish everything you want to on any given day.

Instructions

Form into groups as assigned by the instructor. Have all group members share their lists and their priority classifications. Members should politely "challenge" each other's classifications to make sure that only truly "high-priority" items receive an A rating. They might also suggest that some C items are of such little consequence that they might not be worth doing at all. After each member of the group revises his or her "to do" list based on this advice, go back and discuss the time wasters identified by group members. Develop a master list of time wasters and what to do about them. Have a group spokesperson be prepared to share discussion highlights and tips on beating common time wasters with the rest of the class.

Source: Developed from Roy J. Lewicki, Donald D. Bowen, Douglas T. Hall, and Francine S. Hall, *Experiences in Management and Organizational Behavior*, 3rd ed. (New York: Wiley, 1988), pp. 314–16.

Personal Career Planning

Preparation

Complete the following three activities, and bring the results to class. Your work should be in a written form suitable for your instructor's review.

Step 1: *Strengths and Weaknesses Inventory* Different occupations require special talents, abilities, and skills if people are to excel in their work. Each of us, you included, has a repertoire of existing strengths and weaknesses that are "raw materials" we presently offer a potential employer. Of course, actions can (and should!) be taken over time to further develop current strengths and to turn weaknesses into strengths. Make a list identifying your most important strengths and weaknesses at the moment in relation to the career direction you are most likely to pursue upon graduation. Place a * next to each item you consider most important to address in your courses and student activities *before* graduation.

Step 2. *Five-Year Career Objectives* Make a list of three to five career objectives that are appropriate given your list of personal strengths and weaknesses. Limit these objectiveness to ones that can be accomplished within 5 years of graduation.

Step 3. *Five-Year Career Action Plans* Write a specific action plan for accomplishing each of the five objectives. State exactly what you will do, and by when, in order to meet each objective. If you will need special support or assistance, identify it *and* state how you will obtain it. Remember, an outside observer should be able to read your action plan for each objective and end up feeling confident that (a) he or she knows exactly what you are going to do and (b) why.

Instructions

Form into groups as assigned by the instructor. Share your career-planning analysis with the group; listen to those of others. Participate in a discussion that examines any common patterns and major differences among group members. Take advantage of any opportunities to gather feedback and advice from others. Have one group member be prepared to summarize the group discussion for the class as a whole. Await further class discussion led by the instructor.

Source: Developed in part from Roy J. Lewicki, Donald D. Bowen, Douglas T. Hall, and Francine S. Hall, *Experiences in Management and Organizational Behavior,* 3rd ed. (New York: Wiley, 1988), pp. 261–67. Used by permission.

EXERCISE 11

Decision-Making Biases

Instructions

How good are you at avoiding potential decision-making biases? Test yourself by answering the following questions:

1. Which is riskier:
(a) driving a car on a 400-mile trip?
(b) flying on a 400-mile commercial airline flight?

2. Are there more words in the English language:
(a) that begin with *r*?
(b) that have *r* as the third letter?

3. Mark is finishing his MBA at a prestigious university. He is very interested in the arts and at one time considered a career as a musician. Is Mark more likely to take a job:
(a) in the management of the arts?
(b) with a management consulting firm?

4. You are about to hire a new central-region sales director for the fifth time this year. You predict that the next director should work out reasonably well since the last four were "lemons" and the odds favor hiring at least one good sales director in five tries. Is this thinking
(a) correct?
(b) incorrect?

5. A newly hired engineer for a computer firm in the Boston metropolitan area has 4 years' experience and good all-round qualifications. When asked to estimate the starting salary for this employee, a chemist with very little knowledge about the profession or industry guessed an annual salary of $35,000. What is your estimate?
$ ___ per year

Scoring

Your instructor will provide answers and explanations for the assessment questions.

Interpretation

Each of the preceding questions examines your tendency to use a different judgmental heuristic. In his book *Judgment in Managerial Decision Making,* 3rd ed. (New York: Wiley, 1994), pp. 6–7, Max Bazerman calls these heuristics "simplifying strategies, or rules of thumb" used in making decisions. He states, "In general, heuristics are helpful, but their use can sometimes lead to severe errors. . . . If we can make managers aware of the potential adverse impacts of using heuristics, they can then decide when and where to use them." This assessment offers an initial insight into your use of such heuristics. An informed decision maker understands the heuristics, is able to recognize when they appear, and eliminates any that may inappropriately bias decision making.

Test yourself further. Write next to each item the name of the judgmental heuristic that you think applies (see Chapter 7).

Source: Incidents from Max H. Bazerman, *Judgment in Managerial Decision Making,* 3rd ed. (New York: Wiley, 1994), pp. 13–14. Used by permission.

Strategic Scenarios

Preparation

In today's turbulent environments, it is no longer safe to assume that an organization that was highly successful yesterday will continue to be so tomorrow—or that it will even be in existence. Changing times exact the best from strategic planners. Think about the situations currently facing the following well-known organizations. Think, too, about the futures they may face.

McDonald's
Apple Computer
Yahoo.com
L.L. Bean
Delta Airlines
National Public Radio

Instructions

Form into groups as assigned by your instructor. Choose one or more organizations from the prior list (as assigned) and answer for the organization the following questions:

1. What in the future might seriously threaten the success, perhaps the very existence, of this organization? (As a group, develop at least three such *future scenarios.*)

2. Estimate the probability (0–100 percent) of each future scenario occurring.

3. Develop a strategy for each scenario that will enable the organization to successfully deal with it.

Thoroughly discuss these questions within the group and arrive at your best possible consensus answers. Be prepared to share and defend your answers in general class discussion.

Source: Suggested by an exercise in John F. Veiga and John N. Yanouzas, *The Dynamics of Organization Theory: Gaining a Macro Perspective* (St. Paul, MN: West, 1979), pp. 69–71.

The MBO Contract

Listed below are performance objectives from an MBO contract for a plant manager.

a. To increase deliveries to 98% of all scheduled delivery dates

b. To reduce waste and spoilage to 3% of all raw materials used

c. To reduce lost time due to accidents to 100 work days/year

d. To reduce operating cost to 10% below budget

e. To install a quality-control system at a cost of less than $53,000

f. To improve production scheduling and increase machine utilization time to 95% capacity

g. To complete a management development program this year

h. To teach a community college course in human resource management

1. Study this MBO contract. In the margin write one of the following symbols to identify each objective as an improvement, maintenance, or personal development objective.

  I = Improvement objective
  M = Maintenance objective
  P = Personal development objective

2. Assume that this MBO contract was actually developed and implemented under the following circumstances. After each statement, write "yes" if the statement reflects proper MBO procedures and write "no" if it reflects poor MBO procedures.
(a) The president drafted the eight objectives and submitted them to Atkins for review.
(b) The president and Atkins thoroughly discussed the eight objectives in proposal form before they were finalized.
(c) The president and Atkins scheduled a meeting in 6 months to review Atkins's progress on the objectives.
(d) The president didn't discuss the objectives with Atkins again until the scheduled meeting was held.
(e) The president told Atkins his annual raise would depend entirely on the extent to which these objectives were achieved.

3. Share and discuss your responses to parts 1 and 2 of the exercise with a nearby classmate. Reconcile any differences of opinion by referring back to the chapter discussion of MBO. Await further class discussion.

EXERCISE 14

The Future Workplace

Instructions

Form groups as assigned by the instructor. Brainstorm to develop a master list of the major characteristics you expect to find in the future workplace in the year 2020. Use this list as background for completing the following tasks:

1. Write a one-paragraph description of what the typical "Workplace 2020 *manager's*" workday will be like.

2. Draw a "picture" representing what the "Workplace 2020 organization" will look like.

  Choose a spokesperson to share your results with the class as a whole *and* explain their implications for the class members.

EXERCISE 15

Dots and Squares Puzzle

1. Shown here is a collection of 16 dots. Study the figure to determine how many "squares" can be created by connecting the dots.

2. Draw as many squares as you can find in the figure while making sure a dot is at every corner of every square. Count the squares and write this number in the margin to the right of the figure.

3. Share your results with those of a classmate sitting nearby. Indicate the location of squares missed by either one of you.

4. Based on this discussion, redraw your figure to show the maximum number of possible squares. Count them and write this number to the left of the figure.

5. Await further class discussion led by your instructor.

Leading Through Participation

Preparation

Read each of the following vignettes. Write in the margin whether you think the leader should handle the situation with an individual decision (I), consultative decision (C), or group decision (G).

Vignette I

You are a general supervisor in charge of a large team laying an oil pipeline. It is now necessary to estimate your expected rate of progress in order to schedule material deliveries to the next field site. You know the nature of the terrain you will be traveling and have the historical data needed to compute the mean and variance in the rate of speed over the type of terrain. Given these two variables, it is a simple matter to calculate the earliest and latest times at which materials and support facilities will be needed at the next site. It is important that your estimate be reasonably accurate; underestimates result in idle supervisors and workers, and overestimates result in materials being tied up for a period of time before they are to be used. Progress has been good, and your five supervisors along with the other members of the gang stand to receive substantial bonuses if the project is completed ahead of schedule.

Vignette II

You are supervising the work of 12 engineers. Their formal training and work experience are very similar, permitting you to use them interchangeably on projects. Yesterday, your manager informed you that a request had been received from an overseas affiliate for four engineers to go abroad on extended loan for a period of 6 to 8 months. He argued and you agreed that for a number of reasons this request should be filled from your group. All your engineers are capable of handling this assignment, and from the standpoint of present and future projects there is no particular reason that any one should be retained over any other. The problem is complicated by the fact that the overseas assignment is in what is generally regarded in the company as an undesirable location.

Vignette III

You are the head of a staff unit reporting to the vice president of finance. He has asked you to provide a report on the firm's current portfolio including recommendations for changes in the *selection criteria* currently employed. Doubts have been raised about the efficiency of the existing system in the current market conditions, and there is considerable dissatisfaction with prevailing rates of return. You plan to write the report, but at the moment you are quite perplexed about the approach to take. Your own specialty is the bond market, and it is clear to you that a detailed knowledge of the equity market, which you lack, would greatly enhance the value of the report. Fortunately, four members of your staff are specialists in different segments of the equity market. Together, they possess a vast amount of knowledge about the intricacies of investment. However, they seldom agree on the best way to achieve anything when it comes to the stock market. Whereas they are obviously conscientious as well as knowledgeable, they have major differences when it comes to investment philosophy and strategy. The report is due in 6 weeks, You have already begun to familiarize yourself with the firm's current portfolio and have been provided by management with a specific set of constraints that any portfolio must satisfy. Your immediate problem is to come up with some alternatives to the firm's present practices and select the most promising ones for detailed analysis in your report.

Vignette IV

You are on the division manager's staff and work on a wide variety of problems of both an administrative and technical nature. You have been given the assignment of developing a universal method to be used in each of the five plants in the division for manually reading equipment registers, recording the readings, and transmitting the scoring to a centralized information system. All plants are located in a relatively small geographical region. Until now there has been a high error rate in the reading and/or transmittal of the data. Some locations have considerably higher error rates than others, and the methods used to record and transmit the data vary between plants. It is probable, therefore, that part of the error variance is a function of specific local conditions rather than anything else, and this will complicate the establishment of any system common to all plants. You have the information on error rates but no information on the local practices that generate these errors or on the local conditions that necessitate the different practices. Everyone would benefit from an improvement in the quality of the data because it is used in a number of important decisions. Your contacts with the plants are through the quality control supervisors responsible for collecting the data. They are a conscientious group committed to doing their jobs well but are highly sensitive to interference on the part of higher management in their own operations. Any solution that does not receive the active support of the various plant supervisors is unlikely to reduce the error rate significantly.

Instructions

Form groups as assigned by the instructor. Share you choices with other group members and try to achieve a consensus on how the leader should best handle each situation. Refer back to the discussion of the Vroom–Jago "leader-participation" theory presented in Chapter 13. Analyze each vignette according to their ideas. Do you come to any different conclusions? If so, why? Nominate a spokesperson to share your results in general class discussion.

Source: Victor H. Vroom and Arthur G. Jago, *The New Leadership* (Englewood Cliffs, NJ: Prentice Hall, 1988). Used by permission.

EXERCISE 17

Work vs. Family — You Be the Judge

1. Read the following situation.

Joanna, a single parent, was hired to work 8:15 A.M. to 5:30 P.M. weekdays selling computers for a firm. Her employer extended her workday until 10 P.M. weekdays and from 8:15 A.M. to 5:30 P.M. on Saturdays. Joanna refused to work the extra hours, saying that she had a six-year-old son and that so many work hours would lead to neglect. The employer said this was a special request during a difficult period and that all employees needed to share in helping out during the "crunch." Still refusing to work the extra hours, Joanna was fired. She sued the employer.

2. You be the judge in this case. Take an individual position on the following questions:

Should Joanna be allowed to work only the hours agreed to when she was hired? Or is the employer correct in asking all employees, regardless of family status, to work the extra hours? Why?

3. Form into groups as assigned by the instructor. Share your responses to the questions and try to develop a group consensus. Be sure to have a rationale for the position the group adopts. Appoint a spokesperson who can share results with the class. Be prepared to participate in open class discussion.

Source: This case scenario is from Sue Shellenbarger, "Employees Challenge Policies on Family and Get Hard Lessons," *Wall Street Journal* (December 17, 1997), p. B1.

Compensation and Benefits Debate

Preparation

Consider the following quotations.

On compensation: "A basic rule of thumb should be:pay at least as much, and perhaps a bit more, in base wage or salary than what competitors are offering."

On benefits: "When benefits are attractive or at least adequate, the organization is in a better position to employ highly qualified people."

Instructions

Form groups as assigned by the instructor. Each will be given *either* one of the preceding position statements *or* one of the following alternatives.

On compensation: "Given the importance of controlling costs, organizations can benefit by paying as little as possible for labor."

On benefits: "Given the rising cost of health-care and other benefit programs and the increasing difficulty many organizations have staying in business, it is best to minimize paid benefits and let employees handle more of the cost on their own."

Each group should prepare to debate a counterpoint group on its assigned position. After time is allocated to prepare for the debate, each group will present its opening positions. Each will then be allowed one rebuttal period to respond to the other group. General class discussion on the role of compensation and benefits in the modern organization will follow.

Sources and Uses of Power

Preparation

Consider *the way you have behaved* in each of the situations described below. They may be from a full-time or part-time job, student organization or class group, sports team, or whatever. If you do not have an experience of the type described, try to imagine yourself in one; think about how you would expect yourself to behave.

1. You needed to get a peer to do something you wanted that person to do but were worried he or she didn't want to do it.

2. You needed to get a subordinate to do something you wanted her or him to do but were worried the subordinate didn't want to do it.

3. You needed to get your boss to do something you wanted him or her to do but were worried the boss didn't want to do it.

Instructions

Form into groups as assigned by the instructor. Start with situation 1 and have all members of the group share their approaches. Determine what specific sources of power (see Chapter 13) were used. Note any patterns in group members' responses. Discuss what is required to be successful in this situation. Do the same for situations 2 and 3. Note any special differences in how situations 1, 2, and 3 should be or could be handled. Choose a spokesperson to share results in general class discussion.

After Meeting/Project Review

After participating in a meeting or a group project, complete the following assessment.

1. How satisfied are *you* with the outcome of the meeting project?

   Not at all   Totally
   satisfied   satisfied
      1   2   3   4   5   6   7

2. How do you think *other members of the meeting/project group would rate you* in terms of your *influence* on what took place?

   No   Very high
   influence   influence
      1   2   3   4   5   6   7

3. In your opinion, how *ethical* is any decision that was reached.

   Highly   Highly
   unethical   ethical
      1   2   3   4   5   6   7

4. To what extent did you feel *"pushed into"* going along with the decision.

   Not pushed
      into it   Very pushed
      at all   into it
      1   2   3   4   5   6   7

5. How *committed* are *you* to the agreements reached?

   Not at all   Highly
   committed   committed
      1   2   3   4   5   6   7

6. Did you understand what was expected of you as a member of the meeting or project group?

   Not at all   Perfectly
   clear   clear
      1   2   3   4   5   6   7

7. Were participants in the meeting/project group discussions listening to each other?

   Never   Always
      1   2   3   4   5   6   7

8. Were participants in the meeting/project group discussions honest and open in communicating with one another?

   Never   Always
      1   2   3   4   5   6   7

9. Was the meeting/project completed efficiently?

   Not at all   Very much
      1   2   3   4   5   6   7

10. Was the outcome of the meeting/project something that you felt proud to be a part of?

    Not   Very
    at all   much
       1   2   3   4   5   6   7

Instructions

In groups (actual meeting/project group or as assigned by the instructor) share results and discuss their implications (a) for you, and (b) for the effectiveness of meetings and group project work in general.

Source: Developed from Roy J. Lewicki, Donald D. Bowen, Douglas T. Hall, and Francine S. Hall, *Experiences in Management and Organizational Behavior,* 4th ed. (New York: Wiley, 1997), pp. 195–197.

Why Do We Work?

Preparation

Read the following "ancient story."

In days of old a wandering youth happened upon a group of men working in a quarry. Stopping by the first man, he said, "What are you doing?" The worker grimaced and groaned as he replied, "I am trying to shape this stone, and it is backbreaking work." Moving to the next man, he repeated the question. This man showed little emotion as he answered, "I am shaping a stone for a building." Moving to the third man, our traveler heard him singing as he worked. "What are you doing?" asked the youth. "I am helping to build a cathedral," the man proudly replied.

Instructions

In groups assigned by your instructor, discuss this short story. Ask and answer the question: "What are the lessons of this ancient story for (a) workers and (b) managers of today?" Ask members of the group to role-play each of the stonecutters, respectively, while they answer a second question asked by the youth: "Why are you working?" Have someone in the group be prepared to report and share the group's responses with the class as a whole.

_____

Source: Developed from Brian Dumaine, "Why Do We Work," *Fortune* (December 26, 1994), pp. 196–204.

The Case of the Contingency Workforce

Preparation

Part-time and contingency work is a rising percentage of the total employment in the United States. Go to the library and read about the current use of part-time and contingency workers in business and industry. Ideally, go to the Internet, enter a government database, and locate some current statistics on the size of the contingent labor force, the proportion that is self-employed and part-time, and the proportion of part-timers who are voluntary and involuntary.

Instructions

In your assigned work group, pool the available information on the contingency workforce. Discuss the information. Discuss one another's viewpoints on the subject as well as its personal and social implications. Be prepared to participate in a classroom "dialogue session" in which your group will be asked to role-play one of the following positions:

a. Vice president for human resources of a large discount retailer hiring contingency workers.

b. Owner of a local specialty music shop hiring contingency workers.

c. Recent graduate of your college or university working as a contingency employee at the discount retailer in (a).

d. Single parent with two children in elementary school, working as a contingency employee of the music shop in (b).

The question to be answered by the (a) and (b) groups is "What does the contingency workforce mean to me?" The question to be answered by the (c) and (d) groups is "What does being a contingency worker mean to me?"

The "Best" Job Design

Preparation

Use the left-hand column to rank the following job characteristics in the order most important *to you* (1 = highest to 10 = lowest). Then use the right-hand column to rank them in the order in which you think they are most important *to others*.

___ Variety of tasks ___
___ Performance feedback ___
___ Autonomy/freedom in work ___
___ Working on a team ___
___ Having responsibility
___ Making friends on the job ___
___ Doing all of a job, not part ___
___ Importance of job to others ___
___ Having resources to do well ___
___ Flexible work schedule ___

Instructions

Form work groups as assigned by your instructor. Share your rankings with other group members. Discuss where you have different individual preferences and where your impressions differ from the preferences of others. Are there any major patterns in your group—for either the "personal" or the "other" rankings? Develop group consensus rankings for each column. Designate a spokesperson to share the group rankings and results of any discussion with the rest of the class.

Source: Developed from John M. Ivancevich and Michael T. Matteson, *Organizational Behavior and Management*, 2nd ed. (Homewood, IL: BPI/Irwin, 1990), p. 500. Used by permission.

Upward Appraisal

Instructions

Form into work groups as assigned by the instructor. The instructor will then leave the room. As a group, complete the following tasks:

1. Within each group create a master list of comments, problems, issues, and concerns about the course experience to data that members would like to communicate with the instructor.

2. Select one person from the group to act as spokesperson and give your feedback to the instructor when he or she returns to the classroom.

3. The spokespersons from each group should meet to decide how the room should be physically arranged (placement of tables, chairs, etc.) for the feedback session. This should allow the spokespersons and instructor to communicate while they are being observed by other class members.

4. While the spokespersons are meeting, members remaining in the groups should discuss what they expect to observe during the feedback session.

5. The classroom should be rearranged. The instructor should be invited in.

6. Spokespersons should deliver feedback to the instructor while observers make notes.

7. After the feedback session is complete, the instructor will call on observers for comments, ask the spokespersons for their reactions, and engage the class in general discussion about the exercise and its implications.

Source: Developed from Eugene Owens, "Upward Appraisal: An Exercise in Subordinate's Critique of Superior's Performance," *Exchange: The Organizational Behavior Teaching Journal*, vol. 3 (1978), pp. 41–42.

How to Give, and Take, Criticism

Preparation

The "criticism session" may well be the toughest test of a manager's communication skills. Picture Setting 1—you and a subordinate meeting to review a problem with the subordinate's performance. Now picture Setting 2—you and your boss meeting to review a problem with *your* performance. Both situations require communication skills in giving and receiving feedback. Even the most experienced person can have difficulty, and the situations can end as futile gripe sessions that cause hard feelings. The question is "How can such 'criticism sessions' be handled in a positive manner that encourages improved performance . . . and good feelings?"

Instructions

Form into groups as assigned by the instructor. Focus on either Setting 1 or Setting 2, or both as also assigned by the instructor. First, answer the question from the perspective assigned. Second, develop a series of action guidelines that could best be used to handle situations of this type. Third, prepare and present a mini-management training session to demonstrate the (a) unsuccessful and (b) successful use of these guidelines.

If time permits, outside of class prepare a more extensive management training session that includes a videotape demonstration of your assigned criticism setting being handled first poorly and then very well. Support the videotape with additional written handouts and an oral presentation to help your classmates better understand the communication skills needed to successfully give and take criticism in work settings.

Lost at Sea

Consider This Situation

You are adrift on a private yacht in the South Pacific when a fire of unknown origin destroys the yacht and most of its contents. You and a small group of survivors are now in a large raft with oars. Your location is unclear, but you estimate that you are about 1,000 miles south-southwest of the nearest land. One person has just found in her pockets 5 $1 bills and a packet of matches. Everyone else's pockets are empty. The items at the right are available to you on the raft.

Instructions

1. *Working alone*, rank in Column **A** the 15 items in order of their importance to your survival ("1" is most important and "15" is least important).

	A	B	C
Sextant	___	___	___
Shaving mirror	___	___	___
5 gallons water	___	___	___
Mosquito netting	___	___	___
1 survival meal	___	___	___
Maps of Pacific Ocean	___	___	___
Flotable seat cushion	___	___	___
2 gallons oil-gas mix	___	___	___
Small transistor radio	___	___	___
Shark repellent	___	___	___
20 square feet black plastic	___	___	___
1 quart 20-proof rum	___	___	___
15 feet nylon rope	___	___	___
24 chocolate bars	___	___	___
Fishing kit	___	___	___

2. *Working in an assigned group*, arrive at a "team" ranking of the 15 items and record this ranking in Column **B.** Appoint one person as group spokesperson to report your group rankings to the class.

3. *Do not write in Column* **C** *until further in-structions are provided by your instructor.*

Source: Adapted from "Lost at Sea: A Consensus-Seeking Task," in *The 1975 Handbook for Group Facilitators.* Used with permission of University Associates, Inc.

EXERCISE 27

Work Team Dynamics

Preparation

Think about your course work group, a work group you are involved in for another course, or any other group suggested by the instructor. Indicate how often each of the following statements accurately reflects your experience in the group. Use this scale:

1 = Always 2 = Frequently 3 = Sometimes
4 = Never

____ **1.** My ideas get a fair hearing.

____ **2.** I am encouraged to give innovative ideas and take risks.

____ **3.** Diverse opinions within the group are encouraged.

____ **4.** I have all the responsibility I want.

____ **5.** There is a lot of favoritism shown in the group.

____ **6.** Members trust one another to do their assigned work.

____ **7.** The group sets high standards of performance excellence.

____ **8.** People share and change jobs a lot in the group.

____ **9.** You can make mistakes and learn from them in this group.

____ **10.** This group has good operating rules.

Instructions

Form groups as assigned by your instructor. Ideally, this will be the group you have just rated. Have all group members share their ratings, and make one master rating for the group as a whole. Circle the items over which there are the biggest differences of opinion. Discuss those items and try to find out why they exist. In general, the better a group scores on this instrument, the higher its creative potential. If everyone has rated the same group, make a list of the five most important things members can do to improve its operations in the future. Nominate a spokesperson to summarize the group discussion for the class as a whole.

Source: Adapted from William Dyer, *Team Building,* 2nd ed. (Reading, MA: Addison Wesley, 1987), pp. 123–125.

EXERCISE 28

Feedback and Assertiveness

Preparation

Indicate the degree of discomfort you would feel in each situation below by circling the appropriate number:

1. high discomfort
2. some discomfort
3. undecided
4. very little discomfort
5. no discomfort

1 2 3 4 5   **1.** Telling an employee who is also a friend that she or he must stop coming to work late.

1 2 3 4 5 **2.** Talking to an employee about his or her performance on the job.

1 2 3 4 5 **3.** Asking an employee if she or he has any comments about your rating of her or his performance.

1 2 3 4 5 **4.** Telling an employee who has problems in dealing with other employees that he or she should do something about it.

1 2 3 4 5 **5.** Responding to an employee who is upset over your rating of his or her performance.

1 2 3 4 5 **6.** An employee's becoming emotional and defensive when you tell her or him about mistakes on the job.

1 2 3 4 5 **7.** Giving a rating that indicates improvement is needed to an employee who has failed to meet minimum requirements of the job.

1 2 3 4 5 **8.** Letting a subordinate talk during an appraisal interview.

1 2 3 4 5 **9.** An employee's challenging you to justify your evaluation in the middle of an appraisal interview.

1 2 3 4 5 **10.** Recommending that an employee be discharged.

1 2 3 4 5 **11.** Telling an employee that you are uncomfortable with the role of having to judge his or her performance.

1 2 3 4 5 **12.** Telling an employee that her or his performance can be improved.

1 2 3 4 5 **13.** Telling an employee that you will not tolerate his or her taking extended coffee breaks.

1 2 3 4 5 **14.** Telling an employee that you will not tolerate her or his making personal telephone calls on company time.

Instructions

Form three-person teams as assigned by the instructor. Identify the 3 behaviors with which they indicate the most discomfort. Then each team member should practice performing these behaviors with another member, while the third member acts as an observer. Be direct, but try to perform the behavior in an appropriate way. Listen to feedback from the observer and try the behaviors again, perhaps with different members of the group. When finished, discuss the exercise overall. Be prepared to participate in further class discussion.

Source: Feedback questionnaire is from Judith R. Gordon, *A Diagnostic Approach to Organizational Behavior,* 3rd ed. (Boston: Allyn & Bacon, 1991), p. 298. Used by permission.

- - - - - - **EXERCISE 29** - - - - - - - - - - - - - - - - - - -

Creative Solutions

Instructions

Complete these five tasks while working alone. Be prepared to present and explain your responses in class.

1. Divide the following shape into four pieces of exactly the same size.

2. Without lifting your pencil from the paper, draw no more than four lines that cross through all of the following dots.

3. Draw the design for a machine that will turn the pages of your textbook so you can eat a snack while studying.

4. Why would a wheelbarrow ever be designed this way?

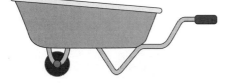

5. Turn the following into words.

(a) ___ program

(b) r\e\a\d\i\n\g

(c) ECNALG

(d)   j
      u
   yousme
      t

(e) stand
    i

Optional Instructions

After working alone, share your responses with a nearby classmate or with a group. See if you can develop different and/or better solutions based on this exchange of ideas.

_____

Source: Ideas 2 and 5 found in Russell L. Ackoff, *The Art of Problem Solving* (New York: Wiley, 1978); ideas 1 and 4 found in Edward De Bono, *Lateral Thinking: Creativity Step by Step* (New York: Harper & Row, 1970); source for 5 is unknown.

EXERCISE 30

Force-Field Analysis

1. Form into your class discussion groups.

2. Review the concept of force-field analysis—the consideration of forces driving in support of a planned change and forces resisting the change.

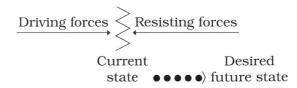

3. Use this force-field analysis worksheet in the assignment:

List of Driving Forces (those supporting the change)

_____
_____ . . . list as many as you can think of

List of Resisting Forces (those working against the change)

_____
_____ . . . list as many as you can think of

4. Apply force-field analysis and make your lists of driving and resisting forces for one of the following situations:

(a) Due to rapid advances in web-based computer technologies, the possibility exists that the course you are presently taking could be in part offered online. This would mean a reduction in the number of required class sessions but an increase in students' responsibility for completing learning activities and assignments through computer mediation.

(b) A new owner has just taken over a small walk-in-and-buy-by-the-slice pizza shop in a college town. There are presently eight employees, three of whom are full-time and five of whom are part-timers. The shop is presently open seven days a week from 10:30 A.M. to 10:30 P.M. each day. The new owner believes there is a market niche available for late-night pizza and would like to stay open each night until 2 A.M.

(c) A situation assigned by the instructor.

5. Choose the three driving forces that are most significant to the proposed change. For each force develop ideas on how it could be further increased or mobilized in support of the change.

6. Choose the three resisting forces that are most significant to the proposed change. For each force develop ideas on how it could be reduced or turned into a driving force.

7. Be prepared to participate in a class discussion led by the instructor.

STUDENT
PORTFOLIO
BUILDER

What Is a Student Portfolio?

A *Student Portfolio* is a paper or electronic collection of documents that summarizes your academic and personal accomplishments in a way that effectively communicates with academic advisors and potential employers.[1] At a minimum, your portfolio should include the following:

Minimum components of a Student Portfolio

- an up-to-date professional résumé.
- a listing of courses in your major and related fields of study.
- a listing of your extra-curricular activities and any leadership positions.
- documentation of your career readiness in terms of skills and learning outcomes.

The purpose of a Student Portfolio is twofold—academic assessment and career readiness.

1. *Academic Assessment Goal* The Student Portfolio serves as an ongoing academic assessment tool that documents your learning and academic accomplishments. As you progress through a curriculum, the portfolio depicts the progress you are making in acquiring the skills and competencies necessary to be successful in lifelong career pursuits. Over time, your portfolio will become increasingly sophisticated in the range and depth of learning and accomplishments that are documented. A well-prepared Student Portfolio is a very effective way of summarizing your academic achievements in consultation with both faculty advisors and professors.

2. *Career Readiness Goal* The Student Portfolio serves as an important means of communicating your résumé and credentials to potential employers, as you search for both internship and full-time job opportunities. The portfolio is an effective career tool that offers value far beyond the standard résumé. Potential employers can readily examine multiple aspects of your accomplishments and skill sets in order to make a desired match. A professional and complete portfolio allows potential employers to easily review your background and range of skills and capabilities. It may convey your potential to a much greater depth and with a more positive impression than a traditional résumé. There is no doubt that a professional and substantive portfolio can help set you apart from the competition and attract the interest of employers.

Planning Your Student Portfolio

Your Student Portfolio should document, in a progressive and clear manner, your credentials and academic work. As you progress through the curriculum in your major and supplementary fields of study, the portfolio should be refined and materials added to display your most up-to-date skills, competencies, and accomplishments. Use of the *Management 8/e* Skill and Outcome Assessment Framework, described shortly, will help you to do this. At my university we ask students to utilize the

---

[1] The value and use of Student Portfolios are described by David S. Chappell and John R. Schermerhorn, Jr., in "Using Electronic Student Portfolios in Management Education: A Stakeholder Perspective," *Journal of Management Education*, vol. 23 (1999), pp. 651–62; and, "Electronic Student Portfolios in Management Education" in Robert deFelippi and Charles Wrankel (eds.), *Educating Managers with Tomorrow's Technology* (Information Age Press, 2003), pp. 101–129.

portfolio to store their coursework. We then review it periodically with them as part of our department's formal advising and outcome assessment programs.

The closer you get to graduation, the entries in your portfolio should become more specific to your job and career goals. In this way, your portfolio becomes a dynamic and evolving career tool with value far beyond that of the standard résumé. I recommend that my students plan their portfolios to serve two immediate career purposes: (1) obtain a professional internship for the junior/senior year period, and (2) obtain their initial full-time job after graduation. A typical student of ours begins his or her portfolio as a sophomore and then refines and adds to it throughout the program of study.

Résumé Writing Guide

The first thing that should go into your Student Portfolio is a professional résumé. Don't worry about how sophisticated or complete it is at first. The important things are to (1) get it started and (2) continue to build it as your experience grows. You will be surprised at how complete it will become with systematic attention and a personal commitment to take full advantage of the professional development opportunities available to you.

The following example should help get you started. It shows both a professional format and the types of things that can and should be included. I have also annotated the sample to show how an internship recruiter or potential employer might respond when reading the résumé for the first time. Wouldn't you like to have such positive reactions to the accomplishments and experiences documented in your résumé?

Interview Preparation Guide

You will know that your Student Portfolio was worthwhile and successful when it helps you land a preferred internship or your first-choice job. But the portfolio only helps get you to the point of a formal interview. The next step is doing well in it. In order to prepare for this step in the recruiting process, consider the following tips on job interviewing.[2]

- *Research the organization* — Make sure you read their recent literature, including annual reports, scan current news reports, and examine the industry and their major competitors.

- *Prepare to answer common interview questions* — Sample questions include: What do you really want to do in life? What do you consider your greatest strengths and weaknesses? How can you immediately contribute to our organization? Why did you choose your college or university? What are your interests outside of work? What was your most rewarding college experience? How would one of your professors describe you? What do you see yourself doing five years from now?

- *Dress for success* — Remember that impressions count, and first impressions often count the most. If you aren't sure what to wear or how to look, get advice from your professors and from career counselors at your college or university.

---

[2] This section and the tips were recommended by my colleague Dr. Robert Lenie Holbrook of Ohio University.

Résumé Sample

Note: The annotations indicate positive reactions by a prospective employer to the information being provided.

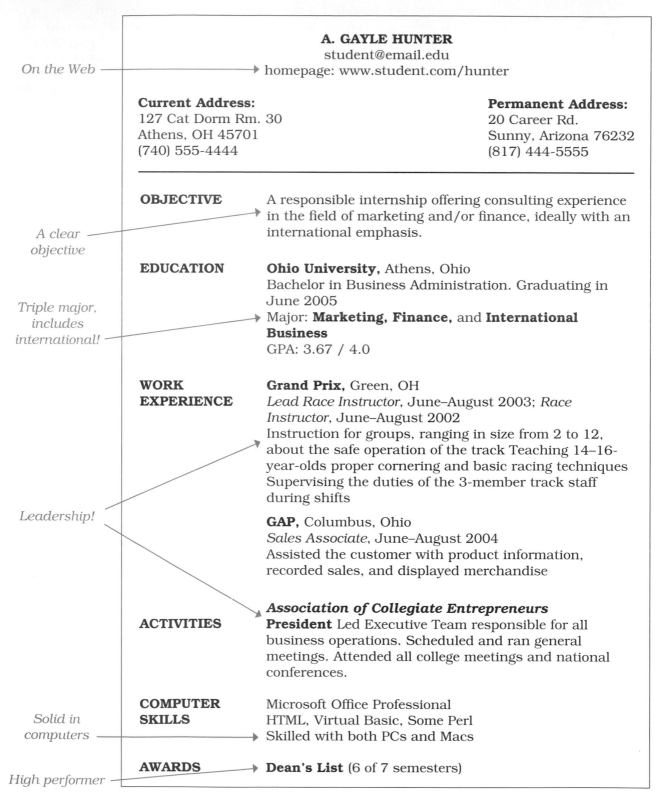

A. GAYLE HUNTER
student@email.edu
homepage: www.student.com/hunter

On the Web

Current Address:
127 Cat Dorm Rm. 30
Athens, OH 45701
(740) 555-4444

Permanent Address:
20 Career Rd.
Sunny, Arizona 76232
(817) 444-5555

OBJECTIVE

A responsible internship offering consulting experience in the field of marketing and/or finance, ideally with an international emphasis.

A clear objective

EDUCATION

Ohio University, Athens, Ohio
Bachelor in Business Administration. Graduating in June 2005
Major: **Marketing, Finance,** and **International Business**
GPA: 3.67 / 4.0

Triple major, includes international!

WORK EXPERIENCE

Grand Prix, Green, OH
Lead Race Instructor, June–August 2003; *Race Instructor*, June–August 2002
Instruction for groups, ranging in size from 2 to 12, about the safe operation of the track Teaching 14–16-year-olds proper cornering and basic racing techniques
Supervising the duties of the 3-member track staff during shifts

GAP, Columbus, Ohio
Sales Associate, June–August 2004
Assisted the customer with product information, recorded sales, and displayed merchandise

Leadership!

ACTIVITIES

Association of Collegiate Entrepreneurs
President Led Executive Team responsible for all business operations. Scheduled and ran general meetings. Attended all college meetings and national conferences.

COMPUTER SKILLS

Microsoft Office Professional
HTML, Virtual Basic, Some Perl
Skilled with both PCs and Macs

Solid in computers

AWARDS

Dean's List (6 of 7 semesters)

High performer

- *Dine for success*—There are no interview "time-outs" for refreshments or meals. The interview is always on. Make sure that you know how to dine in the presence of others. If you don't, get help before the interview.

- *Follow-up*—After the interview, send a "thank you" letter, ideally no longer than a week later. In the letter be sure to mention specific things about the organization that are important/insightful to you, and take the opportunity to clarify again where and how you believe you would fit as a valuable employee. Be prompt in providing any additional information requested during the interview.

Skill and Outcome Assessment Framework

Skill and outcome assessment is an increasingly important part of management education. It allows you to document key academic accomplishments and career readiness for faculty review and for review by potential employers. Following guidelines of the AACSB, the International Association for Management Education, I suggest integrating into your portfolio specific documentation of your accomplishments in the following six areas of professional development.

Six components of the Skill and Outcome Assessment Framework

1. *Communication*—Demonstrates ability to share ideas and findings clearly in written and oral expression, and with technology utilization.

2. *Leadership*—Demonstrates ability to influence and support others to perform complex and ambiguous tasks.

3. *Teamwork*—Demonstrates ability to work effectively as a team member and as a team leader.

4. *Critical Thinking*—Demonstrates ability to gather and analyze information for creative problem solving.

5. *Ethics/Social Responsibility*—Demonstrates ability to make morally responsible choices and be a good citizen.

6. *Self-Management*—Demonstrates ability to evaluate oneself, modify behavior, and meet obligations.

7. *Professionalism*—Demonstrates ability to sustain a positive impression, instill confidence, and advance in a career.

The many learning resources and activities in this *Management Learning Workbook* — cases, projects, exercises, and self-assessments—relate to these skills and outcome assessment areas. There is no better time than the present to start participating in the learning experiences and documenting your results and accomplishments in your student portfolio.

Getting Started with Your *Student Portfolio*

The basic Student Portfolio consists of (1) a professional résumé and (2) a compendium of coursework samples that displays your career readiness skills and capabilities.

Communication - Demonstrates ability to share ideas and findings clearly in written and oral expression.

- Writing
- Oral presentation
- Giving and receiving feedback
- Technology utilization

Teamwork - Demonstrates ability to work effectively as a team member and a team leader.

- Team contribution
- Team leadership
- Conflict management
- Negotiation and consensus building

Self-Management - Demonstrates ability to evaluate oneself, modify behavior, and meet obligations.

- Ethical understanding/behavior
- Personal flexibility
- Tolerance for ambiguity
- Performance responsibility

Leading - Demonstrates ability to influence and support others to perform complex and ambiguous tasks.

- Diversity awareness
- Global awareness
- Project management
- Strategic leadership

Critical Thinking - Demonstrates ability to gather and analyze information for creative problem solving.

- Problem solving
- Judgment and decision making
- Information gathering/interpretation
- Creativity and innovation

Professionalism - Demonstrates ability to sustain a positive impression, instill confidence, and advance in a career.

- Personal presence
- Personal initiative
- Career management
- Unique "value added"

Ethics/Social Responsibility - Demonstrates ability to make morally responsible choices and be a good citizen.

- Personal integrity
- Ethical leadership
- Community building
- Service

Portfolio Format

The easiest way to organize a paper portfolio is with a three-ring binder. This binder should be professional in appearance and have an attractive cover page that clearly identifies it as your student portfolio. The binder should be indexed with dividers that allow a reader to easily browse the résumé and other materials to gain a complete view of your special credentials.

In today's age of information technology and electronic communication, it is also highly recommended that you develop an online or *electronic portfolio*. This format allows you to communicate easily and effectively through the Internet with employers offering potential internship and job placements. An online version of your student portfolio can be displayed either on your personal website or on one provided by your university. Once you have created an electronic portfolio, it is easy to maintain. It is also something that will impress reviewers and help set you apart from the competition. At the very least, the use of an electronic portfolio communicates to potential employers that you are a full participant in this age of information technology.

Career Development Plan — A Portfolio Project

A very good way to enhance your Student Portfolio is by completing the following project as part of your introductory management course, or on your own initiative. Called the "Career Development Plan," the objective of this project is to identify professional development opportunities that you can take advantage of while in college and to advance your personal career readiness.

Deliverable: Write and file in your Student Portfolio a two-part career development memorandum that is written in professional format and addressed to your instructor or to "prospective employer." The memorandum should do the following.

- *Part A.* Answer the question: "What are my personal strengths and weaknesses as a potential manager?"

    It is recommended that you utilize the *Management 8/e* Skill & Outcome Assessment Framework in structuring your analysis. It is also recommended that you support your answer in part by analysis of results from your work with a selection of experiential exercises and self-assessments from this workbook. You can also supplement the analysis with other relevant personal insights.

- *Part B.* Answer the question: "How can I best take advantage of opportunities remaining in my undergraduate experience to improve my managerial potential?"

    Make this answer as specific as possible. Describe a clear plan of action that encompasses the time available to you between now and graduation. This plan should include summer and intercession activities, as well as academic and extracurricular experiences. Your goal should be to build a résumé and complete portfolio that will best present you as a skilled and valuable candidate for the entry-level job that you would like in your chosen career field.

Evaluation: Your career development memorandum should be professional and error-free, and meet the highest standards of effective written communication. It should be sufficiently analytical in Part A to show serious consideration of your personal strengths and weaknesses in managerial potential at this point in time. It should be sufficiently detailed and in-depth in Part B so that you can objectively evaluate your progress step-by-step between now and graduation. Overall, it should be a career development plan you can be proud to formally include in your Student Portfolio. It should serve as a positive indicator of your professionalism.

Sample Portfolio Components

The following samples are taken from portfolios built by my students. They document a range of accomplishments and capabilities. As with the sample résumé presented earlier, I have shown them here with illustrative comments (written in red) that indicate how a prospective employer might react when reading them in print or viewing them online. As you look at these samples, ask: "How can I best display my course and academic accomplishments to document my learning and career readiness?"

Written Assignment in French

Second language skill!! →

La Conception de L'Amour Pendant toute L'Histoire

La conception de l'amour pendant toute l'histoire est tres interresant de voir. Pendant l'histoire, les formes de l'mouront ont change un peu, mais l'idee le plus de base reste la meme. Dans les ouvrages au XVIeme siecle, on peut trouver les idees de l'amour qui sont semblable a la conception de l'amour dans notre societe moderne. Avec un comparaison entre la poesie de Louise Labe et Ronsard au XVIeme siecle, et le film Indochine, que Regis Wargnier a realise a 1992, on peut voir la conception de l'amour pendant l'histoire.

International Virtual Teamwork Project

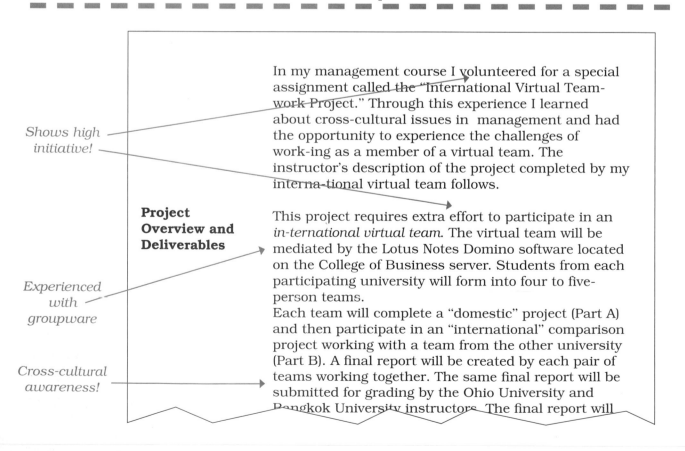

Shows high initiative!

In my management course I volunteered for a special assignment called the "International Virtual Team-work Project." Through this experience I learned about cross-cultural issues in management and had the opportunity to experience the challenges of work-ing as a member of a virtual team. The instructor's description of the project completed by my interna-tional virtual team follows.

Project Overview and Deliverables

Experienced with groupware

Cross-cultural awareness!

This project requires extra effort to participate in an *in-ternational virtual team*. The virtual team will be mediated by the Lotus Notes Domino software located on the College of Business server. Students from each participating university will form into four to five-person teams.

Each team will complete a "domestic" project (Part A) and then participate in an "international" comparison project working with a team from the other university (Part B). A final report will be created by each pair of teams working together. The same final report will be submitted for grading by the Ohio University and Bangkok University instructors. The final report will

CASES FOR CRITICAL THINKING

CASE 1

Apple Computer, Inc.: People and Design Create Apple's Future

Apple Computer paradoxically exists as both one of America's greatest successes and one of its greatest failures to achieve potential. It ignited the personal computer industry in the 1970s,[1] bringing such behemoths as IBM and Digital Equipment almost to their knees. At the same time, Apple is an example of opportunities lost. It represents a fascinating microcosm of American business as it continues to utilize its strengths while reinventing itself.

Corporate History [2]

The history of Apple Computer is a history of passion among its founders, employees, and loyal users. A pair of Stevens, who from an early age had an interest in electronics, started it. Steven Wozniak and Steven Jobs initially utilized their skills at Hewlett Packard and Atari, respectively. Wozniak constructed his first personal computer, the Apple I, and, along with Jobs, created Apple Computer on April 1, 1976.

However, it wasn't until 1977 and the introduction of the Apple II, with its plastic case and color graphics, that Apple really took off. The addition of a floppy drive in early 1978 added to the popularity of the new computer. By 1980, the release of the Apple III found the company with several thousand employees and Steven Jobs at the helm.

Early on, Apple Computer exhibited an extreme emphasis on new and innovative styling in its computer offerings. Jobs took a personal interest in the development of new products, including the Lisa and the legendary MacIntosh, with its graphical interface and 3.5-inch floppy disk.

The passion that Apple is so famous for was clearly evident in the design of the MacIntosh (Mac). Project teams worked around the clock to develop the machine and its graphical user interface (GUI) operating system (Mac OS), based loosely on a design developed by the Xerox Palo Alto Research Center. The use of graphical icons to create simplified user commands was immensely popular.

When IBM entered the personal computer market, Jobs recognized the threat posed and realized that it was time for Apple to "grow up" and be run in a more business-like fashion. In early 1983, he persuaded John Sculley, then president of Pepsi-Cola, to join Apple as president. The two men clashed almost from the start, with Sculley eventually ousting Jobs from the company.

The launch of the Mac, with its increased speed from a Motorola chip and its expandability, reinvigorated Apple's sales once again. In tandem with the LaserWriter, the first affordable PostScript laser printer for the Mac, and Pagemaker, one of the first desktop publishing programs, the Mac was an ideal solution for inexpensive publishing.

However, by the 1990s IBM PCs and clones were saturating the personal computer market. In addition, Microsoft launched Windows 3.0, a greatly improved version of the Wintel operating system for use on IBM PCs and clones. While in 1991 Apple had contemplated licensing its Mac operating system to other computer manufacturers and making it run on Intel-based machines, the idea was nixed by then chief operating officer (COO) Michael Spindler.

Innovative Design to the Rescue

Apple continued to rely on innovative design to remain competitive. In the 1990s, Apple introduced a very popular notebook computer line, along with the unsuccessful Newton personal digital assistant. Sculley, having lost interest in the day-to-day operations of Apple, was eventually forced out and replaced with Michael Spindler.

Spindler oversaw a number of innovations, including the PowerMac family, the first Macs to be based on the PowerPC chip, an extremely fast processor that was co-developed with IBM and Motorola. The PowerPC processor allowed Macs to compete with, and in many cases surpass, the speed of Intel's newer processors. In addition, Apple finally licensed its operating system to a number of Mac-cloners, but never in significant numbers.

After a difficult time in the mid-1990s, Spindler was replaced with Gil Amelio, the former president of National Semiconductor. This set the stage for one of the most famous returns in corporate history.

Jobs's Return

After leaving Apple, Steven Jobs started NeXT computer, an advanced personal computer with a sleek, innovative design. However, with its proprietary software, the device never gained a large following. Jobs then co-founded Pixar computer-animation studios in the late 1980s. It co-produced a number of movies with Walt Disney Studios, including the popular *Toy Story*.[3]

In late 1996, Apple announced the purchase of NeXT and Jobs returned to Apple in an unofficial capacity as advisor to the president. However, when Gil Amelio resigned, Jobs accepted the role of "interim CEO" (i CEO) of Apple Computer and wasted no time in making his return felt.

Jobs announced an alliance with Apple's former rival, Microsoft. In exchange for $150 million in Apple stock, Microsoft and Apple would have a five-year patent cross-license for their graphical interface operating systems. He revoked licenses allowing the production of Mac clones and started offering Macs over the Web through the Apple Store.

In addition to many new product offerings, Jobs introduced the iMac, with a revolutionary see-through design that has proved popular among consumers. This was followed shortly by the iBook, a similar-type portable computer. Apple once again was viewed as an industry innovator, with its revolutionary designs and innovations.[4]

Unfortunately, Apple remains a relatively small player in the computer industry. While its products are wildly popular among a dedicated set of users, it still commands only a little over 5 percent of the total computer market. It remains locked in constant boom-or-bust cycles, dependent on its ability to turn out a stream of new product hits.

What Does the Future Hold?

Apple is faced with a stark reality: Can it continue to offer both hardware and software solutions in a rapidly changing technology environment? Its early decision to keep its technology proprietary, as opposed to IBM's decision to support an open architecture system, has proved to be a costly strategy to support in the long run.

Some argue that Apple should reinvent itself once again and this time concentrate on software. Apple is gradually admitting that it can no longer afford to fight the Wintel system, the combination of Microsoft's Windows operating system and the Intel processor. Apple's new product introductions fail to attract many present non-Mac users—just 15 percent of its revenues come from Wintel customers.[5]

Apple is betting that its new operating system, the Mac OS X, will be a big hit with computer users. It is the largest update in the operating system since it was first released in the mid-1980s. Recognizing the need to attract new Mac users rather than just recycle present Ap-

ple enthusiasts, Apple is emphasizing the compatibility of its system with Windows. "The transition to a Mac is easy in part because you'll continue to use the same applications you already know . . . Word, PowerPoint and Excel, . . . And, thanks to exclusive features, the Mac versions improve on their Windows counterparts. Office documents are fully compatible between Mac and Windows, so you can share everything from spreadsheets to presentations. . . . [T]he Mac is at home on PC networks . . . making the business of sharing files and printers with PCs entirely painless."[6]

Part of Apple's new corporate strategy, developed in the face of a massive slowdown in the technology industry, involves taking advantage of the explosion of personal electronic devices—CD players, MP3 players, digital cameras, DVD players, and so on —by initially building Mac-only applications that add value to those devices. Just as iMovies adds tremendous value to digital cameras, iDVD adds value to DVD players and iTunes adds value to CD and MP3 players. However, Apple recognizes the size of the PC market that is not being reached and has made iPod and iTunes into Windows-compatible products. In its first week, iTunes sold 1.5 million songs and captured 80 percent of the market share of legal music down-

loads. It is Apple's hope that making Apple products the "digital hub" of the new "digital lifestyle" will revitalize Apple's sales and guarantee the long-term security of the company.[7]

Apple is also eyeing the global market and in November 2003 opened its first store in Japan. With five floors of Apple products and applications located in Japan's Ginza, it offers an experience to rival that of the Sony store in the same shopping area. Apple is hoping to develop a global presence and to attract new users internationally.[8]

Review Questions

1. Why is Apple not a dominant provider of personal computers?
2. Evaluate Apple in the context of the new economy. Can Apple survive?
3. Should the firm enable its operating system to run on both Apple and PC systems?
4. What would you suggest Apple do to popularize the Apple computer line?

You Do the Research

1. Look at the Apple home page's Top 10 reasons to switch. What do these indicate about Apple's strategy?
2. Locate five sources on the Web that discuss Apple and the history of the personal computer market.

CASE 2

The Coca-Cola Company: Coke Gets Back to Business

With production facilities in over 200 countries in the world, there are few products as internationally recognized as the ubiquitous Coke bottle.[1] To put this in perspective, another American icon, McDonald's, has locations in only 119 countries.[2] As one of the world's best-known brands, Coca-Cola has capitalized on opportunities and thrived. However, the process has not been without some upheavals.

When Roberto Goizueta, its CEO for 17 years, passed away on October 18, 1997, after a short bout with lung cancer, the future looked uncertain. During Goizueta's tenure at Coca-Cola, the market value of the company had dramatically increased from $4 billion to nearly $150 billion. This made him one of the greatest value creators in history. While the appointment of CFO Douglas Ivester as his replacement did not immediately allay the concerns of the financial market, the value of Coke stock continued to increase until mid-1998. Since then, the value of the stock has declined and as of late November 2003, the market value of Coca-Cola was $115 billion. Douglas Daft, president and chief operating officer, with 30 years of Coke experience, replaced Ivester as chairman and CEO in 2000.[3] The question, then and now, on many investors' minds remains: "Can Coke recapture its previous growth pace and stock value without Goizueta's legendary leadership?"

Coca-Cola's Global Dominance

The larger a company is, the harder it is to continue to grow at a steady pace. This remains the major challenge facing the Coca-Cola Company. The U.S. market is already well developed, with an average consumption per person of one serving per day of Coke products in both 2001 and 2002. The European and Eurasian market grew slightly from 2001 to 2002, with average consumption increasing from one and a half to two servings per week. The Latin American, Asian, and African markets' consumption levels were unchanged from 2001 to 2002 at four servings per week, two servings per month, and three servings per month, respectively.[4] However, even given the much lower consumption rate internationally than in the United States, more than 70 percent of Coca-Cola's income is generated outside the United States. This is primarily due to population differentials.

Coca-Cola, recognizing the importance of international sales, has been very sensitive to local market conditions. Products are developed to meet the varied taste preferences of consumers. In fact, Coca-Cola produces more than 300 brands worldwide in addition to its flagship brands, Coke and Diet Coke. The bottling and distribution system is also adapted to local needs. For instance, all bottlers are local companies either independently owned or only partially owned by the Coca-Cola Company. In this way, Coca-Cola gains the benefits of intrinsic local knowledge. The distribution systems range from boats in Indonesia to four-legged power in the Andes to fleets of trucks in the United States. In each case, local conditions are considered. Coca-Cola prides itself on acting as a local citizen in a global marketplace.

Coke's Dominance

Coca-Cola has achieved its dominance in the global marketplace through its consistent loyalty to the Coke heritage and the image and standards that it conveys. Coca-Cola historically has not been a company noted for innovation; it was almost 100 years after the introduction of Coke that it introduced Diet Coke. After the disastrous introduction of New Coke, there was reluctance to tamper with Coke. As Douglas Daft, chairman and CEO, put it in his 2002 letter to share owners, "Responsibility for the world's most beloved and valuable brand requires extreme care in how, when, and why we extend it. We don't risk consumer loyalty to the brand or seek an artificial bump in volume by spinning out product after product to chase the latest fad."[5] However, 2002 represented a period of unprecedented innovation—Vanilla Coke, Diet Vanilla Coke, and Diet Coke with lemon attracted new consumers.

Historically, carbonated beverages have been the backbone of the Coca-Cola Company; in 2002 they accounted for 85 percent of sales. Coca-Cola acknowledgment of changing consumer tastes has fostered a continued expansion of its line of noncarbonated beverages. Growth in sales of noncarbonated beverages was 28 percent from 2001 to 2002. This growth has been fueled both internally and through acquisitions and licensing agreements. Coca-Cola is hoping to achieve profitability through economies of scale and by capitalizing on its existing distribution system.

The Coca-Cola Company has positioned itself for growth by moving key decision making closer to local markets and by fostering deeper connections to con-

sumers. It has also restructured, with a management team coordinating a new, nimble, and entrepreneurial network. As one of his first acts as CEO, Daft axed 6,000 employees, many of them middle and senior managers in Atlanta. The new structure reflects his continuing commitment to a leaner, more entrepreneurial organization. Under him, there is a 10-person executive management team composed of:

- President and chief operating officer of the Coca-Cola Company
- Senior vice president and chief marketing officer
- Senior vice president and worldwide public affairs and communications officer
- Executive vice president and chief financial officer
- Executive vice president and general counsel and secretary
- Five executive vice presidents of the Coca-Cola Company who are presidents and chief operating officers for North America; Europe, Eurasia, and the Middle East; Latin America; Asia; and Africa

Twenty-four division and operations presidents report to the chief operating officers. This group of individuals, along with Coca-Cola employees and partners worldwide, are responsible for implementing the six strategic priorities that are laid out in the 2002 Annual Report:[6]

1. "Accelerate carbonated soft-drink growth, led by Coca-Cola."
2. "Selectively broaden our family of beverage brands to drive profitable growth."
3. "Grow system profitability and capability together

with our bottling partners. Our drive for profitability throughout our system brought us even closer to our bottlers in 2002."
4. "Serve customers with creativity and consistency to generate growth across all channels."
5. "Direct investments to highest-potential areas across markets. Our business approach is tailored to each market based on its stage of development. In rural areas of China, we direct our efforts toward expanding availability of affordable packages, while in cities such as Shanghai and Beijing, we execute more sophisticated image-building promotions, activating points of purchase so that consumers have greater connections with our brands."
6. "Drive efficiency and cost effectiveness everywhere. We continue to drive efficiency throughout our system, establishing disciplined routines and gaining economies of scale in material and ingredient purchasing."

Will the restructuring and the new strategic initiatives help Coca-Cola achieve its mission of "benefiting and refreshing everyone it touches" and regain the growth and value experienced under Roberto Goizueta?

Review Questions

1. Apply Henri Fayol's five rules of management to the Coca-Cola case.
2. Consider the following quote from Coca-Cola's statement on diversity: "We embrace our commit-

ment to diversity in all its forms at The Coca-Cola Company as a core value. Diversity—of race, gender, sexual orientation, ideas, ways of living, cultures and business practices—provides the creativity and innovation essential to our economic well-being. Equally important is a highly motivated, healthy and productive workforce that achieves business success through superior execution and superb customer satisfaction."[7]

Relate this quote to the case and to the behavioral approaches to management.

3. How does Coca-Cola score on the eight attributes of performance excellence?

4. Do you think Douglas Daft will be successful in regaining the growth and value experienced under Roberto Goizueta?

You Do the Research

1. While stock prices have declined since 1998, what has happened to revenues and income over the same period?

2. What are Coca-Cola's underlying beliefs? See the following website: www2.coca-cola.com/ ourcompany/ ourbeliefs.html.

3. Read Coca-Cola's statement on diversity. What insights does it provide? See the following website: www2.coca-cola.com/ ourcompany/ourdiversity.html.

CASE 3

Tom's of Maine: At Tom's, "Doing Business" Means "Doing Good"

Tom's of Maine represents one of the first natural health care companies to distribute its products beyond the normal channels of health food stores. With its continued growth, the owners, Tom and Kate Chappell, still emphasize the values that got them started more than three decades ago. The experiences of Tom and Kate Chappell in meeting the challenges they have encountered provide considerable insight into how a small firm can stay true to its founding principles and continue to grow in a fiercely competitive environment.

Getting Tom's of Maine Going

For its first 15 years, Tom's of Maine looked a lot like many other new businesses. Tom and Kate Chappell had an idea they believed in and felt others would buy into as well. Based on this idea, and with financing from a small loan, the Chappells started the company in 1970. As is the case with many business startups, the company's first product was not successful. Its phosphate-free detergent was environmentally friendly

but, according to Tom Chappell, "it didn't clean so well."[1] Consumers did appear to be interested in "green," or environmentally friendly, products, however, and the fledgling company's next products, toothpaste and soap, were more successful.

All Tom's of Maine products were made with all-natural ingredients and were packaged using recycled materials whenever possible. New personal care products, including shampoo and deodorant, were developed

while avoiding the controversial practice of animal testing.[2] This refusal caused Tom's to wait seven years and spend about ten times the usual sum to get the American Dental Association's seal of approval for its fluoride toothpastes.

In 1992, Tom's deodorant accounted for 25 percent of its business. Chappell reformulated the product for ecological reasons (replacing petroleum with vegetable glycerin), but the new formulation "magnified the human bacteria that cause odor" in half its customers. After much agonizing, Chappell ordered the deodorant taken off the shelves at a cost of $400,000, or 30 percent of the firm's projected profits for the year. Dissatisfied consumers were sent refunds for the new product, along with a letter of apology.

Tom's of Maine recovered from this experience, but founder Tom Chappell was not happy. The company's products were a success in health food stores, and Chappell was beginning to think in terms of national distribution. He had hired a team of marketing people with experience at major companies. At the same time, he felt that something was missing; he was "tired of creating new brands and making money."[3]

One pivotal event was the introduction of baking soda toothpaste. The product was gritty and didn't have the sweet flavor typical of commercial toothpastes, and the marketing manager told Chappell, "In all candor I don't know how we're going to sell it."[4] Chappell insisted that the product be test-marketed. It proved to be a best-seller and was quickly copied by Arm and Hammer and Procter & Gamble.[5] It also appeared that the new product's sales potential had become more important to the company than the qualities of the product itself. "We were working for the numbers, and we got the numbers. But I was confused by success, unhappy with success" said Chappell.[6] He later wrote, "I had made a real go of something I'd started. What more could I do in life except make more money? Where was the purpose and direction for the rest of my life?"[7] As a result of this line of thinking, the successful businessman Tom

Chappell entered Harvard Divinity School in the fall of 1986.[8]

Sharpening the Company's Focus

The years that Chappell spent as a part-time student at the divinity school brought him to a new understanding of his role. "For the first time in my career, I had the language I needed to debate my bean-counters" he explained.[9] He realized that his company was his ministry. "I'm here to succeed. But there's a qualifier. It's not to succeed at all costs, it's to succeed according to my principles."[10]

One tangible result was the development of a mission statement for the company that reflected both the company's business aspirations and its commitment to social responsibility. This document spelled out the values that would guide the company in the future. It covered the types of products ordered and the need for natural ingredients and high quality. It also included respect for employees and the need for meaningful work as well as fair pay. It pointed out the need to be concerned with the community and even the world. Finally, it called for Tom's of Maine "to be a profitable and successful company, while acting in a socially responsible manner."[11] Some of the company's programs were the result of decisions made by top management. The company began donating 10 percent of its pretax profits to charities ranging from arts organizations to environmental groups. These included funds donated to state and local curbside recycling programs as well as a pledge of $100,000 for the Rainforest Alliance.

The company also urged its employees to get involved in charitable causes. It set up a program that allowed employees to donate 5 percent of their work time to volunteer activities. Employees enthusiastically took advantage of the opportunity. When one employee began teaching art classes for emotionally disturbed children, others became interested, until almost all of the company's employees were involved.[12] Other employees worked in soup kitchens and homeless shelters. Employees formed their own teams to work on projects or used the company's matching service. Tom's even created the position of vice president of community life.

The volunteer program did have its costs, however. Other employees had to pitch in to cover volunteers' absences, which amounted to the equivalent of 20 days a month. However, Colleen Myers, the vice president of community life, believed that the volunteer activities were valuable to the company as well as the community. "After spending a few hours at a soup kitchen or a shelter, you're happy to have a job. It's a morale booster, and better morale translates pretty directly into better productivity."[13] Sometimes the company even benefitted directly from these activities. Chappell explained, "The woman who headed up those art classes—she discovered she's a heck of a project manager. We found that out, too."[14]

Employee benefits were not strictly psychological. The company offered flexible four-day scheduling and subsidized day care. Even coffee breaks were designed with employee preferences in mind, providing them with fresh fruit. The company also helped individual employees earn their high school equivalency degrees and develop skills for new positions.[15]

By 1993, Tom's of Maine was moving beyond health food stores and into supermarkets and drugstores, where 70 percent of toothpaste is purchased. Even as Tom's product distribution expanded nationwide, the company's marketing strategy was low key. Katie Shisler, vice president of marketing, says: "We just tell them our story. We tell them why we have such a loyal base of consumers who vote with their dollars every day. A number of trade accounts appreciate our social responsibility and are willing to go out on a limb with us."[16] Tom Chappell agreed: "We're selling a lot more than toothpaste; we're selling a point of view—that nature is worth protecting."[17]

By the mid-1990s, Tom's of Maine was facing increasing competition. Its prices were similar to those of its national competitors for baking soda toothpaste but 20 to 40 percent higher for deodorant and mouthwash. Tom Chappell did not appear worried, however. He believed that "you have to understand from the outset that they have more in the marketing war chest than you. That's not the way you're going to get market share, you're going to get it by being who you are."[18] He explained his philosophy: "A small business obviously needs to distinguish itself from the commodities. If we try to act like commodities, act like a toothpaste, we give up our souls. Instead, we have to be peculiarly authentic in everything we do."[19] This authenticity is applied to both ingredients and advertising decisions. "When you start doing that customers are very aware of your difference. And they like the difference."[20]

Tom's of Maine: A Different Kind of Company?

Tom's of Maine distinguishes itself from other companies by stressing the "common good" in all of its endeavors. The company is passionately concerned about corporate wellness, customer wellness, product wellness, community and environmental wellness, and employee wellness. In late 2000 the company launched Tom's Online Wellness Store to make its full product line available to customers around the globe. Among other customer-oriented activities, Tom's utilizes the services of a wellness advisory council and provides wellness education. Tom's of Maine practices stewardship through its commitment to natural, sustainable, and responsible ingredients, products, and packaging. In embracing the philosophy of "doing well by doing good," Tom's has continued to produce impressive business results that attest to an ongoing stream of corporate wellness. In fiscal year 2001, Tom's sales exceeded $35 million, which directly reflects the continued strengthening of its various product lines.[21]

Throughout the 1990s Tom's of Maine was repeatedly recognized for providing a model of ethical business standards for others to follow. Among other awards, Tom and Kate Chappell have received the Corporate Conscience Award for Charitable Contributions from the Council of Economic Priorities, the New England Environmental Leadership Award, and the Governor's Award for Business Excellence.[22] Clearly, Tom's of Maine demonstrates that "common-good capitalism" can work and that businesses can be operated to simultaneously earn a profit and serve the common good. In an effort to pass these lessons on to other businesspeople, Tom Chappell has authored two books, *The Soul of a Business: Managing for Profit and the Common Good* and *Managing Upside Down: Seven Intentions for Values-Centered Leadership*, and created the Saltwater Institute, a nonprofit organization that provides training in the Seven Intentions.[23]

Chappell's Seven Intentions for seeking and achieving a values–profits balance are:

1. Connect with goodness. Non-work discussions with an upbeat spin usually draw people to common ground, away from hierarchical titles.
2. Know thyself, be thyself. Discovering and tapping people's passions, gifts and strengths generates creative energy.
3. Envision your destiny. The company is better served if its efforts are steered by strengths instead of following market whims.
4. Seek counsel. The journey is long, and assistance from others is absolutely necessary.
5. Venture out. The success of any business hinges

on pushing value-enhanced products into the market.

6. Assess. Any idea must be regularly reviewed and refined if necessary.

7. Pass it on. Since developing and incorporating values is a trial-and-error process, sharing ideas and soliciting feedback allows for future growth.[24]

Review Questions

1. Which way of thinking about ethical behavior best describes Tom's of Maine and its founder, Tom Chappell?

2. What potential dilemma did Tom Chappell face in the mid-1980s?

3. How important were Tom Chappell's personal views in helping Tom's of Maine to be successful?

You Do the Research

1. Should Tom's stay independent, or should it merge with a larger firm?

2. Can Chappell's approach to ethical management work at larger firms?

3. Find five Internet sites that discuss ethics and social responsibility, and identify an important ethical lesson or insight that is provided on each site.

CASE 4

United Parcel Service: UPS Hits the Road with Technology

United Parcel Service (UPS), the world's largest package distribution company, transports more than 4 billion parcels and documents annually. With more than 360,000 employees, 1,750 operating facilities, 2,000 daily flights, 88,000 vehicles, and the world's largest private communication system, UPS provides service in more than 200 countries.[1] How does UPS control such a vast and extended enterprise and still fulfill its commitment to serving the needs of the global marketplace?

Corporate History

In 1907, there was a great need in America for private messenger and delivery services. Only a few homes had private telephones, and luggage, packages, and personal messages had to be carried by hand. The U.S. Postal Service did not yet have the parcel post system. To help meet this need, an enterprising 19-year-old, James E. ("Jim") Casey, borrowed $100 from a friend and established the American Messenger Company in Seattle, Washington. Despite stiff competition, the company did well, largely because of Jim Casey's strict policies on customer courtesy, reliability, round-the-clock service, and low rates. These principles, which guide UPS even today, are summarized by Jim's slogan: "Best Service and Lowest Rates."[2]

Obsessed with efficiency from the beginning, the company pioneered the concept of consolidated delivery—combining packages addressed to certain neighborhoods onto one delivery vehicle. In this way, manpower and motorized equipment could be used more efficiently. The 1930s brought more growth. By this time, UPS provided delivery services in all major West Coast cities, and a foothold had been established on the other coast with a consolidated delivery service in the New York City area. Many innovations were adopted, including the first mechanical system for package sorting. During this time, accountant George D. Smith joined the firm and helped make financial cost control the cornerstone of all planning decisions. The name United Parcel Service was adopted—"United" to emphasize the unity of the company's operations in each city, "Parcel" to identify the nature of the business, and "Service" to indicate what was provided to customers.[3]

In 1953, UPS resumed air service, which had been discontinued during the Depression, offering two-day service to major cities on the East and West Coasts. Packages flew in the cargo holds of regularly scheduled airlines. Called UPS Blue Label Air, the service grew, until by 1978 it was available in every state, including Alaska and Hawaii. The demand for air parcel delivery increased in the 1980s, and federal deregulation of the airline industry created new opportunities for UPS. But deregulation caused change, as established airlines reduced the number of flights or abandoned routes altogether. To ensure dependability, UPS began to assemble its own jet cargo fleet—the largest in the industry. With growing demand for faster service, UPS entered the overnight air delivery business, and by 1985 UPS Next Day Air service was available in all 48 contiguous states and Puerto Rico. Alaska and Hawaii were added later. That same year, UPS entered a new era with international air package and document service, linking the United States and six European nations.

UPS Today

In 1988, UPS received authorization from the Federal Aviation Administration (FAA) to operate its own aircraft, thus officially becoming an airline. Recruiting the best people available, UPS merged a number of different organizational cultures and procedures into a seamless opera-

tion called UPS Airline. UPS Airline was the fastest-growing airline in FAA history, formed in little more than one year with all the necessary technology and support systems. UPS Airline has become one of the 10 largest airlines in the United States. UPS Airline features some of the most advanced information systems in the world to support flight planning, scheduling, and load handling.

Today, the UPS system moves more than 13.3 million packages and documents daily around the globe. UPS picks up from 1.8 million customers per day and delivers to 6.1 million customers per day. Packages are processed using advanced information technology and are transported by the company's own aircraft, chartered aircraft, and a fleet of delivery vehicles.[4] U.S. and international package delivery operations constitute a substantial segment of UPS's business. Another growing and important segment is the company's nonpackage unit, which focuses on supply chain solutions for UPS customers.[5] Today, UPS emphasizes its customer service orientation with the advertising slogan: "What can brown do for you?"

Innovations at UPS

Known for its technological innovations, UPS keeps its package delivery and nonpackage operations on the cutting edge. Tom Weidemeyer, chief operating officer, says that UPS likes to take the really long-term view about investments in its infrastructure. Technology at UPS spans an incredible

range, from specially designed package delivery vehicles to global computer and communications systems. For example, UPSnet is a global electronic data communications network that provides an information-processing pipeline for international package processing and delivery. UPSnet, which has more than 500,000 miles of communications lines and a satellite, links more than 1,300 distribution sites in 46 countries. The system tracks 821,000 packages daily.[6]

UPS Worldport™ is the latest example of technology being used to increase efficiency and quality in the company's package operations. Located in Louisville, Kentucky, Worldport is a 4-million-square-foot facility outfitted with "overhead cameras to read smart labels and process documents, small packages, and irregular-shaped objects with astounding speed. Equipped with more than 17,000 high-speed conveyors, Worldport is capable of processing some 84 packages every second and can be expanded to handle nearly 140 packages per second—or more than 500,000 packages per hour."[7] Worldport can also consolidate more volume at a single location, thereby enabling the company to use larger and more efficient aircraft and streamlining sorting at regional hubs throughout the world.[8]

UPS Supply Chain Solutions—the company's nonpackage operation—is targeted toward a variety of supply chain challenges faced by customers, including but not limited to helping customers in managing overseas suppliers, post-sales servicing of parts logistics, and order processing. This operation also coordinates transportation, vendors, contracts, and shipments, and simplifies international trade and regulatory compliance.

UPS Supply Chain Solutions relies on a physical and virtual infrastructure for managing the flow of goods, information, and funds for different customers. For example, UPS developed an integrated supply chain with advanced automation to enable Honeywell to provide efficient and rapid order processing and delivery to the North American automotive aftermarket. Another supply chain solution was provided to TeddyCrafters, thereby enabling it to better manage the transportation and distribution of supplies from Asian and U.S. vendors. UPS designed a comprehensive inbound distribution system for TeddyCrafters that improved inventory management and provided for weekly restocking of the chain's retail stores. Still another supply chain challenge was solved for Tokyo Electron America. UPS implemented a field restocking network that provided real-time inventory management. In all these cases, and many others, UPS uses its own technological expertise in the transportation and distribution of documents and packages to help other companies achieve efficient, rapid, and low-cost solutions for all stages of their supply chains.[9]

Three Trends Driving the Industry

Frederick Smith of FedEx, a UPS competitor, identifies three trends driving the package delivery business: globalization, cost cutting, and Internet commerce. *Globalization* will cause the world express-transportation market to explode to more than $150 billion. While DHL Worldwide Express is a major player in the international market, UPS and Fed Ex are expanding at a rapid pace. Lee Hibbets of Air Cargo Management Group in Seattle states that: "FedEx is seen as more aggressive, whereas UPS is a little bit more methodical and long term." *Cost cutting* among customer firms—primarily by cutting inventory—fits into the package firms' delivery systems. Technology plays a significant part in package delivery companies' capabilities to assist customers in cutting their inventories. UPS and FedEx are competing fiercely in using technology to facilitate cost-cutting efforts. *Internet commerce*, the third trend, generates a huge need for shipping. Package delivery companies hope to capture the lion's share of the Internet commerce shipping business.[10]

It remains to be seen who will win out in the package delivery wars, but FedEx and UPS are both leaders in the market. Their ability to track packages around the world is a testament to the value of technology in the workplace. With technological innovations generating higher productivity, the future for package delivery remains bright. Moreover, with attention being given to the challenges of supply chain management, package delivery companies can apply their technological expertise in developing additional business opportunities.

Review Questions

1. Describe UPS's competitive advantage.
2. How does UPS approach customer relationship management?
3. How does technology enable UPS to be a quality-driven organization?

You Do the Research

1. Describe the general environmental factors that affect UPS and its competitors in the package delivery industry.
2. Identify the stakeholders for UPS, and explain how those stakeholders potentially influence the company.
3. Describe the organizational culture at UPS and the role that it plays in the company's success.

Harley-Davidson: Harley Style and Strategy Have Global Reach

With a celebration of almost legendary proportions, Harley-Davidson marked a century in business with a year-long International Road Tour from July 2002 to July 2003. The party finally culminated in August 2003 in hometown Milwaukee.[1] Brought back from near death, Harley-Davidson represents a true American success story. Reacting to global competition, Harley has been able to reestablish itself as the dominant maker of big bikes in the United States. However, success often breeds imitation, and Harley faces a mixture of domestic and foreign competitors encroaching on its market. Can it meet the challenge?

Harley-Davidson

When Harley-Davidson was founded in 1903, it was one of more than 100 firms producing motorcycles in the United States. The U.S. government became an important customer for the company's high-powered, reliable bikes, using them in both world wars. By the 1950s, Harley-Davidson was the only remaining American manufacturer.[2]

But British competitors were beginning to enter the market with faster, lighter-weight bikes. Honda Motor Company of Japan began marketing lightweight bikes in the United States, moving into middleweight vehicles in the 1960s. Harley initially tried to compete by manufacturing smaller bikes but had difficulty making them profitably. The company even purchased an Italian motorcycle firm, Aermacchi, but many of its dealers were reluctant to sell the small Aermacchi Harleys.[3]

American Machine and Foundry Co. (AMF) took over Harley in 1969, expanding its portfolio of recreational products. AMF increased production from 14,000 to 50,000 bikes per year. This rapid expansion led to significant problems with quality, and better-built Japanese motorcycles began to take over the market. Harley's share of its major U.S. market—heavyweight motorcycles—fell to 23 percent.[4]

In 1981, a group of 13 managers bought Harley-Davidson back from AMF and began to turn the company around with the rallying cry "The Eagle Soars Alone." As Richard Teerlink, former CEO of Harley, explained: "The solution was to get back to detail. The key was to know the business, know the customer, and pay attention to detail."[5] The key elements in this process were increasing quality and improving service to customers and dealers. Management kept the classic Harley style and focused on the company's traditional strength—heavyweight and super-heavyweight bikes.

In 1983, Harley-Davidson asked the International Trade Commission (ITC) for tariff relief on the basis that Japanese manufacturers were stockpiling inventory in the United States and providing unfair competition. The tariff relief was granted on April 1, 1983, and a tariff for five years was placed on all imported Japanese motorcycles that were 700cc or larger. In 1987, Harley petitioned the ITC to have the tariff lifted because the company felt capable and confident in its ability to compete with foreign imports. Also in 1983, the Harley Owners Group® (H.O.G.®) was formed. H.O.G. membership soared to more than 90,000 by 1989 and by 2003 exceeded 750,000 members.[6]

Once Harley's quality image had been restored, the company slowly began to expand production. The company made only 280 bikes per day in January 1992, increasing output to 345 bikes per day by the end of that year. Despite increasing demand, production was scheduled to reach only 420 per day, approximately 100,000 per year, by 1996.[7] However, in 1996 Harley recognized the demand and the first of many grander expansion plans began with the opening of a new distribution center in Franklin, Wisconsin. In 1997, Harley began production in new facilities in Milwaukee, Wisconsin, Menomonee Falls, Wisconsin, and Kansas City, Missouri. In 1998, a new assembly plant was opened in Manaus, Brazil and Harley acquired the remaining interest in Buell motorcycles. In 2001, expansions were announced for the Milwaukee, Wisconsin, Tomahawk, Wisconsin, and York, Pennsylvania plants.[8]

As indicated by the expansions, the popularity of the motorcycles continued to increase throughout the 1980s. The average Harley purchaser was in his late thirties, with an average household income of over $40,000. Teerlink didn't like the description of his customers as "aging" baby-boomers: "Our customers want the sense of adventure that they get on our bikes. . . . Harley-Davidson doesn't sell transportation, we sell transformation. We sell excitement, a way of life."[9] However, the average age and income of Harley riders has continued to increase. In 2002, the median age of a Harley rider was 47 and the median income was just under $80,000.[10]

Although the company had been exporting motorcycles ever since it was founded, it was not until the late 1980s that Harley-Davidson management began to think seriously about international markets. In 1987, the company acknowledged its ability to compete with foreign imports and started to consider competing more seriously in the international market. Traditionally, the company's ads had been translated word for word into foreign languages.

Now, ads were developed specifically for different markets, and rallies were adapted to fit local customs.[11] The company also began to actively recruit and develop dealers in Europe and Japan. It purchased a Japanese distribution company and built a large parts warehouse in Germany to support its European operations. Harley-Davidson continued to look for ways to expand its activities. Recognizing that German motorcyclists rode at high speeds—often more than 100 mph—the company began to study ways to give Harleys a smoother ride. It also began to emphasize accessories that would give riders more protection.[12]

The company also created a line of Harley accessories available through dealers or by catalog, all adorned with the Harley-Davidson logo. These jackets, caps, T-shirts, and other items became popular with nonbikers as well. In fact, the clothing and parts had a higher profit margin than the motorcycles; nonbike products made up as much as half of sales at some dealers.

International Efforts

Harley continues to make inroads in overseas markets. In 2002, Harley had 30 percent of the worldwide market for heavyweight motorcycles—chrome-laden cruisers, aerodynamic rocket bikes mostly produced by the Japanese, and oversize touring motorcycles. In the United States, Harley had the largest market share, 46.4 percent, followed by Honda with 20.2 percent. In Europe,

Harley ranked sixth, with only 6.6 percent of the market share behind Honda, Yamaha, BMW, Suzuki, and Kawasaki. However, in the Asia/Pacific market, where it might be expected that Japanese bikes would dominate, Harley had the largest market shares for 2000, 2001, and 2002. Harley had 21.3 percent of the market share compared to 19.2 percent for Honda.[13]

Harley motorcycles are among America's fastest-growing exports to Japan. Harley's Japanese subsidiary adapted the company's marketing approach to Japanese tastes, even producing shinier and more complete tool kits than available in the United States. Harley bikes have long been considered symbols of prestige in Japan. Before World War II, a small company called Rikuo built them under a licensing arrangement. Consistent with their U.S. counterparts, many Japanese enthusiasts see themselves as rebels on wheels.[14]

Another recent effort by Harley to expand its buyer base involves the development of its Blast motorcycle from its Buell division. Fifty percent of Blast sales are to women, raising the overall percentage of women buying Harleys from 2 percent in 1987 to 9 percent by 1999. That 9 percent figure remained constant through 2002. With 17 consecutive years of increased production as well as record revenues and earnings, the future for Harley appears bright.[15]

Review Questions

1. Describe Harley-Davidson's international busi-

ness strategy. Would you consider Harley to be a multinational corporation?

2. If you were Harley's top management, in which regions of the world would you consider expanding?

3. Evaluate Harley-Davidson's decision not to produce overseas. What would be the advantages of overseas production? What problems might the company encounter if it

does manufacture abroad?

4. Harley appears to have moved from providing a product (motorcycles) to providing a service (a way of life). Discuss how this movement from products to services may have affected the company.

You Do the Research

1. How successful have competitors been against

Harley in the United States?

2. Should Harley alter its image as the U.S. population ages?

3. Should businesses like Harley receive protection from overseas competition? Can you find another instance where a company asked that a tariff against imports be eliminated early?

CASE 6

Domino's Pizza: Great Ideas Bring Domino's to Your Door

As of 2002, Domino's Pizza had more than 7,300 company-owned and franchised stores in the United States and more than 50 other countries. *Pizza Today* named it "Chain of the Year" for 2003. With sales in 2002 of more than 400 million pizzas and revenues of nearly $4 billion, it represents an impressive success story. Starting in 1960 with one store in Ypsilanti, Michigan, Tom Monaghan redefined the pizza industry and, in so doing, built a corporate powerhouse. It entered the international market in 1983 with its first store outside the United States, which was in Winnipeg, Canada. At the end of 2003, 2,500 of the stores were international and revenues generated in those stores exceeded $1 billion.[1] Could you be another Tom, given the chance?

The Domino Story

Tom Monaghan and his brother, James, borrowed $500 in 1960 to purchase "DomiNick's," a pizza store, in Ypsilanti, Michigan. The following year Tom bought out his brother's half interest for a used Volkswagen Beetle. In 1965, Tom changed the name of the establishment to "Domino's Pizza" and two years later opened the first franchise

location in Ypsilanti.[2]

Growing up in orphanages, Tom dreamed of succeeding in a big way. In his first 13 years in the business, he worked 100-hour weeks, seven days a week. He only had one vacation, and that was for six days when he got married to his wife, Margie.[3] The following quote exhibits his high need to be the best at whatever he does:

I was distracted by some of the rewards of

success, which was hurting my business. I put all of those distractions aside, and focused solely on Domino's Pizza. I decided to take a "millionaire's vow of poverty." I am focusing on God, family and Domino's Pizza.[4]

The pizza industry is highly fragmented, with more than 61,000 pizzerias and $30 billion in sales per year. More than 3 billion pizzas are sold each year in America, representing annual consumption of over 23 pounds of pizza per capita.[5] The issue for any pizzeria is how to create an advantage and differentiate its product.

Monaghan decided to concentrate only on pizzas and developed the strategy of delivering a hot pie in 30 minutes or less. He chose to locate his early franchises in college towns and near military bases, whose populations are both high consumers of pizzas. This strategy proved to be very successful, and Domino's passed 200 locations in the late 1970s.[6]

Monaghan is credited with developing many of the pizza practices now taken for granted within the industry, including dough trays, the corrugated pizza box, insulated bags to transport pizzas, and a unique system of internal franchising. "Tom Monaghan made pizza delivery what it is today," says Eric Marcus, a 46-unit Domino's franchisee based in Dayton, Ohio. "The one thing about Tom is that he knew what he wanted, and he knew how to stay focused on what he wanted. He had a vision that pizza should be delivered in 30 minutes or less."[7]

The 1980s proved to be a huge time for Domino's growth, as it closed out the decade with more than 5,000 locations and $2 billion in sales.[8] During that time, Monaghan purchased the Detroit Tigers baseball team and developed significant philanthropic activities in various Domino's communities.

However, the road to success was not entirely smooth, and Domino's did have to face hurdles and challenges along the way. In 1968, the firm's commissary and company headquarters were destroyed by fire. In 1976, Amstar Corp., maker of Domino Sugar, filed a trademark infringement lawsuit against the firm that was settled in Domino's favor in 1980. In 1993, responding to concerns for drivers' safety, the firm discontinued the "30-minute guarantee" and replaced it with the total satisfaction guarantee: "If for any reason you are dissatisfied with your Domino's Pizza dining experience, we will re-make your pizza or refund your money."[9]

In 1998, Monaghan sold "a significant" portion of his ownership in Domino's to Bain Capital Inc., a Massachusetts investment firm. While he remained on the board of directors, he was no longer engaged in the day-to day activities of the firm. Instead, he wanted to devote his time to religious pursuits, including the building of educational facilities in Ann Arbor, Michigan.[10]

David Brandon, formerly of Procter & Gamble and Valassis Communications, was hired as president. In his first full year as president, Domino's achieved a 4.4 percent growth in sales. Now chairman and CEO, Brandon has been recognized as the visionary who led Domino's to win the coveted "Chain of the Year" award for 2003 given by *Pizza Today*. Jeremy White, editor-in-chief of the monthly trade publication, observed: "Domino's had an impressive year. Between solid product introductions, savvy advertising and a 'People First' mentality that has trickled down from Chairman and CEO Dave Brandon to store employees, the chain managed to post positive financial results in a time of economic instability."[11]

Domino's Future

With a history of innovations in the pizza industry, Domino's constantly looks for new ways to enhance customer value. *Pizza Today* honored the company for outstanding sales, strong leadership, innovation, brand image, and customer satisfaction.[12] In Domino's early years, Tom Monaghan set the stage for the company's later successes with his innovations and brand development strategies. He even recognized how important it was to adapt to local culture in order to achieve success overseas. "Culture comes first. Some early attempts to open Domino's stores internationally faltered because the company tried to establish in markets that had cultures unaccustomed to pizza or the convenience of home delivery. Understanding cultures and adapting to them was the first step in the process of global expansion."[13] Can Domino's continue to be innovators in the pizza business?

Monaghan displayed the drive and determination representative of many entrepreneurs in today's dynamic market. He had what it took to succeed. Could *you* do what Tom Monaghan did?

Review Questions

1. What allowed Tom Monaghan to develop Domino's into a worldwide enterprise?

2. Why do you think Tom Monaghan chose to get out of the day-to-day operations of Domino's?

3. How do you think the characters of Tom Monaghan and David Brandon differ? How are they similar?

Why was each the right person for the company at the time?

You Do the Research

1. What are pizza parlors presently doing to differentiate their products?

2. Look at the profiles of other successful entrepreneurs. Do they have some character attributes in common?

CASE 7

Kate Spade: Risk Turns Niches into Opportunities

- -

After graduating from college in 1986, Katherine (Kate) Noel Brosnahan was employed by *Mademoiselle* magazine, working her way up to senior fashion editor/head of accessories before her departure in 1991. During this time, Kate concluded that the women's fashion accessories market lacked stylish, practical handbags. Kate, along with her then boyfriend and now husband, Andy Spade, saw an opportunity and capitalized on it.[1] How did Kate and Andy capitalize on this opportunity?

The Startup

Kate and Andy set out "to develop a well-edited line of fashionable, but not 'trendy' handbags."[2] Kate developed design sketches for six handbags with simple shapes that emphasized utility, color, and fabric. Kate also investigated production costs. Andy contributed the marketing expertise, drawing on his experience at several advertising agencies. In January 1993, Kate and Andy launched Kate Spade Handbags.[3]

Kate worked full time to get the new company firmly established while Andy initially worked only part time. From January 1993 until September 1996, Andy worked nights and weekends on behalf of the new company and continued to work full time for an advertising agency. Andy began working full time with Kate Spade Handbags in September 1996, becoming its president and creative director.

Early on, Kate and Andy recognized the crucial need for recruiting talented people to help them grow the business. In late 1993, Pamela Simotas joined the company to assist Kate with the sourcing of materials and the manufacturing of the handbags. In 1994, Elyce Arons joined the company to focus on sales and public relations. The addition of Simontas and Arons led to the creation of a partnership that now numbers seven persons, each of whom brings special expertise and talents to the company.[4]

Growing into the Future

Kate Spade's vision focused on developing product lines and appropriately positioning the company in both the domestic and global marketplace. Kate Spade's original design philosophy relied on simplicity, elegance, and enduring quality "to create products that combined great personal style with long-lasting utility." This design philosophy has been consistently applied to growing the company's product lines. In addition to the original six nylon tote bags, Kate Spade's product lines now include leather handbags and accessories, evening bags, baby bags, a luggage collection, shoes, glasses, paper products (e.g., personal organizers, address books, and journals), and beauty products. In 1999, Jack Spade, an accessories line for men, was launched under Andy's tutelage. Jack Spade products include messenger bags, briefcases, and utility bags, among other items.[5]

In mid-1996, Kate Spade opened its first retail shop in New York City's Soho neighborhood. Expansion of the retail operation soon followed, with stores being opened in Boston, Los Angeles, Greenwich, Manhasset, San Francisco, Georgetown, and Chicago. Numerous Kate Spade outlets now exist in several Japanese cities, including Tokyo, Kyoto, and Osaka. International distribution of Kate Spade products has also expanded to Australia, the Bahamas, Bermuda, Canada, England, Guam, Hong Kong, Ireland,

Korea, the Philippines, Puerto Rico, Saipan, Singapore, and Taiwan. An e-commerce operation is currently under development.[6]

In just over a decade, Kate Spade has grown from the germ of an idea about how to fill a void in the women's fashion accessories market into a multi–product line business with distribution in several U.S. and international locations. A future challenge for Kate Spade is how to build on its phenomenal success of the past decade. Continued expansion will be a key element in accomplishing this. Growth of the fledgling Jack Spade business may be another important element of the company's continued growth. Perhaps the Jack Spade line will be the company's growth engine of the next decade? Kate and Andy Spade recognize that their biggest challenge in the future will be to continue differentiating themselves from their competition while creating a passionate following

among customers who have numerous choices.[7]

Review Questions

1. Describe the key decisions that Kate and Andy faced in the startup of their company.
2. What were the key elements of Kate Spade's growth in the first decade of its operations? What specific business decisions were made in implementing these key elements of growth?
3. What key decisions will Kate Spade need to make during the second decade of its operations?

You Do the Research

1. What options are available to Kate Spade in developing an e commerce operation?
2. How might Kate Spade utilize information technology to help fuel continuing global expansion?

CASE 8

Wal-Mart: Planning for Superstore Competition

Wal-Mart, first opened in 1962 by Sam Walton in Rogers, Arkansas, has become the largest retailer in the world, with more than 4,600 store locations and approximately 1.25 million associates worldwide. Despite the death of Sam Walton in 1992, Wal-Mart continues to be successful, reaching record annual sales of $244.5 billion and earnings of $8.0 billion in fiscal 2003.[1] Maintaining this phenomenal growth presents an important challenge to Wal-Mart's current leadership.

Carrying on Sam Walton's Legacy

In his 1990 letter to Wal-Mart stockholders, then-CEO David Glass laid out the company's philosophy: "We approach this new exciting decade of the '90s much as we did in the '80s—focused on only two main objectives, (a) providing the customers what they want, when they want it, all at a value, and (b) treating each other as we would hope to be treated, acknowledging our total dependency on our associate-partners to sustain our success."[2] Following in Sam Walton's footsteps, Glass believed that the traditional format of organization, employee commitment, cost control, carefully planned locations for new stores, and attention to customer needs and desires would enable Wal-Mart to enjoy continued success.

Wal-Mart grew by paying careful attention to its market niche of customers who were looking for quality at a bargain price. Customers did not have to wait for a sale to realize savings. Many of its stores were located in smaller towns, primarily throughout the South and Midwest. As Glass looked ahead at the 1990s, he recognized the opportunities and threats that confronted Wal-Mart. While the traditional geographical markets served by Wal-Mart were not saturated, growth in these areas was limited. Any strategy to achieve continuing growth would have to include expansion into additional geographical regions. Glass recognized that continued growth might also have to include new product lines and higher-priced products to allow existing stores to achieve year-to-year sales growth.

In 1993, the company added the 91-store Pace Membership Warehouse chain, which it had purchased from Kmart.[3] Competition was increasing as smaller regional chains such as Costco and Price Club merged and opened stores in many of the same markets as Wal-Mart.[4] The company began to experiment with one-stop shopping in 1987, when it opened Hypermart USA, a Wal-Mart/supermarket combination. Experimentation with different retailing formats continued in subsequent years.

Wal-Mart is now made up of five retail divisions and five specialty divisions. The retail divisions include Wal-Mart Stores, SAM's Clubs (membership warehouse clubs), Neighborhood Markets (selling groceries, pharmaceuticals, and general merchandise), International Division, and Walmart.com (an online version of the neighborhood Wal-Mart store). Three of the specialty divisions—Tire & Lube Express, Wal-Mart Optical, and Wal-Mart Pharmacy—are commonly operated in conjunction with the Wal-Mart Stores and Supercenters and SAM'S Club outlets.[5]

Wal-Mart subscribes to the corporate policy "buy American whenever possible." Nonetheless, it has a global procurement system that enables it to effectively coordinate its entire worldwide supply chain and to share its buying power and merchandise network with all its operations throughout the world.[6] The company has set up an extensive inventory control procedure based on a satellite communication system that links all stores with the Bentonville, Arkansas, headquarters. The satellite system is also used to transmit messages from headquarters, training materials, and communications among stores, and can even be used to track the company's delivery trucks. In addition, Wal-Mart has an online system that links the company's computer systems with its suppliers. Because of its use of innovative technology, Wal-Mart has gained a competitive advantage in the speed with which it delivers goods to its customers.

While each new Wal-Mart brings in new jobs, it can also bring detrimental effects to the community as well. A 1991 *Wall Street Journal* article noted that many small retailers are forced to close after Wal-Mart opens nearby.[7] In one Wisconsin town, even J.C. Penny lost 50 percent of its Christmas sales and closed down when Wal-Mart opened up. In an Iowa town, four clothing and shoe stores, a hardware store, a drug store, and a dime store all went out of business. In 1994, the voters in Green field, Massachusetts, forced Wal-Mart to withdraw its building plans by using a few simple rules of engagement. It also had to give up plans to build in Bath, Maine; Simi Valley, California; and two towns in Pennsylvania. Vermont successfully resisted all Wal-Mart plans to locate in that state.

Even Wal-Mart's "Bring it home to the USA" buying program produced controversy when an NBC news program found clothing that had been made abroad hanging on racks under a "Made in the USA" sign in 11 Wal-Mart stores. In addition, the program showed a tape of children sewing at a Wal-Mart supplier's factory in Bangladesh. Wal-Mart insisted that its supplier was obeying local labor laws, which allowed 14-year-olds to work. A company official had also paid a surprise visit to the factory and had not found any problems. Then-CEO David Glass stated: "I can't tell you today that illegal child labor hasn't happened someplace, somewhere. All we can do is try our best to prevent it."[8]

Meanwhile, Wal-Mart began considering international expansion. In March 1994, the company bought 122 Canadian Woolco stores, formerly owned by Woolworth Corp., the largest single purchase Wal-Mart had made.[9] This international expansion continued, and in 2003, Wal-Mart's international division was the second largest with respect to sales and earnings. The almost 1,200 international locations had $41 billion in sales and an operating profit of $2 billion.[10]

Sam's Cultural Legacy

Wal-Mart's success is built upon its culture. Rob Walton, the company's current chairman of the board, says: "Although Wal-Mart has grown large, we still focus daily on the culture and values established by my father, Sam Walton."[11] Sam Walton founded and built Wal-Mart around three basic beliefs: *respect for the individual, service to our customers*, and *striving for excellence*. Wal-Mart's slogan that "our people make the difference" reflects the company's respect for and commitment to its associates (employees). Diversity is also highly valued. Wal-Mart's philosophy of customer service emphasizes the lowest possible prices along with the best possible service to each and every customer. Lee Scott, Wal-Mart Stores' current president and CEO, observes: "Sam was never satisfied that prices were as low as they needed to be or that our product's quality was as high as they deserved—he believed in the concept of striving for excellence before it became a fashionable concept."[12]

Three critical elements in Wal-Mart's approach to customer service are the *sundown rule*, the *ten-foot rule*, and *every day low prices*. The *sundown rule* means Wal-Mart sets a standard of accomplishing tasks on the same day that the need arises—in short, responding to requests by sundown on the day it receives them. The *ten-foot rule* promises that if an employee comes within ten feet of a customer, the employee must look the customer in the eye and ask if the person would like to be helped.

Every day low prices is another important operating philosophy. Wal-Mart believes that by lowering markup, it will earn more because of increased volume, thereby bringing consumers added value for the dollar every day.[13]

While Wal-Mart has enjoyed phenomenal success, there is no guarantee that it will continue to do so in the future. As the company's 2003 Annual Report points out, preserving and advancing the *every day low prices* concept and helping thousands of new associates to embrace the customer-centered Wal-Mart culture are essential for the company to continue growing.[14]

Review Questions

1. What are Wal-Mart's key objectives?
2. How have Wal-Mart's managerial philosophies and principles enabled it to pursue these key objectives?
3. How do planning and controlling seem to be linked at Wal-Mart?

You Do the Research

1. Explain how the various elements of Sam Walton's cultural legacy contribute to the company's ethical orientation.
2. Sam Walton's 1992 book *Made in America* identifies 10 key factors in building a business. These factors are identified on the company's website, www.walmartstores.com. How do these factors relate to Wal-Mart's culture and success?

Virgin Group: Reaching for the Sky in a New Economy

S ir Richard Branson has assembled a collection of companies under the umbrella brand of "Virgin." Branson has repeatedly confounded analysts with his ability to spot emerging trends and profit from them. One senior executive at Virgin describes the company as a "branded venture-capital firm."[1] Branson has continually redefined Virgin's business operations, branching out into a variety of ventures but always capitalizing on his exuberant entrepreneurial spirit.

Richard Branson: Young Entrepreneur

Born in 1950, Branson began his first entrepreneurial venture when he was a 16-year-old student at a boarding school. He founded a magazine called *Student* to address contemporary issues of the time, such as the Vietnam War and the Paris student uprising. While raising about $6,000 over a six-month period to fund the magazine, Branson recruited well-known celebrities—like Jean-Paul Sarte and Vanessa Redgrave, among others—to be interviewed in or to write for the publication.[2] Branson, with his brashness, extraordinary ambition, and passion for success, went on to become a billionaire entrepreneur.

The magazine was followed in 1970 with a venture into discount records. Branson and Company ran ads in a mail-order catalog, and an increasing number of individuals purchased discounted records from it. Then his group from the magazine found an old shop, cleaned it up, and started a discount record store. Searching for a name for the business, they came up with three options: "Slipped Disc," "Student," and "Virgin." Since they were all virgins at business, the name Virgin was selected.[3] It quickly became the largest discount music megastore chain in the world.

In 1972 Branson branched out into the music recording business with Virgin Records. His first recording artist, Mike Oldfield, released "Tubular Bells," which went on to sell more than 5 million copies. When punk rock became popular, Branson signed the Sex Pistols, a group no other recording studio would touch. Other groups included Genesis, Simple Minds, Culture Club, Phil Collins, and the Rolling Stones.

Moving on to Other Ventures

Other people might have been content with their early success, but Richard Branson was not finished. Running his business interests out of a houseboat on the Thames River, he launched Virgin Airways in 1984 (now Virgin Atlantic) with a single jumbo jet. Taking on British Airways, he sued them for alleged dirty tricks and won. The airline is famous for its offbeat perks, including massages and premium first-class service.

Branson also refuses to follow the industry leaders. As many airlines drop fares and cut service in order to compete for passengers, Branson keeps Virgin Atlantic focused on reasonable fares and unique customer service, including ice cream with movies, private bedrooms, showers, and exercise facilities.

Looking back on his various business ventures, Branson says, "I started the magazine because I had a passion for what I was doing. That's also why I went into the airline business, even though everybody I talked to told me that there was no money to be made there. I felt that I could make a difference. That's the best reason to go into business—because you feel strongly that you can change things."[4] Branson's business objectives from the start have been to be noticed, have fun, and make money by constantly starting new firms.[5]

Over the years, Virgin Group Ltd. has created more than 200 new businesses, employing more than 25,000 people, with revenues exceeding £3 billion (US$5 billion) annually.[6] Virgin Group

Ltd. currently has business interests in planes, trains, finance, soft drinks, music, mobile phones, holidays, cars, wines, publishing, bridal wear—and more.[7] Virgin doesn't represent a business so much as it represents a business-making machine.[8]

When Virgin starts a new business, it is based on solid research and analysis. The company reviews the industry and puts itself in the customer's shoes. Virgin asks several fundamental questions: "Is this an opportunity for restructuring a market and creating competitive advantage? What are the competitors doing? Is the customer confused or badly served? Is this an opportunity for building the Virgin brand? Can we add value? Will it interact with our other businesses? Is there an appropriate trade-off between risk and reward?"[9]

Not everything touched by Branson turns to gold. He was forced in the early 1990s to sell his beloved Virgin Records to Thorn EMI to secure the survival of his Virgin Airlines. As a result, Branson now employs a strategy of using wealthy partners to provide the bulk of the cash necessary to run a business, with Virgin providing the brand-name recognition in exchange for a controlling interest in the venture. Rather than mixing with investment bankers, he has a habit of keeping his companies private—preferring to sell off chunks of his empire to fund new business startups. His sale of a 49 percent share of Virgin Atlantic to Singapore Airlines for $979 million provided him the needed cash to plow into his Internet ventures.[10]

Although Virgin represents a late arrival to the Internet, Branson has attacked the venture with the same enthusiasm displayed in his previous business startups. Many of his business interests already had a presence on the Web, including Thetrainline.com, a joint venture with the British transport company Stagecoach. The site sells tickets for Britain's 23 train operators, has more than 1.8 million users and purchases of more than $2.5 million weekly, and is adding 55,000 new users each week.[11] By transferring an airline-type reservation system onto the Net, Virgin earns 9 percent of every ticket booked. Virgin will sell competitors' services right alongside its own. What Branson is hoping to do is leverage his presence into a "cyberbrand" with a premium presence on the Web.

"Virgin's approach to the Net has been very clever," claims Simon Knox, professor of brand marketing at the Cranfield University School of Management in Bedford. "Each launch of a new business builds upon the one before, rather than developing isolated branded businesses."[12] Others, like Michael Arnbjerg, with the market research firm IDC in Copenhagen, disagree. He argues that "Virgin can leverage its brand in certain market sectors, but that's not enough to become a major player."[13]

Expanding the Business Portfolio

The Virgin Group's main focus is on providing services rather than on producing products. To help fuel its services growth, Virgin actively seeks business proposals from the public via its website. "If you have a fantastic idea for us, then we're all ears! We're always on the lookout for fresh ideas to improve our current companies and to create brand new ones."[14]

In soliciting proposals, the company emphasizes that "Virgin is famous for its down-to-earth good value and service, so all new ideas will need to reflect these values. We also have a great sense of fun, and we like to do things just a little bit differently from the rest."[15] Virgin asks people who submit business proposals to address the following issues: the nature of the product or service idea; the business sector into which this idea fits; the idea or project's current stage of development; the proposal submitter's involvement in the project, as well as the role he/she/they would like to maintain; the reason for approaching Virgin and the anticipated role of Virgin in the project; and an assessment of the venture's potential.[16]

Virgin says that it respects the intellectual property rights of all new business proposals that it receives. The company notes, however, that it receives "hundreds of proposals which are often similar to those suggested by others, or to ideas which we have developed internally."[17] While only a few submitted proposals actually move forward in the business development process, the ones that are most likely to be successful are already well developed, have large-scale potential, and can be implemented quickly.[18]

What does the future hold for Sir Richard and the Virgin Group? If history is any predictor, the company's portfolio will continue to embrace a wide range of businesses that have the potential for providing quality service in a fun and different way.

Review Questions

1. What are the key strategic questions that the Virgin Group asks when starting a new business venture?

2. How has the Virgin Group established a competitive advantage?

3. How would you characterize the corporate strategy of Branson's Virgin Group?

4. What are the main advantages and disadvantages associated with Virgin's solicitation of business proposals from the public to help grow the business?

You Do the Research

1. Examine the range of businesses that fall under the Virgin Group's corporate umbrella. Does investment in these different businesses make sense from a business strategy perspective? Why or why not?

2. Do a SWOT analysis for Virgin Group Ltd.

3. How dependent is the success of Virgin on Richard Branson? If something happened to him, would the company be able to survive?

CASE 10

Krispy Kreme: Where Growth Is Really Sweet

At Krispy Kreme's 324th store opening in late October 2003, a crowd began gathering early outside the store. Close to 100 people huddled under a tent and umbrellas on that cold, rainy morning waiting for the store's opening. With the local media present, the store opened at 5:30 A.M. to the crowd's chanting "Doughnuts! Doughnuts!" One customer who had been in line since 3:00 A.M. admitted to getting up early to see presidents and governors—and now to purchase Krispy Kreme doughnuts. As admirable—or crazy—as this may seem, it's tame compared to the doughnut dedication shown by others. Some people will even camp out at the stores in the final days of construction and set up before the opening. Rob Perugini camped outside of the 324th Krispy Kreme for 17 days before the opening, breaking the old record of 13 days.[1] What does Krispy Kreme do to produce such devotion to its doughnuts?

The Founding and Early Growth of Krispy Kreme

Krispy Kreme Doughnuts, founded in 1937, has grown from a small doughnut shop in a rented building into "a leading branded specialty retailer, producing more than 5 million doughnuts a day and over 1.8 billion a year."[2] After purchasing a yeast-raised doughnut recipe from a French chef in New Orleans, Vernon Rudolph, Krispy Kreme's founder, began making doughnuts in a rented building in Winston-Salem, North Carolina, and selling them to local grocery stores. Soon Rudolph began selling hot doughnuts directly to customers.[3] In the ensuing years, Krispy Kreme grew into a small chain of stores, all using the same recipe. Product quality varied, however, and the company established a dry-mix plant and distribution system to ensure a consistent product. Krispy Kreme continued to expand and enjoyed steady growth until the mid-1970s, when the company was sold to Beatrice Foods subsequent to Rudolph's death.[4]

The sale to Beatrice Foods ushered in an era in which Krispy Kreme stores sold ice cream, sausage biscuits, and other food products in addition to doughnuts. Even the doughnut recipe was changed. Horrified by what was happening, a group of Krispy Kreme franchisees repurchased the company from Beatrice foods a few years later.[5]

With the 1982 repurchase, Krispy Kreme refocused on making the hot doughnut experience a company priority. The company continued expanding throughout the southeastern United States, and then in 1996 it opened its first unit outside the Southeast. This store was in New York City. In 1999, Krispy Kreme opened its first store in California. National expansion has accelerated rapidly since then. In December 2001, the company opened a store in Canada, its first outside the United States.[6]

Growth Through Excellence

Krispy Kreme has a strategic philosophy that is oriented toward growth through excellence. The company's strategic philosophy revolves around the following beliefs:

- "All products we make in our stores will have a taste and quality that are second to none."
- "The starting point in controlling product quality is controlling the quality and freshness of the ingredients."
- "We will be thoroughly prepared to execute growth initiatives when they become needed."
- "We view quality, service, and innovation as keys to creating and maintaining a competitive advantage."
- "We view our company as a set of capabilities, not just a product or brand."
- "We view our growth and success as a company as a natural result of the growth and success of our people."[7]

Krispy Kreme's growth has been partly fueled by the company's obsession with product consistency. Krispy Kreme strives for such consistency that a doughnut purchased anywhere in the world at any time will taste exactly the same. This is accomplished by testing all raw ingredients before delivery is accepted. If a test sample of a shipment does not meet the company's standards, the entire shipment is rejected. Krispy Kreme also makes sample doughnuts from every single 2,500-pound batch of mix to ensure that each batch is blended correctly.[8]

Krispy Kreme is more like a factory than a bakery. Krispy Kreme stores typically operate around the clock, producing doughnuts for walk-in customers as well as for wholesale purchase by supermarkets and grocery stores.[9]

National expansion through franchising has driven a good portion of Krispy Kreme's growth, particularly since the mid-1990s. Significant growth has occurred even though a Krispy Kreme franchise is the most costly food franchise available—being about five times the standard cost for most operations, as estimated by the International Franchise Association. A Krispy Kreme franchise, costing $2 million per location on average, is both extraordinarily difficult to obtain and in great demand. Krispy Kreme requires its franchisees to have "$5 million in net worth to apply and . . . ownership and operating experience with multi-unit food service operations."[10] Krispy Kreme also seeks "area developers"—franchisees who will open at least 10 stores in a region.

Krispy Kreme stores are high-volume operations with higher profit margins than other fast-food business. A typical McDonald's franchise has revenues of about $1.5 million annually and a typical Dunkin' Donuts averages about $744,000.[11] In fiscal 2001, Krispy Kreme franchisees had average revenue of $2.2 million per location. This jumped to $2.8 million in fiscal 2002 and $3 million in fiscal 2003. Company stores had even higher annual sales volume, reaching about $4 million in fiscal 2003.[12]

"Krispy Kreme now takes an ownership stake in all new franchisees, claiming anywhere from 33% to 75%," a strategy that increasingly is being adopted by other franchising companies. "The parent companies engage in such partnerships because they lead to higher earnings and faster expansion." Krispy Kreme takes an ownership stake even though franchisees "have the money and desire to open as many stores as the company will allow."[13]

While fueling growth, this joint-partnership strategy has not been a smooth road. A lawsuit over the terms of an alleged contract was filed by two franchisees in northern California. An equity fund that was formed by 35 Krispy Kreme executives to invest in franchise stores was disbanded in the aftermath of the Enron scandal so "that no individual's personal gain would conflict with the overall good of the company."[14]

Krispy Kreme's rapid growth has also been facilitated by its use of information technology. The company uses the Internet as well as a corporate intranet to aid national and international expansion. Using its information technology, Krispy Kreme has made more and more of its services and information accessible to corporate staff, stores, franchisees, and suppliers. The vast majority of orders from individual units are placed over the company's intranet. Using the Internet and intranet, individual stores from anywhere in the world can train employees around the clock.[15]

Krispy Kreme continues to expand into new markets, both in the United States and overseas. In fiscal 2003, the company entered 17 new U.S. markets as well as one in Canada. It also opened its first store outside of North America, which is in Sydney, Australia. At the end of fiscal 2003, the company is also preparing for a store opening in London. In addition, the company acquired Montana Mills Bread Company and successfully introduced Krispy Kreme Signature Coffees—an outgrowth of its earlier acquisition of Digital Java, Inc. Krispy Kreme has developed a roasting process for coffee beans that ensures the same high level of quality and consistency with its coffees as it has with its doughnuts.[16]

In line with its emphasis on product consistency, Krispy Kreme's opening of a new store engenders highly consistent customer behavior. A Krispy Kreme store opening attracts a lot of attention. The experience of James Consentino, a West Palm Beach, Florida, franchisee is typical on the morning of a store opening and in the ensuing days. "At 5:30 A.M. that morning, he'll let in a mob of people who've been waiting outside for hours for the warm doughnuts streaming from his ovens at a rate of 2,640 per hour. The event will probably be covered by a TV news crew—most Krispy Kreme openings are—and in his first week Consentino will take in almost as much in revenue as the typical Dunkin' Donuts store makes in a year."[17]

Review Questions

1. What are the key elements of Krispy Kreme's strategic philosophy? How do these elements relate to the organizing trend of balancing decentralization with centralization?
2. What type of organizational structure does Krispy Kreme appear to be using?
3. What is the potential for developing a network structure at Krispy Kreme?

You Do the Research

1. Based on its recent growth history, what would you predict for Krispy Kreme in the next five years? What type of organizational structure should be used to accommodate whatever growth you predict?
2. Suppose that you decide to exercise your entrepreneurial motivation and want to look into franchising opportunities. What key elements would you look for in a franchising relationship?
3. Does Krispy Kreme present a better franchise opportunity than those provided by other franchising companies? Why or why not?

BET Holdings: World-Class Entrepreneur Places BET on Future

Robert Johnson, born the ninth of ten children in Hickory, Mississippi, is a true rags-to-riches success story. His father, Archie, chopped wood while his mother taught school. Ultimately, their search for a better life led them to Freeport, Illinois, a predominantly white working-class neighborhood. Archie supplemented his factory jobs by operating his own junkyard on the predominantly black east side of town. Edna Johnson got a job at Burgess Battery, and although she eventually secured a job for her son, Robert, at the battery firm, he knew it wasn't for him.[1]

Robert Johnson's Journey to Becoming an Entrepreneur

Bobby Johnson showed an enterprising nature at an early age, delivering papers, mowing lawns, and cleaning out tents at local fairs. At Freeport High School, he was an honors student and entered the University of Illinois upon graduation. Virgil Hemphill, his freshman roommate, commented: "He was not overly slick, overly smooth. He was kind of innocent and naive. His strength was being able to talk to different types of people. I went to Freeport with him, and he could communicate with the regular people and with the suit-and-tie people."[2]

Johnson did well at Illinois, studying history, holding several work-study jobs, and participating in Kappa Alpha Psi, a black fraternity. After graduation in 1968, he was admitted to a two-year program at Princeton University's Woodrow Wilson School of Public and International Affairs. He had a full scholarship plus expenses but dropped out after the first semester to marry his college sweetheart, Sheila Crump, a

former cheerleader and a gifted violinist. He eventually returned to Princeton to earn his master's degree in public administration in 1972.[3]

He moved on to Washington, D.C., to work at the Corporation for Public Broadcasting, followed by the Washington Urban League, where the director, Sterling Tucker, was leading the struggle for District home rule. Tucker appreciated Johnson's ability to think both "micro-ly and macro-ly" while still "thinking like a visionary" in pursuing larger goals.[4] Moving on to work for the Congressional Black Caucus, Johnson became impressed with the possibilities for black power that lay in television—and cable, in particular. In 1976, he began working as a lobbyist for the National Cable Television Association (NCTA), where he gained invaluable insight into the cable industry.

At the NCTA's 1979 convention, Johnson met Bob Rosencrans, president of UA-Columbia Cablevision. While Bob Johnson had a strong idea for providing cable programming to minority audiences, he had no satellite time. Rosencrans, on the

other hand, was looking for programs to support his local franchises and to fill some unused slots on one of the cable TV satellites. "I just said, 'Bob, you're on. Let's go.' I don't think we even charged him. We knew he couldn't afford much, and for us, it was a plus because it gave us more ammunition to sell cable. The industry was not attracting minority customers."[5]

With $15,000 from a consulting contract that he received upon his departure from NCTA, Robert Johnson launched Black Entertainment Television (BET) at 11:00 P.M. on January 8, 1980. The first BET show was a 1974 African safari movie, *Visit to a Chief's Son.* Initially, BET aired for only two hours on Friday nights. The first show bounced off an RCA satellite and into 3.8 million homes served by Rosencrans's franchises. Johnson received his first crucial financing from John Malone of TCI in the form of a $380,000 loan plus $120,000 for a 20 percent ownership in BET.[6]

To raise capital in the 1980s, Johnson sold off pieces of BET to Time Inc.

and Taft Broadcasting for more than $10 million. However, controversy over programming followed Johnson from the start, with his heavy reliance on music videos (60 percent of total programming), gospel and religious programs, infomercials, and reruns of older shows such as *Sanford and Son* and *227*.[7] After a decade of learning the finer points of the cable industry, Johnson went public with BET.

BET suffered from low fees compared to other cable offerings. Early on BET was earning only 2 cents per subscriber, while major networks such as TNT and USA were getting 15 to 20 cents. Johnson won the battle for higher fees, which jumped from 2.5 cents to 5 cents in 1989 and eventually to 15.5 cents over the next five years.[8]

The Growth of BET Holdings

Robert Johnson had grand plans for BET, seeking to turn the enterprise into what marketers call an umbrella brand.[9] The firm published two national magazines that reached 250,000 readers: *Young Sisters and Brothers* for teens and *Emerge* for affluent adults, and it had interests in film production, electronic retailing, and radio.[10] The first BET Sound-Stage restaurant opened in suburban Washington and another in Disney World in Orlando. With Hilton as a partner, Johnson explored opening a casino in Las Vegas, Nevada.[11]

Johnson wanted to capture some of the black consumers' disposable income—valued at $425 billion annually. To do this, he partnered primarily with big names as such Disney, Hilton, Blockbuster, Microsoft, and others. "You simply cannot get big anymore by being 100 percent black-owned anything," Johnson claimed.[12] His Black Entertainment Television cable station provided the perfect medium to influence this increasingly affluent black audience.

BET, Inc. aims to become "the leading African-America multi-media entertainment company. BET is committed to establishing the most valued consumer brand within the African-American marketplace."[13] Black Entertainment Television, distinctly targeted toward serving the African-American community, remains at the core of the BET business empire. As of late 2003, Black Entertainment Television reached more than 74 million cable subscribers in the United States.[14] Included among this subscriber base are more than 90 percent of all black households that have cable hookups. BET's related digital cable businesses include BET on Jazz, BET Gospel, BET Classic Soul, BET International, and BET Hip Hop. BET Books publishes literature on African-American themes written by African-American authors. BET Pictures produces documentaries on African-American themes and made-for-TV movies. BET Interactive, a partnership among BET, Microsoft, Liberty Digital Media, News Corporation, and USA Net-

works, has the Internet portal BET.com, which is the leading online site for African-Americans.[15]

BET Holdings II, Inc. has grown into such a success story that Viacom, Inc. purchased it for $3 billion in November 2000. Robert Johnson remains as chairman and CEO of the Viacom subsidiary, reporting to Viacom's president and chief operating officer, Mel Karmazin.[16] Karmazin describes the acquisition of BET Holdings as "a strategically perfect fit. . . . Viacom is home to the industry's most creative and distinctive branded programming, the perfect environment for BET's television and online business to grow and prosper."[17]

Review Questions

1. Is a mechanistic organizational design or an organic organizational design more appropriate for BET? Explain your answer.
2. How might environment and strategy influence BET's organizational design?
3. As a multifaceted, multimedia entertainment company, what challenges regarding differentiation and integration does BET likely face?

You Do the Research

1. Was Robert Johnson correct in selling his BET Holdings II to Viacom?
2. Will BET Interactive become a major force on the Web?
3. What's next for Robert Johnson?

SAS Institute: Systems Help People Make a Difference

Founded in 1976 by Dr. James Goodnight and Dr. John Sall, both professors at North Carolina State University, SAS Institute, Inc. provides business intelligence (BI) software and services at more than 40,000 customer sites worldwide, including 90 percent of the *Fortune* 500 companies. SAS, which stands for "statistical analysis software," is headquartered in Cary, North Carolina. It is the world's largest privately held software company, having more than 100 offices worldwide with approximately 10,000 employees. With an unbroken record of growth and profitability, SAS had revenue of $1.18 billion in 2002 and invested about 25 percent of revenues into research and development.[1] The phenomenal success story of SAS is, in no small part, due to its human resources strategy, policies, and practices. How do the HR strategy, policies, and practices contribute so much to the success of SAS?

Human Resources Policies and Practices at SAS

Fast Company metaphorically describes the SAS Institute as a modern company that is like a kingdom in a fairy-tale land. "Although this company is thoroughly modern (endowed with advanced computers, the best child care, art on almost every wall, and athletic facilities that would make an NBA trainer drool), there is something fairy-tale-like about the place. The inhabitants are happy, productive, well rounded—in short, content in a way that's almost unheard-of today. They are loyal to the kingdom and to its king, who in turn is the model of a benevolent leader. The king—almost unbelievably—goes by the name Goodnight."[2]

SAS is strongly committed to its employees. The company strives to hire talented people and goes to extraordinarily lengths to ensure that they are satisfied. James Goodnight, the CEO of SAS, says: "We've made a conscious effort to ensure that we're hiring and keeping the right talent to improve our products and better serve our customers. To attract and retain that talent, it's essential that we maintain our high standards in regards to employee relations."[3]

SAS has been widely recognized for its work-life programs and emphasis on employee satisfaction. The company's various honors include being recognized by *Working Mothers* magazine as one of "100 Best Companies for Working Mothers" and by *Fortune* magazine as one of the "100 Best Companies to Work for in America." The *Working Mothers* recognition has been received 13 times, and the *Fortune* recognition has occurred for six consecutive years.[4]

SAS pays its employees competitively, targeted at the average for the software industry. It does not provide stock options like other companies in the industry.[5] Instead of relying on high salaries and stock options to attract and retain workers like many software companies do, SAS takes a very different approach. It focuses on providing meaningful and challenging work, and it encourages teamwork. SAS also provides a host of benefits that appeal to the employees and help keep them satisfied. As one employee who took a 10 percent pay cut to join SAS said: "It's better to be happy than to have a little more money."[6]

Employees are given the freedom, flexibility, responsibility, and resources to do their jobs, and they are also held accountable for results. Managers know what employees are doing and they work alongside them, writing computer code.[7] "The company employs very few external contractors and very few part-time staff, so there is a strong sense of teamwork throughout the organization."[8] SAS employees are clearly involved in their work. One employee, Kathy Passarella, notes: "When you walk down the halls here, it's rare that you hear people talking about anything but work."[9]

Included among the various employee benefits that SAS provides are an employee fitness and recreational center, an employee laundry service, a heavily subsidized employee cafeteria, live piano music in the employee cafeteria, subsidized on-site child care, and a free health center.[10] All of these benefits are geared toward employees having a better work experience and/or a better balance between their work lives and their personal lives. The company's commitment to work-life balance is evident in SAS's 35-hour workweek, which clearly recognizes the importance of employees' personal lives.[11]

In reflecting on the company's generous benefits package, David Russo, SAS's head of human resources, says: "To some people, this looks like the Good Ship Lollipop, floating down the stream. It's not. It's part of a soundly designed strategy." That strategy is intended "to make it impossible for people not to do their work."[12]

Extraordinary Employee Benefits: At What Cost?

While SAS goes to extraordinary lengths to ensure that employees are satisfied, the company expects and demands productivity and performance results in return. The owners of SAS want employees to be satisfied because they believe satisfied employees will be excellent performers and will provide exceptional service to the company's customers. "If you treat employees as if they make a difference to the company, they will make a difference to the company. . . . Satisfied employees create satisfied customers."[13] This viewpoint might be described as a form of enlightened realism and enlightened self-interest on the part of the company. Satisfied employees make for satisfied customers, and satisfied customers make for an ongoing stream of revenue and profits for SAS.

SAS's leaders recognize both the benefits and costs associated with keeping employees satisfied. One of the most significant benefits for SAS is a very low annual turnover rate, which is less than 4 percent, as compared to approximately 25 percent for the industry as a whole. This low turnover saves the company about $70 million annually in employee replacement costs.[14] On the cost side, of course, is the company's monetary outlay for the various programs. David Russo, the human resources director, argues that the employee replacement cost saving more than pays for the company's generous benefits. "That's the beauty of it," says Russo. "There's no way I could spend all the money we save."[15]

Perhaps of more concern on the "cost side" is the potential for employees failing to perform. In commenting on the company's performance expectations for employees, Goodnight says: "I like to be around happy people, but if they don't get that next release out, they're not going to be very happy."[16] Pondering the likelihood that SAS employees would take advantage of the company's relaxed atmosphere, John Sall, co-owner of SAS, observes: "I can't imagine that playing Ping-Pong would be more interesting than work."[17] David Russo adds some additional perspective. He says: "If you're out sick for six months, you'll get cards and flowers, and people will come to cook dinner for you. If you're out sick for six Mondays in a row, you'll get fired. We expect adult behavior."[18]

Clearly, human resource management at SAS is a two-way street. SAS has an HR strategy and related policies and practices that attract, motivate, and retain highly capable workers who make significant contributions to the ongoing success of the company. Goodnight and the other SAS leaders expect nothing less than superior performance from the employees, and they continue to get it. The employees are loyal and committed to the company, and they are productive—so loyal, committed, and productive, in fact, that only a small percentage of the employees ever leave once they have been hired at SAS. Having quality employees who want to stay—isn't this the human resources goal that should challenge all companies?

Review Questions

1. What is the basic management philosophy that governs employee relationship management at SAS Institute?

2. Explain how the SAS human resources strategy, policies, and practices affect the company's ability to attract, develop, and maintain a quality workforce.

3. What impact have the SAS human resources strategy, policies, and

practices had on the company's financial success?

You Do the Research

1. Compare SAS with Trilogy Software, a competitor in the computer software industry, in terms of approaches to attracting, developing, and maintaining a quality workforce.

2. Why does Trilogy take the approach that it does? Why does SAS take the approach that it does?

3. Would the SAS approach to attracting, developing, and maintaining a quality workforce be adaptable to any company in any industry? Why or why not?

CASE 13

Southwest Airlines: How Herb Kelleher Led the Way

The U.S. airline industry experienced problems in the early 1990s. From 1989 through 1993, the largest airlines, including American, United, Delta, and USAir, lost billions of dollars. Only Southwest Airlines remained profitable throughout that period. Herb Kelleher, co-founder of Southwest in 1971 and until recently its CEO, pointed out that "we didn't make much for a while there. It was like being the tallest guy in a tribe of dwarfs."[1] Nevertheless, Southwest Airlines has grown to the point of having operating revenue of $5.5 billion in 2002, which also was its 30th consecutive year of profitability. This is particularly noteworthy since Southwest flies to only 58 cities in 30 states, and its average flight length is 537 miles.[2] How did a little airline get to be so big? Its success is due to its core values, developed by Kelleher and carried out daily by the company's 35,000 employees. These core values are humor, altruism, and "luv" (the company's stock ticker symbol).[3]

Southwest Airlines's Unique Character and Success

One of the things that make Southwest Airlines so unique is its short-haul focus. The airline does not assign seats or sell tickets through the reservation systems used by travel agents. Many passengers buy tickets at the gate. The only foods served are peanuts, pretzels, and similar snacks, but passengers don't seem to mind. In fact, serving Customers (at Southwest, always written with a capital C) is the focus of the company's employees. When Colleen Barrett, currently Southwest's president and chief operating officer (COO), was the executive vice president for customers, she said, "We will never jump on employees for leaning too far toward the customer, but we come down on them hard for not using common sense."[4] Southwest's core values produce employees who are highly motivated and who care about the customers and about one another.

One way in which Southwest carries out this philosophy is by treating employees and their ideas with respect. As executive vice president, Colleen Barrett formed a "culture committee," made up of employees from different functional areas and levels. The committee continues and meets quarterly to come up with ideas for maintaining Southwest's corporate spirit and image. All managers, officers, and directors are expected to "get out in the field," meet and talk to employees, and understand their jobs. Employees are encouraged to use their creativity and sense of humor to make their jobs and the customers' experiences more enjoyable. Gate agents, for example, are given a book of games to play with waiting passengers when a flight is delayed. Flight agents might do an imitation of Elvis or Mr. Rogers while making announcements. Others have jumped out of the overhead luggage bins to surprise boarding passengers.[5]

Kelleher, currently chairman of the board and chairman of the executive committee, knows that not everyone would be happy as a Southwest employee: "What we are looking for, first and foremost, is a sense of humor. Then we are looking for people who have to excel to satisfy themselves and who work well in a collegial environment." He feels that the company can teach specific skills but that a compatible attitude is most important. When asked to prove that she had a sense of humor, Mary Ann Adams, hired in 1997 as a finance executive, recounted a practical joke in which she turned an unflattering picture of her boss into a screen saver for her department.[6]

To encourage employees to treat one another as well as they treat their customers, departments examine linkages within Southwest to see what their "internal customers" need. The provisioning department, for example, whose responsibility is to provide the snacks and drinks for each flight, selects a flight attendant as "customer of the month." The provisioning department's own board of directors makes the selection decision, as well as other departmental managerial decisions. Other departments have sent pizza and ice cream to their "internal customers." Employees write letters commending the work of other employees or departments, and these letters are valued as much as those from "external customers."

When problems do occur between departments, the employees work out solutions in supervised meetings.

Employees exhibit the same attitude of altruism and "luv" (Southwest's term for its relationship with its customers) toward other groups as well. A significant portion of Southwest employees volunteer their time at Ronald McDonald Houses throughout Southwest's service territory. When the company purchased a small regional airline, employees personally sent cards and company T-shirts to their new colleagues to welcome them to the Southwest family. They demonstrate similar caring toward the company itself. As gasoline prices rose during the period of the Gulf War in the early 1990s, many of the employees created the "Fuel from the Heart Program," donating fuel to the company by deducting the cost of one or more gallons from their paychecks.

Acting in the company's best interests is also directly in the interest of the employees. Southwest has a profit-sharing plan for all eligible employees; and unlike many of its competitors, Southwest consistently has profits to share. Employees can also purchase Southwest stock at 90 percent of market value; at least 13 percent of Southwest's employees own company stock. Although approximately 81 percent of employees are unionized, the company has a history of good labor relations.[7]

Southwest Airlines is a low-cost operator. According to Harvard University professor John Kotter, setting the standard for low costs in the airline industry does not mean Southwest is *cheap*. "Cheap is trying to get your prices down by nibbling costs off everything . . . [firms like Southwest Airlines] are thinking 'efficient,' which is very different. . . . They recognize that you don't necessarily have to take a few pennies off of everything. Sometimes you might even spend more."[8] By buying one type of plane— the Boeing 737—Southwest saves on both pilot training and maintenance costs. The *cheap* paradigm would favor used planes; Southwest's choice results in the youngest fleet of airplanes in the industry because the model favors high productivity over lower capital expenditures.

Southwest currently operates a fleet of 381 Boeing 737 jets with the configuration shown in the table below.[9]

By utilizing each plane an average of 12 hours per day, Southwest is able to make more trips with fewer planes than any other airline. Since May 1988, Southwest Airlines has won the monthly "Triple Crown" distinction of airline service— Best On-Time Record, Best Baggage Handling, and Fewest Customer Complaints—more than 30 times. From 1992 through 1996, Southwest won the annual "Triple Crown" every year.[10]

Type of 737	Number of Aircraft	Seats per Aircraft
737-200	26	122
737-300	194	137
737-500	25	122
737-700	136	137

Southwest's Ongoing Challenges

Despite its impressive record of success, Southwest Airlines has pressing concerns to address. Management worries about the effects on morale of limited opportunities for promotion. The company has created "job families" with different grade levels so that employees can work their way up within their job category. However, after five or six years employees begin to hit the maximum compensation level for their job category.

Another issue is how to maintain the culture of caring and fun while expanding rapidly into new markets. Southwest's success has been built with the enthusiasm and hard work of its employees; as Kelleher said, "The people who work here don't think of Southwest as a business. They think of it as a crusade."[11] Cultivating that crusading atmosphere is a continuing priority for the company.

As Herb Kelleher prepared to relinquish his role as Southwest's CEO, a major concern for investors was whether the company's success could be maintained because so much of Southwest's success was attributable to Kelleher's unique management and leadership style. Recent events, however, seem to demonstrate that Kelleher's successors—longtime Southwest employees Jim Parker (currently vice chairman of the board and CEO) and Colleen Barrett (currently president and COO)—were well prepared to handle the challenges of maintaining Southwest's culture and success. As Barrett wrote in the company's *Spirit Magazine*: "Air travel changed forever two years ago, but our steadfast determination remains unbroken to provide the high-spirited Customer Service, low fares, and frequent nonstop flights that Americans want and need."[12] Not even terrorist attacks can derail the company that Herb Kelleher led to success. Southwest Airlines continues to be recognized by *Fortune* magazine as America's most admired airline as well as one of the most admired companies in America. In 2003 *Air Transport World* magazine selected Southwest as the "Airline for the Year." The reasoning: 30 consecutive years of profitability, while providing affordable fares for millions of passengers. Other recognitions of Southwest culture and success continue to pile up.[13]

2002 Fun Facts

- Southwest received 243,657 resumes and hired 5,042 new employees.
- Southwest booked approximately 83 million reservations.
- Southwest served 32.8 million cans of soda and juice and 11.7 million cans of water.
- Southwest served 162.4 million bags of peanuts.
- Southwest purchased 1.1 billion gallons of jet fuel.
- Southwest has 1,000 married couples working for the company.
- Southwest received requests for service from 140 destinations.[14]

Review Questions

1. What role has leadership played in the success of Southwest Airlines?
2. Explain the role of employee empowerment at Southwest Airlines and how it can act as a substitute for leadership.
3. Describe Kelleher's leadership style.
4. What is the key to Southwest's continued success under leaders other than Herb Kelleher?

You Do the Research

1. How did Herb Kelleher use power and exercise influence at Southwest Airlines?
2. Which of the leadership theories described in Chapter 13 seem to provide the most useful explanation for Herb Kelleher's success in leading Southwest Airlines?
3. Find examples that show how Herb Kelleher and other leaders at Southwest Airlines have acted with integrity. What lessons do these examples provide for future managers and leaders?

NASCAR: Fast Cars, Passion Motivate Top Drivers

In only his second full year of NASCAR Winston Cup Series racing, the young Ryan Newman was rapidly becoming a racing phenomenon. He had a spectacular 2002 racing season and was on target to surpass it in 2003. As of mid-October 2003, Newman had competed in 34 Winston Cup races, finishing among the top ten 19 times while winning eight pole positions and eight races.[1] Ryan Newman appears driven to succeed. What motivates someone like Ryan Newman?

Ryan Newman's Racing Passion

A self-admitted car buff, Ryan Newman loves to drive cars and work on them.[2] His passion for fast cars developed at an early age. Encouraged by his parents, he started racing quarter midgets when he was only four-and-a-half years old. Newman amassed more than 100 midget car victories. Later he raced midget cars and sprint cars, achieving extraordinary success there as well. He won Rookie of the Year honors in 1993 for the All-American Midget Series, in 1995 for the USAC National Midget Series, in 1996 for USAC Silver Crown Racing, and in 1999 for sprint cars.[3]

In 2000, Newman began driving for the Penske Racing Team, competing in five Automobile Racing Club of America (ARCA) races and one NASCAR Winston Cup Series race. He won two of the ARCA races. In 2001, Newman competed in a total of 26 ARCA, Busch Grand National Series, and Winston Cup races, finishing in the top ten on 11 occasions with two first-place finishes.[4] In 2002, Newman raced full time in the Winston Cup Series, earning six pole positions, 22 top-ten finishes, 14 top-five finishes, and one first-place finish in 36 starts. Finishing in sixth place in the 2002 Winston Cup rankings, Newman won Rookie of the Year honors.[5]

In the off-season, Newman pursued his college degree in mechanical engineering at Purdue University, with the intent of gaining an advantage in his racing career. He crafted a plan of study that enabled him to focus on vehicle dynamics—vehicle design, materials strength, and so on—that would complement his interest in racing.[6]

Joining the Penske Racing Team

When Newman joined the Penske Racing Team in late 1999, the team's co-owners hired Buddy Baker, a former race car driver and subsequently a race car driving instructor, to work with Newman. Being very selective about the drivers he works with, Baker insisted on meeting Newman and his family before accepting the job offer. Baker says: "When I started talking to Ryan, I could feel the energy that he had, and the passion he had for the sport. Then, I met his dad, and right there I knew, OK, he's got a good background. His father's been with him in go-carts, midgets. He turned the wrenches for his son. It was an automatic fit for me." Baker thinks of Newman as though he were one of his own sons, both of whom briefly tried racing but neither of whom had a passion for it. Baker says that he never wanted to do anything but race, and Newman is just like him. Referring to Newman, Baker says: "From the time he was 5 years old until now, he's never wanted to be anything else."[7]

Referring to his pre–Winston Cup racing days, Newman says: "I always worked on my own cars and maintained them, did the set-ups, things like that. Obviously, I also drove them so I was always a hands-on, involved, seat of the pants driver." As a Winston Cup driver, Newman acknowledges that he misses working on the cars, "but when you have great guys doing that work, you don't feel like you have to do it yourself."[8] "For all my life, my family has been my crew. To come to an organization like Penske, and have so many more people behind you fighting for the same goals, it's like being in a bigger family. When you're with people you like, you have the confidence to do things well."[9]

Most of the people who work on Newman's crew are engineers, and all of them are computer whizzes—significant talents for building and maintaining today's race cars.[10] Newman and the crew, lead by Matt Borland, try to learn from the problem situations that they encounter so they can "keep the freak things from happening."[11]

Challenges of the 2033 Racing Season

In anticipation of the Daytona 500 near the beginning of the 2003 NASCAR season, Newman said: "I love racing at Daytona. Sure I won an ARCA race at Daytona, but I don't really have much experience there. It's a track that is just incredible to be at. The minute you drive through the tunnel, you feel overwhelmed." Newman enters every race with the attitude that he can and will win it.[12]

Newman had a spectacular crash at the Daytona 500 in which his car became airborne. He walked away sore but uninjured. When asked about the potential impact of the crash on him and the Penske racing team, Newman simply replied that such events make them fight back harder and stronger.[13] Just a few weeks later, a cut tire sent Newman into the wall at Talladega Superspeedway, triggering a fiery 27-

car wreck. Newman walked away uninjured.[14]

Newman's success seems to be part racing talent, part drive and determination, and part engineering expertise. In the Kansas 400 in early October 2003, Newman made his last pit stop with 79 laps remaining while many other drivers made pit stops with 65 laps to go. Newman won the race, his eighth Winston Cup victory of the 2003 season and his third in his last five outings. Some drivers questioned how Newman could have gone the 79 laps without refueling. Jeremy Mayfield, who finished third, said: "I'm not an engineer. But I know that if you've got 22 gallons of fuel in your car, and everybody's got the same length fuel line and everybody's got so much horsepower, it takes so much fuel to make that." Although hinting that Newman had cheated, Mayfield used the same type of car and a similar race strategy. Mayfield drove a Dodge, just like Newman and the second-place finisher. Mayfield also stayed out of the pits, just as Newman did.[15] Moreover, several other drivers made fuel stops with 78 laps to go and did not return to the pits for the remainder of the race.[16]

Driver Bill Elliot, who led on 115 laps of the race, was upset about the situation and refused to attend the post-race news conference. While asserting that it's very difficult to get both fuel mileage and power, Mike Ford, the crew chief for Elliot, nonetheless said any wrongdoing by Newman's team was purely speculative. Responding to the insinuation that cheating had occurred, Newman and his

crew chief, Matt Borland, maintained that no NASCAR rules were broken.[17]

In the ensuring days, Jeff Gordon and Tony Stewart, both Winston Cup champions, expressed suspicions about Newman's fuel usage. Other drivers and crew chiefs viewed Newman's critics as sore losers. Rookie driver Jamie McMurray commented: "Each time you win, somebody accuses you of cheating. That's just a sore loser. We want to be Ryan Newman. We want to go out and win eight races next year. We hope everybody accuses us of cheating." McMurray's veteran crew chief, Donnie Wingo, added: "I wouldn't take anything way from those guys. They've worked real hard. I don't think it's anything they're doing wrong that they shouldn't be doing." Veteran driver Bobby LaBonte pointed out that young drivers and crew chiefs, like Ryan Newman and Matt Borland, build their racing strategies around science and track position. Noting that technological advances have changed the competitive climate in racing, LaBonte said: "There are a lot of smart people working on race teams lately. You have people that are looking at all different ways to win races." Adamantly maintaining that he and his crew have done nothing wrong, Newman asserts that his racing team does the best job it can with what they have. "When there's an opportunity to try and stretch it to the end, we're going to try to stretch to the end," says Newman.[18]

Review Questions

1. What are the key factors that motivate Ryan Newman?

2. Using the fundamental ideas of the content theories of motivation, explain Ryan Newman's racing success.
3. How can the expectancy theory of motivation help in understanding Ryan Newman's passion for racing?
4. How can goal-setting theory help in understanding Ryan Newman's passion for racing?

5. Use equity theory to explain the various reactions to Ryan Newman's win at the Kansas 400 in early October 2003.

You Do the Research

1. What is passion in the context of work? In the context of a person's life outside of work?
2. What are you passionate about? How can you incorporate your true passion into your work-life?
3. Follow up on the controversy regarding Ryan Newman's win of the Kansas 400 in early October 2003. How did this controversy unfold? What are the motivational implications for Newman? For his racing crew? For other drivers and their crews?

CASE 15

Steinway & Sons: Craftwork, Tradition, and Time Build Grand Pianos

Steinway & Sons remains one of the best-known producers of concert pianos in the world. Throughout its great history, the company has shown a distinctive talent at innovation, as evidenced by its more than 100 patents, and is known for quality workmanship. In an age of mass production, Steinway continues to manufacture a limited number of handmade pianos in a unique testament to individual craftsmanship. However, some rival piano makers have tried to challenge Steinway's dominance of the concert piano market.[1] Can Steinway continue its cherished ways, or will it need to adjust to new circumstances?

A Long and Golden History

German immigrant Henry Enghelhart Steinway founded Steinway & Sons in 1853. Henry was a master cabinetmaker who built his first piano in the kitchen of his home in Seesen, Germany. He had built 482 pianos by the time he established Steinway & Sons. The first piano produced by the company, number 483, was sold to a New York family for $500. It is now displayed at New York City's Metropolitan Museum of Art.

Steinway's unique quality became obvious early in the history of the firm, as proven by its winning gold medals in several American and European exhibitions in 1855. The company gained international recognition in 1867 at the Paris Exhibition when it was awarded the prestigious Grand Gold Medal of Honor for excellence in manufacturing and engineering.[2] Henry Steinway developed his pianos with emerging technical and scientific research, including the acoustical theories of the renowned physicist Herman von Helmhotz.

Steinway was owned in the 1970s by CBS, and many concert artists complained that the quality of the pianos had suffered as a result of that ownership. Pianists talked of the "Teflon controversy," when Steinway replaced some fabric innards with Teflon (it now coats the Teflon with fabric). Steinway was sold by CBS in 1985, and many experts voiced the opinion that Steinway's legendary quality was returning. Larry Fine, a piano expert, argued that "a Steinway has a kind of sustained, singing tone that a Yamaha doesn't have. Yamaha has a more brittle tone in the treble that some jazz pianists prefer."[3]

The Steinway Factory

Today, the making of a Steinway piano follows the Steinway tradition. Every grand piano takes more than a year to complete and incorporates more than 1,000 details that set a Steinway apart from its competitors. A tour of the Steinway factory is a trip back through time, as many of the manufacturing techniques have not changed since 1853. The key steps in the process of crafting a Steinway piano are described below.[4]

Using a method that was patented in 1878, the piano manufacturing process begins with the creation of the inner and outer piano rims that give a grand piano its distinctive shape—this is known as the piano case. Eighteen layers of hard-rock maple, each 22 feet in length, are laminated together and then formed into shape on a giant piano-shaped vise. The rim-bending team centers the wood on the vise and forces it into place with the aid of wood clamps.

Meanwhile the soundboard is formed by hand, being "expertly tapered by a craftsman to be slightly thinner at the edges so that it can vibrate properly once it is glued to the piano's inner rim." The bridge of the soundboard must be notched for the piano strings before the soundboard can be placed into the piano case. A highly skilled crafts-

man, with years of training, performs this operation because precision is so essential to the quality of the piano's sound.

The veneer for a piano is cut from a single tree to ensure a uniform appearance of the wood finish. It is cut to size and matched for grain, to be applied subsequently to the designated piano.

A wooden brace assembly is then crafted to fit within the piano case and to help support the 340-pound cast-iron plate that provides the rigid and stable foundation for approximately 40,000 pounds of tension from the piano strings. This brace assembly is secured to the rim of the piano with fine carpentry joinery and maple dowels. The cast-iron plate is then fitted to the piano case and any needed adjustments are made before final installation of the plate.

After the soundboard and cast-iron plate are properly fitted in the piano case, the piano wires are installed, using both a machine-guided stringer and appropriate hand tools. Next, the felt hammers are formed into the proper shape, using glue and a copper forming tool. The felt hammers are then put on the hammershanks and dampers are installed to prevent unintentional vibration of the piano strings. A master technician painstakingly matches the damper felts to the strings; reaching underneath the piano while looking in mirrors, the master technician adjusts the levers that control each of the dampers.

Next, the keyboard is calibrated by inserting lead weights into the body of each

key so that the pressure required to push a key down is the same for every key. Subsequently, a master voicer will adjust the tone quality of each key. This is done by sticking the hammer's felt with a small row of needles to reduce stiffness of the felt, resulting in a mellower tone, or by applying a small amount of lacquer to the felt to achieve the opposite effect. Finally, a tone regulator adjusts string tension by turning the tuning pins.

Steinway's process of making a grand piano is complex, requiring numerous processes and procedures that must be performed by highly skilled craftsmen. True craftsmen produce the world's finest-quality concert pianos. However, not everyone wants or can afford a Steinway piano. What has Steinway & Sons done to reach other markets while maintaining the Steinway reputation for product quality?

Expansion Beyond the Classic Steinway Pianos

In recent years, Steinway developed Boston Piano in an attempt to broaden its market. Steinway & Sons designed Boston pianos using the latest computer technology and then outsourced the manufacturing to Kawai, the second-largest Japanese piano maker. By transferring its quality and knowledge of building pianos to the Boston Piano operation, Steinway was able to open up a whole new market. The Boston Piano venture demonstrated that Steinway's core competence of hand craftsmanship could be applied in a newer, high-technology manner to a lower-priced market niche.[5]

In early 2001, Steinway & Sons introduced a third line of pianos, called the Essex, to complement its Steinway and Boston lines. The Essex line offers two grand and two upright models ranging in price from $5,200 to $17,800. With the Essex, Steinway now provides pianos for every level of musical ability and budget.[6]

The question remains: Can Steinway continue to operate in the way that has proved successful over the past 150 years? At the moment, the answer appears to be—YES.

Review Questions

1. The equation specifying that Performance = Ability × Support × Effort is known as the individual performance equation. Using this equation, explain the exceptional performance that is required of and exhibited by the craftsmen at Steinway.
2. Use the core job characteristics model to explain the implications of Steinway's piano manufacturing process for work motivation and behavior.
3. How does Steinway's piano manufacturing process exhibit the need for teamwork? How does this relate to job enrichment?

You Do the Research

1. How does Steinway continue its emphasis on craftsmanship in this age of mass production?
2. Can any of Steinway's processes be transferred to other companies?
3. What other consumer products appear to be using a Steinway approach to producing its products?

CASE 16

Callaway Golf: Big Bertha's Team Hits a Long Ball

"Callaway Golf Company designs, creates, builds and sells Demonstrably Superior and Pleasingly Different golf products. That means that any club, ball or putter in the Callaway Golf family must be a significant improvement not only upon the products of our competitors, but also our own."[1] How does Callaway Golf achieve its goals of manufacturing and distributing demonstrably superior and pleasingly different golf products?

Callaway's DSPD Philosophy

In 1982, after a long business career in textiles and wine making, Ely Callaway purchased and bought a 50 percent interest in Hickory Stick USA, a small pitching wedge and putter manufacturing operation. Callaway's goal was to build demonstrably superior and pleasingly different (DSPD) golf clubs. The DSPD phi-losophy was based on his previous business experiences and served as the primary guiding principle for Callaway Golf, the company that grew out of Hickory Stick.[2]

The DSPD philosophy provides an important foundation for Callaway Golf's corporate mission. According to the company's 2002 Annual Report, the mission is as follows: "Callaway Golf Company is driven to be a world class organization that designs, develops, makes and delivers demonstrably superior and pleasingly different golf products that incorporate breakthrough technologies, backs those products with noticeably superior customer service, and generates a return to our shareholders in excess of the cost of capital. We share every golfer's passion for the game, and commit our talents and technology to increasing the satisfaction and enjoyment all golfers derive from pursuing that passion."[3]

Implementing the DSPD Philosophy

Callaway Golf's numerous innovations "revolutionized the industry with friendly clubs that helped golfers of all abilities find more enjoyment and a few more great shots in their game."[4] These innovations included the 2-Ball putter and the HX aerodynamic cover pattern on golf balls. Perhaps the company's most publicized innovation was the Big Bertha Driver with a large stainless steel head.

Capitalizing on its design and manufacture of "demonstrably superior and pleasingly different golf products," Callaway Golf continued to grow. It went public with its stock in 1992, the year in which it also acquired Odyssey Putters. Callaway entered the golf ball market in 2000.[5] Today Callaway Golf is the "number one manufacturer of drivers, fairway woods, irons, and putters."[6]

Callaway Golf operates in 107 countries, building on Ely Callaway's vision of helping the average golfer to find more enjoyment from the game. Ely Callaway, now deceased, retired from the company in 2001. His vision continues to be carried out under the leadership of his handpicked successor, Ron Drapeu, and the various teams that are the backbone of Callaway's operations.[7]

Teamwork at Callaway Golf

Teamwork at Callaway Golf is built around five different teams: research and development, information systems, manufacturing, sales, and general/administrative. The *research and development team*—which draws on engineering, analytical, and computer skills from people trained in a wide range of industries—is responsible for designing, building prototypes, and testing the company's innovative, premium golf equipment. The *information systems team* uses various computer applications to supply the company's information needs around the clock. The *manufacturing team* uses the latest manufacturing and assembly techniques to achieve levels of efficiency, innovation, and safety that are at the top of the golf industry. Among other fields, the manufacturing team members have backgrounds in industrial, mechanical, electrical, and process engineering, as well as in chemistry and aerodynamics. The *sales team* spans the world to provide golf retailers with the latest innovations in golf equipment and the highest-quality service. The *general/administrative team*—consisting of accountants, legal experts, artists, human resource generalists, receptionists, writers, and others—helps to build and grow the company by supporting the activities of the other teams.[8]

While the members of these teams reflect considerable diversity of backgrounds, all of the team members share some common characteristics. Callaway Golf looks for "integrity, honesty, daring, enthusiasm, accountability and hard work" in its employees. In addition, the company seeks to keep a "healthy balance between career and play," recognizing that this results in "happier people who are more productive in every aspect of their lives."[9] Thus far, Callaway Golf has used both similarities and differences among it employees to forge five very effective teams. Will Callaway be able to maintain this balance in the future, or will diversity be sacrificed for commonality, or commonality for diversity?

Review Questions

1. What is the DSPD philosophy? Explain how the operations of the different teams reflect the DSPD philosophy.
2. What team member characteristics does Callaway Golf consider to be important? Why do these characteristics seem to be important?
3. Consider the question at the very end of the case: "Will Callaway be able to maintain this balance in the future, or will diversity be sacrificed for commonality, or commonality for diversity?" What is the most reasonable answer to this question? Why?

You Do the Research

1. Identify a competitor of Callaway Golf. How does Callaway Golf's DSPD philosophy compare to the fundamental management philosophy of the competitor? What managerial insights do you gain from making this comparison?
2. Use the Callaway Golf competitor that you identified for the

previous question. How does Callaway Golf's emphasis on teamwork compare to the competitor's approach to organizing and utilizing the talents of its employees? What insights about teamwork does this comparison provide?

CASE 17

The United Nations: Conflict and Negotiation in the Global Community

The United Nations (UN),[1] like its precursor the League of Nations, was established after a devastating World War in order to promote cooperation, peace, and security among countries. UN members are sovereign nations—the organization is not a world government and does not make laws. On October 24, 1945, the UN officially came into existence with 51 member countries. It now has over 190 members, including most countries in the world.

Members accept the obligations of the UN Charter, an international treaty that sets out basic principles of international relations. It is an organization that truly embraces the concepts of diversity, cooperation, and conflict resolution and prevention. However, the UN does much more than resolve conflict. Looking at the major headings on its home page, you find, in addition to peace and security, emphases on economic and social development, human rights, humanitarian affairs, and international law.

A World Order—How Does It Work?

The United Nations is made up of six main branches:

- The General Assembly: This body considers pressing international problems, and each member has one vote. Key decisions require a two-thirds majority; for others, a simple majority is sufficient. In recent years, in an effort to promote harmony, there has been a striving for consensus.
- The Security Council: The 15-member council has primary responsibility for maintaining international peace and security. Five of the member countries (China, France, the Russian Federation, the United Kingdom, and the United States of America) are permanent members; the other ten are elected for two-year terms. Under the UN charter, UN members are obligated to follow the Security Council's directives. Decisions require nine "yes" votes, and any permanent member can veto a decision. The Security Council tries to exhaust all possibilities for resolution prior to authorizing the use of force. The possibili- ties short of force include negotiation, mediation, reference to the International Court of Justice, and economic pressure.
- The Economic and Social Council: The 54-member council coordinates the economic and social work of the UN system. Members are elected for three-year terms.
- The Trusteeship Council: The council was formed to administer 11 trust territories. When the final territory became self-governing in 1994, the rules of procedure were changed. The current council is composed of the five permanent mem-

bers of the Security Council and meets only if needed.

- The International Court of Justice: Often called the World Court, this body is responsible for deciding disputes between countries when the countries agree to participate. The 15 judges, elected jointly by the General Assembly and Security Council, make decisions that those appearing before them are obligated to accept. It is based in The Hague and is the only UN body not headquartered in New York.
- The Secretariat: The Secretariat, the staff of the UN headed by the elected Secretary-General, handles the administrative work of the United Nations.

In addition, there are 14 other independent organizations, such as the International Monetary Fund and the World Health Organization, that are linked to the UN through cooperative agreements. These organizations, along with the UN's six branches, subunits, programs, and funds, form the UN system. The UN system promotes human rights, protects the environment, fights disease, fosters economic development, and reduces poverty, in addition to preserving world peace and security.

The UN offers the most opportunity in its ability to influence international public opinion. World conflicts are discussed on a world stage with a world audience. However, that does not guarantee that conflict can be prevented or that peacekeeping is a simple exercise.

In fact, one of its most inclusive experiences to date involved engaging in conflict.

The UN served as a focal point in arranging a coalition of nations to counter Iraq's invasion and occupation of Kuwait in the early 1990s. Thirty-four nations, under the auspices of the Security Council, provided the military forces necessary for Operation Desert Storm and drove Saddam Hussein's forces out of Kuwait. President George H. W. Bush's claim of a "New World Order" as a result of the outcome did not come to pass.

Peacekeeping can be a very dangerous enterprise and can be of short duration or last for decades. As of October 2003, 1,841 peacekeepers had died since the inception of the UN; 252 of those deaths occurred in 1993. In October 2003, there were thirteen peacekeeping missions in operation: two in Asia, three in the Middle East, three in Europe, and five in Africa. Two of those had been in operation for decades—the one at the India Pakistan border began in 1949, and UN peacekeepers have been in Cyprus since 1964. It seems that the goal of durable peace may be hard to achieve.

Other Conflicts

While the Security Council has the primary responsibility for maintaining international peace and security, the Security Council itself is not entirely peaceful. After the September 11, 2001, terrorist attacks on the World Trade Center and the Pentagon, the Security Council speedily adopted a resolution that obligated member countries to ensure that terrorists would be brought to justice. However, the dissension among Security Council members regarding the ap-

propriate action to take against Iraq subsequent to September 11 was newsworthy and unresolved. Some members wished to continue to try to settle the matter peacefully through diplomatic means. However, in the end the United States and its allies took nonsanctioned action against Saddam Hussein. It remains to be seen whether this has caused an irreparable breach in relations or damaged the power and prestige of the UN. The UN Security Council has implicitly accepted the situation by adopting resolutions indicating their willingness to become involved in the process of stabilizing a postwar Iraq.

The structure of the Security Council, funding, and priorities are also a source of conflict within the UN. While the UN provides an infrastructure system that transcends national borders, thereby encouraging international solutions to world problems, many smaller countries argue against domination by the larger nations, particularly by the Security Council's permanent membership.

In reaction to pressure from a number of nations, including the United States, the UN launched a reform movement in the late 1990s. Discussions on financing, operations, and Security Council makeup continue, but many times to the frustration of the smaller countries. These frustrations are best expressed by quotations taken from the speeches made during the September 22 to October 7, 1997, debate of the General Assembly on UN reform.[2] The following quotes illustrate the frustration with the power of the Security Council, the use of the veto, and the lack of transparency in its actions:

> If reform of the [Security] Council is to be truly comprehensive and consistent with the spirit and realities of our time, then we must seek to remove—or at least, as a first step, restrict—the use of the veto power. Democracy in the United Nations is a mockery if the voice of the majority is rendered meaningless by the narrow interests of the dominant few. (Minister for Foreign Affairs of Malaysia, HE Dato' Seri Abdullah bin Haji Ahmad Badawi)

> We also believe that real reform of the Security Council should aim above all at ensuring that decision-making machinery and processes have the transparency, effectiveness and pluralism that must characterize every democratic institution. This includes, among other specific measures, the limitation of the veto power of the Council's permanent members, and for timelier and more effective action to prevent international conflicts at the request of any State Member of the Organization. (President of the Republic of Ecuador, HE Mr. Fabian Alarcon Rivera)

> We would similarly like to see certain restrictions placed on the use of the veto. We understand that all efforts at restructuring and reform in the United Nations, however, should be focused on economic growth and development. In addition, my country is calling for

a reversal in the diminishing role of the General Assembly. The accountability of the Security Council to the General Assembly must be re-emphasized, and the General Assembly should more actively assert its role in the maintenance of international peace and security. (Chair of the delegation of Antigua and Barbuda, HE Mr. Patrick Albert Lewis)

> In the era of democracy, transparency and proper management that we are claiming for our countries, there is nothing more normal than to insist, together, on the same values and principles in this Organization which unites us. (Minister for Foreign Affairs of Algeria, HE Mr. Ahmed Attaf)

> Belgium, together with a number of like-minded countries that share the general concern with regard to strengthening the authority of the Security Council, . . . advocate[s] an increase in both permanent and non-permanent members, greater regional representativeness, enhanced Council efficiency and a limitation of the right of veto. The right of veto is incompatible with the general interest. It should be possible to modify the decision-making mechanism so as to avoid recourse to this instrument, which has become entirely obsolete. Belgium also pleads for more transparency and closer cooperation between the Security Council and countries contributing to

peacekeeping operations. (Minister for Foreign Affairs of Belgium, HE Mr. Erik Derycke)

Another source of dissension among UN members is the direction of the UN toward goals than are not so directly related to maintaining peace and security. The United States withheld its dues for a number of years in protest regarding UN policies and charges of administrative waste within its programs. The dissension concerning the funding and priorities of the UN is illustrated in the following quotes drawn from the same debate, in which implicit reference also is made to the United States and other member countries withholding of funds from the UN:[3]

> The situation of the United Nations social sphere is the most worrisome. The greatest burden of the Organization's budgetary crisis has fallen upon the bodies involved, whose financing has dropped by many millions of dollars during the present decade. . . . In a world where 1.3 billion people still survive on less than a dollar a day, in a world where, for the price of one combat plane, 57,000 children in Africa can be fed for a year, it is impossible to conceive of a reform of the United Nations whose priority is not to strengthen the work of its institutions and programmes dedicated to social issues. (President of the Republic of Colombia, HE Mr. Ernesto Samper Pisano, also Chair of the Non-Aligned Movement)

. . . the eradication of poverty throughout the world should be the main goal of the international community's coordinated efforts in the coming years. The globalization of the economy cannot be limited to the use of cheap labour in the developing world, the proliferation of profitable investments and the exploitation of certain markets. It should also aim at providing coordinated and systematic assistance to immense populations whose only experience of globalization has been their poverty and frustration. (President of the Republic of Ecuador, HE Mr. Fabian Alarcon Rivera)

While we are deeply engaged in this process of reform we must not lose sight of the fundamental goals that impelled us to undertake it in the first place: to enhance the Organization's ability to foster development and to address the root causes of poverty and conflict. Reform should not become a euphemism for budget slashing or an excuse for certain Member States to renege on their financial obligations to the Organization. (Minister for Foreign Affairs of Indonesia, HE Mr. Ali Alatas)

Jamaica also endorses the need for measures to improve efficiency, and we have no quarrel with reform to streamline and rationalize the system. In welcoming these steps, we must however emphasize that reform is not synonymous with cost cutting. Reform is not about doing less; it is about doing better. (Prime Minister of Jamaica, The Right Honourable Percival James Patterson)

The current financial situation has no link with the assessment system. The way to deal with it is by making full, timely and unconditional payments of the assessments the General Assembly assigns to Member States. . . . The financial crisis of the Organization should not lead us to take decisions that distort the spirit of reform we share. Carried to the extreme, this logic would call for the designation of Ted Turner as a permanent member of the Security Council, with the right of veto. By the way, we appreciate Mr. Turner's generosity. (Minister for Foreign Affairs of Mexico, HE Mr. Angel Gurria)

It cannot be justified that some countries unilaterally pay less than their legally binding share, or nothing at all. Non-payment is unacceptable. How can those of us who always make a point of paying in full and on time, without conditions, expect our citizens and taxpayers to continue financing free riders? (Minister for Foreign Affairs of Norway, HE Mr. Bjorn Tore Godal)

If the United Nations is to be reformed and made effective, then adequate financing is a matter of top priority. We therefore appeal to all Member States to pay their dues in full, on time, and without conditions. (First Deputy Prime Minister and Minister for Foreign Affairs of Uganda, HE The Honourable Iriya Kategaya)

Reform should not become a euphemism for budget slashing or an excuse for certain Member States to renege on their financial obligations to the Organization. (Minister for Foreign Affairs of Indonesia, HE Mr. Ali Alatas)

It is apparent that considerable concern exists over the funding, the organization, and the role of the UN. But does that mean that it has failed?

The Future

Even in the face of frustration, it appears that most members continue to believe that the UN still represents the world's best opportunity to create a climate of communication and dispute resolution across national borders, and to promote worldwide well-being. They recognize that the UN has had notable success in a variety of areas, including both the Nuclear Non-Proliferation Treaty (1968) and the Comprehensive Nuclear-Test-Ban Treaty (1996), the promotion of democracy, the improvement of world health, and the resolution of conflicts within and between member nations. The Millennium Declaration of 2000 set out goals for the UN in key areas including, among others, peace, security and disarmament, economic development and poverty eradication, environmental protection, and human rights.

The following quotes,

drawn from the same debate as the previous quotes, illustrate the ongoing commitment to and belief in the UN as the best chance for effective international cooperation:[4]

The General Assembly is a unique body in international institutional machinery. In it, representativity is practically universal. States participate on an equal footing without regard for their size or power, and the ideal of international democracy attains its clearest expression, at least in formal terms. The decisions of this body have great moral and political force and accordingly, it is essential to formulate them better and make them more timely. (Minister for Foreign Affairs of Uruguay, HE Mr. Alvaro Ramos)

The United Nations has an irreplaceable role in a world that still combines forces of integration and cooperation with forces of disintegration and aggression. (Minister of External Relations of Brazil, HE Mr. Luiz Felipe Lampreia)

Where else but at the United Nations can we deal with the truly global issues such as the new security threats of uncivil society, environmental degradation, violations of human rights and poverty? Given the nature of these issues, unilateral, bilateral or even regional efforts are of course good, but not enough. Not even the most prosperous and powerful nations on earth can successfully solve them alone. Only the United Nations has a global mandate and global legitimacy. (Minister for Foreign Affairs of Finland, HE Ms. Tarja Kaarina Halonen, now president of Finland)

Will the members continue to support the UN, join forces, and seize the opportunities to revitalize the UN—a "unique and universal instrument for concerted action in pursuit of the betterment of humankind" as Kofi Annan requested[5]—or allow it to go the way of the League of Nations?

Review Questions

1. What is the difference between mediation and negotiation? Can you find an effective use of each by the UN?

2. Based on the quotes given, how would you classify the *General Debate on Reform* in terms of conflict management styles?

3. If reform does occur, how do you think the reform will be perceived—lose–lose, win–lose, or win–win?

4. What suggestions might you make to the UN to improve communication and conflict resolution?

You Do the Research

1. What does the most recent Security Council resolution about Iraq indicate regarding the UN's involvement in that area?

2. In how many peacekeeping operations is the UN currently involved?

3. Has there actually been any reform of the Security Council since the *General Debate on Reform* in 1997?

4. How many member countries are currently in arrears in their payments to the UN?

5. What are the current issues on the UN agenda?

The Walt Disney Company: The Art of Brand Building Keeps Disney Center Stage

The Walt Disney Company has evolved from a wholesome family-oriented entertainment company into a massive multimedia conglomerate. Not only is Disney a producer of media but it also distributes its and others' media products through a variety of channels; operates theme parks and resorts; and produces, sells, and licenses consumer products based on Disney characters and other intellectual property. CEO Michael Eisner has been instrumental in many of these changes. How can such extensive changes occur while trying to maintain the Disney brand?

Disney Through the Years

After his first film business failed, artist Walt Disney and his brother Roy started a film studio in Hollywood in 1923. The first Mickey Mouse cartoon, *Plane Crazy*, was completed in 1928. *Steamboat Willie*, the first cartoon with a soundtrack, was the third production. The studio's first animated feature film was *Snow White* in 1937, followed by *Fantasia* and *Pinocchio* in the 1940s. Disneyland, the theme park developed largely by Walt, opened in 1955 in Anaheim, California. The television series the *Mickey Mouse Club* was produced from 1955 to 1959, and the Disney weekly television series (under different names, including *The Wonderful World of Disney*) ran for 29 straight years.[1]

Walt Disney died in 1966 of lung cancer. Disney World in Orlando, Florida, opened in 1971, the same year that Roy Disney died. His son, Roy E., took over the organization. However, the creative leadership of brothers Walt and Roy Dis-

ney was noticeably absent. Walt's son-in-law, Ron Miller, became president in 1980. Many industry watchers felt that Disney had lost its creative energy and sense of direction because of lackluster corporate leadership and nepotism. In 1984, the Bass family, in alliance with Roy E. Disney, bought a controlling interest in the company. Their decision to bring in new CEO Michael Eisner from Paramount and a new president, Frank Wells, from Warner Bros., ushered in a new era in the history of Disney.[2]

Work the Brand

Michael Eisner has been involved in the entertainment industry from the start of his career (ironically, beginning at ABC television in the 1960s). He exhibits a knack for moving organizations from last place to first through a combination of hard work and timely decisions. For example, when he arrived at Paramount Pictures in 1976, it was dead last among the six major

motion picture studios. During his reign as the company's president, Paramount moved into first place with blockbusters such as *Raiders of the Lost Ark*, *Trading Places*, *Beverly Hills Cop*, and *Airplane*, along with other megahits. By applying lessons he learned in television at ABC to keep costs down, he kept the average cost of a Paramount picture during his tenure at $8.5 million, while the industry average was $12 million.[3]

Eisner viewed Disney as a greatly underutilized franchise identifiable by millions throughout the world. In addition to reenergizing film production, Eisner wanted to extend the brand recognition of Disney products through a number of new avenues. Examples of his efforts over the years include the Disney Channel (cable), Tokyo Disneyland (Disney receives a management fee only), video distribution, Disney stores, Broadway shows (e.g., *Beauty and the Beast*), and additional licensing arrangements for the Disney characters.

However, in the early 1990s problems began emerging for Disney. An attempt to build a theme park in Virginia based on a Civil War theme was defeated by local political pressure. EuroDisney, the firm's theme park in France, resulted in over $500 million in losses for Disney due to miscalculations on attendance and concessions. In 1994, Eisner underwent emergency open-heart bypass surgery and Frank Wells, long working in the shadows of his boss but increasingly viewed as integral for the success of Disney, died in a helicopter crash. Eisner's choice to succeed Wells, Michael Ovitz from Creative Artists Agency, did not work out, and Ovitz soon left. Stories of Eisner's dictatorial management style brought succession worries to shareholders.

Capital Cities/ABC

Once again, Eisner ushered in a new era at Disney by announcing the $19 billion takeover of Capital Cities/ABC on July 31, 1995. The deal came in the same week as Westinghouse Electric Corporation's $5.4 billion offer for CBS Inc. Disney represented one of several consolidations of media conglomerates that increasingly control the distribution of entertainment programming in the United States. Disney ranked as the third-largest media conglomerate behind AOL Time Warner and Viacom.

Eisner appreciated the importance of both programming content and the distribution assets needed to deliver it.[4] As a result of many of Eisner's decisions, the Walt Disney Company has been transformed from a sleepy film production studio into a major entertainment giant, with its revenues of over $2 billion in 1987 increasing to $22 billion in 1997.[5] Its stock price has multiplied over 15 times, creating enormous wealth for both stockholders and executives of Disney.

One of the biggest questions arising from the ABC deal is whether Disney paid too dearly for declining network assets. Viewership among all the major networks was declining. According to Michael Jordan, the CEO of CBS, "the pure network television business is basically a low-margin to breakeven business."[6] The networks were squeezed by having to pay extravagantly for programming and were attracting an audience of older viewers who were scorned by advertisers.

However, another way to look at networks is as the lifeblood of the global, vertically integrated entertainment giants that own them and as loss leaders that act to promote their parent company's more lucrative operations. In this scenario, ABC acts as Disney's megaphone to tell the masses about Disney movies, theme parks, Disney-made shows, and toys. Another financial advantage occurs when the network owns and syndicates a hit show, something that could not be done before the networks were deregulated in the mid-1990s. By owning more of their own shows, the networks avoid the increasing licensing fees from the production companies.[7]

A potential risk is that a network will miss out on a hit by favoring its own shows. Disney has blocked out certain parts of the week for its own shows. Fox and Disney appear best situated to exploit their platforms, with Fox injecting new life into an old brand, and Disney providing diverse production assets to feed its network.[8] This strategy works as long as networks remain big. During the 1990s, however, network viewership declined; the various networks have cushioned this problem by investing more in their cable holdings.

Hard Times and Brand Investment

Not everything Disney touches turns to gold. For example, in early 2001, the company was forced to downscale its go.com Internet site as it continued to lose hundreds of millions of dollars.[9] Moreover, from fiscal 1998 through fiscal 2000, net income declined by half, from $1.85 billion to $920 million, while operating revenue grew from $22.98 billion to $25.4 billion.[10] In fiscal 2001 the company had a net loss of $158 million on operating revenue of $25.2 billion.[11]

Nonetheless, Disney remained committed to integrating its various operations into the greater Disney picture and to developing its brands. As Michael Eisner said in the late 1990s: "It sounds funny, but I am thinking about the millennium change. I've got to protect the Disney brand well into the future."[12]

As of fiscal 2002, the Walt Disney Company's businesses included *media networks*, *studio entertainment*, *Walt Disney parks and resorts*, and *consumer products.* Among the various *media network* holdings are (1) broadcasting networks such as ABC Television Network, Disney-owned and -operated television stations and radio stations, and Touchstone Television and Buena Vista productions, and (2) cable networks such as the ESPN-branded businesses, the Disney Channel, Toon Disney, SOAPnet, and a variety of online commerce, broadband, and wireless subscription services.[13] Disney's *studio entertainment* segment produces and/or acquires animated and live-action films, musical recordings, live stage plays, and animated television products.[14] *Walt Disney parks and resorts* include the company's theme park and resort operations (e.g., Walt Disney World, Disneyland, and the Disney Cruise Line) and ESPN Zone sports-theme restaurants, among others. Walt Disney parks and resorts also receives licensing royalties and/or management fees from the Paris and Tokyo Disneyland resorts.[15] The *consumer products* segment produces books and magazines, operates Disney retail stores, and licenses

Disney's characters and other intellectual property to manufacturers, retailers, publishers, and promoters.[16]

The Walt Disney Company has been very careful in maintaining brand identity and family values. However, the company recognizes that not everything is a Disney cartoon. For example, when the company goes outside its tradition, it produces its films under the Pixar or Buena Vista labels. Such movies are still family oriented in a broadly defined manner but are not the typical Disney film.

In his letter to shareholders in Disney's 2002 annual report, Michael Eisner wrote: "The past years have been disappointing in terms of earnings and stock price, but they have also been an exciting period of investment in our key brands . . . investment that I am confident will pay off well in the years ahead."[17] The company's competitive advantage is rooted in "maintaining strong and differentiated brands, most notably the Disney and ESPN brands." These brands are powerful from a business perspective because they are unique, thereby differentiat-

ing the products, and they are relevant to consumers.[18] This competitive advantage has helped return the Walt Disney Company to financial success. In fiscal 2002, the Walt Disney Company's net income was $1.2 billion on operating revenue of $25.3 billion.

Review Questions

1. Examine the internal and external forces for change faced by Disney.
2. How have external forces in the entertainment industry affected Disney's need for change?
3. What changes do you foresee in the entertainment industry in the next five years?

You Do the Research

1. Disney has apparently turned its fortunes around. What are the prospects that the company will maintain this success in the future?
2. Has the Walt Disney Company really moved past its reputation as a children's movie and theme park provider?
3. Are media conglomerates headed for trouble?

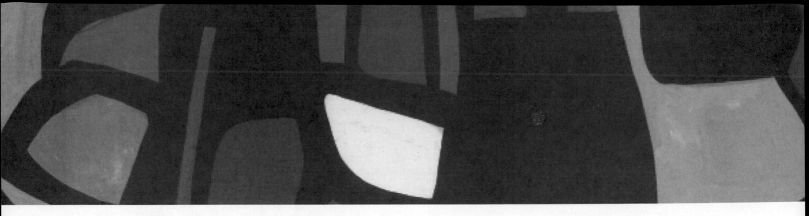

INTEGRATING
CASES

Outback Steakhouse, Inc.
Fueling the Fast-Growth Company

- -

Marilyn L. Taylor, D.B.A., Gottlieb-Missouri, Distinguished Professor of
Business Strategy, Henry W. Bloch School of Business and Public
Administration, University of Missouri—Kansas City,
Kansas City, MO 64110

Krishnan Ramaya, Ph.D., Henry W. Bloch School of Business and
Public Administration, University of Missouri—Kansas City,
Kansas City, MO 64110

George M. Puia, Ph.D., School of Business,
Indiana State University, Terre Haute, IN 47809
Tel: (812) 237-2090

*Support for the development of this case and its accompanying video
were provided by*

Center for Entrepreneurial Leadership
Ewing Marion Kauffman Foundation
Kansas City, MO

- - - - - - - - - - - - - - - - - - - MANAGEMENT LEARNING WORKBOOK **W-159**

The authors express deep appreciation to the following individuals at the Ewing Marion Kauffman Foundation: Dr. Ray Smilor, vice president of the Center for Entrepreneurial Leadership Inc.; Ms. Pam Kearney, communications specialist, Communications Department; and Ms. Judith Cone, ETI professional with the Center for Entrepreneurial Leadership Inc. In addition, the authors wish also to express appreciation to Outback executives Chris Sullivan, chairman and CEO; Bob Basham, president and COO; Tim Gannon, sr. vice president; Bob Merritt, sr. vice president, CFO, and treasurer; Nancy Schneid, vice president of marketing; Ava Forney, assistant to the chairman and CEO; as well as the other Outback officers, executives, and employees who gave so enthusiastically and generously of their time, knowledge, and skills to make this case study possible.

Contact Person: George M. Puia, Ph.D.

Exhibits may be found in the Instructor's Manual.

Outback Steakhouse: Fueling the Fast-Growth Company

Since the company's initial public offering in June of 1991, Wall Street observers had continually predicted a downturn in the price of Outback's stock. Indeed, most analysts viewed Outback as just another fad in an intensely competitive industry where there are plenty of imitators. They continued to caution that Outback was in a saturated market and that the company could not continue growing at its existing pace. The December 1994 issue of *Inc.* magazine declared Outback's three founders as winners of the coveted Entrepreneur of the Year award. The company was profiled in 1994 and early 1995 by the business press as one of the biggest success stories in corporate America in recent years.[1]

At 5:00 P.M. on a Saturday in early 1995 in Brandon, a suburb outside Tampa, the lines had already begun to form in a strip mall outside Outback Steakhouse. Customers waited anywhere from half an hour to almost two hours for a table.

The firm's founders, Chris Sullivan, Bob Basham, and Tim Gannon, organized Outback in August 1987 with the expectation of building five restaurants and spending increased leisure time on the golf course and with their families. In 1988 the company had sales of $2.7 million from its two restaurants. By year-end 1994 the chain exceeded all of the founders' expectations, with over 200 restaurants and $549 million in systemwide sales (see Exhibits 1 and 2 for financial data) and had formed a joint venture partnership with Texas-based Carrabbas Italian Grill to enter the lucrative Italian restaurant segment, currently dominated by General Mills' Olive Garden. A 1994 national survey of the country's largest restaurant chains ranked Outback first in growth (52.9%), second by sales per unit ($3.3 million), sixth by market share (5.9%), and tenth by number of units (205), all of which was accomplished in less than six years (see Exhibit 3).[2]

The founders expected that Outback could grow into a 550–600-unit chain in the continental United States. During 1995 alone, the company expected to add 65 to 70 new restaurants, maintain overall sales growth comparable to 1994, and continue to increase its same-store sales. In spite of the company's past success and future plans, however, analysts and other industry observers questioned how long Outback could continue its astounding growth, whether the company could maintain its strong momentum while pursuing multiple major strategic thrusts to propel its growth, and whether and how the culture of the company could be maintained. Skepticism about Outback's continued growth was clearly evident in the way Wall Street analysts viewed the company. By the end of 1994, Outback's stock was one of the most widely held stocks on the short sellers' list.[3] Adjusted for stock splits, Outback's share price rose from $3.50 to almost $30 over a three-year period. Exhibits 4 and 5 provide information on Outback's stock performance as well as samples of analysts' perspectives on Outback's continued growth during 1994.

The French Restaurant Legacy

The French coined the term *restaurant*, meaning "a food that restores," and were the first to create a place that could be defined as a restaurant by modern standards.[4] Before the French Revolution most culinary experiences were the exclusive domain of the nobility. The French Revolution dispersed the nobility and their chefs. The chefs, denied the patronage of the nobles, scattered throughout Europe, taking the restaurant concept with them.

In contrast, American restaurants grew up in response to the need to serve the burgeoning 19th-century U.S. workforce. The rapid growth of U.S. cities, fueled by the influx of European immigrants, provided the initial impetus for the American restaurant industry. Initially, restaurants were single family-owned operations and consisted of two broad categories.[5] The first category, fine dining, had facilities that were affordable only to the wealthy and were located primarily in major cities. The second category catered primarily to industrial workers. This latter category included concepts such as lunch wagons and soda fountains, which later evolved into coffee shops and luncheonettes. These grew rapidly in response to the continuous expansion of urban areas. The American obsession with efficiency propelled yet another restaurant concept, the self-service restaurant, to become a central theme for 20th-century American restaurants.

Retail and theater chains emerged with the new century. The first large U.S. restaurant chain organization was the brainchild of Frederick Henry Harvey, an English immigrant.[6] After his Harvey House opened in 1876 in Topeka, Kansas, restaurant chains too quickly became part of the American scene.

The restaurant industry's $290 billion revenues in 1993 accounted for 4.3 percent of U.S. GDP.[7] The industry's 100 largest chains accounted for 40 percent of total industry sales. U.S. restaurants in the latter part of the twentieth century could broadly be classified into three segments—fast-food, casual dining, and fine dining. However, within these three broad categories were highly fragmented sub-segment markets. The fast-food segment was primarily catered to by major chains such as McDonald's, Wendy's, Burger King, Hardee's, and Kentucky Fried Chicken. Casual dining catered to the cost conscious and typically priced menu entrees between fastfood and fine dining restaurants. Fine dining establishments catered to affluent customers and were located primarily in major metropolitan areas. Fine dining establishments were mostly single-unit businesses. In the early 1990s 75 percent of all casual dining establishments were still mom-and-pop operations.[8] The industry was characterized by high failure rates. Approximately 75 percent of all establishments failed within the first year; 90 percent within five years. Failure in the restaurant industry was attributed to a plethora of factors, including undercapitalization, poor location, poor food quality, underestimation of the effort needed to be successful, the effect of changing demographics segments, and government regulations.[9]

Restaurant operations are highly labor-intensive businesses. However, aspiring restaurant owners often seriously underestimated their capitalization require-

ments, that is, the funds needed for leasehold improvements and equipment. Indeed, new restaurants are often seriously undercapitalized. The owners might also fail to plan for other startup funds such as the first year's working capital, preopening expenses, advertising, and inventory costs.

Location choice was another common error. A restaurant location had to attract sufficient traffic to sustain operations. The demographics required for appropriate fine dining restaurant sites were different from those required for casual dining establishments, which differed again from fast-food establishments such as McDonald's. The availability of suitable locations especially in major cities had become an important factor in the success or failure of restaurants.

Aspiring restaurant owners also often underestimated *the effort required* to make a restaurant successful. Running a restaurant was hard work and could easily involve 80 to 100 hours of work each week. *Changing demographics* affected not only location choices but also the theme and type of restaurant. What had once been easily definable segments had fundamentally changed. It had become increasingly difficult to clearly define targetable segments. *American Demographics* magazine referred to the current situation as "particle markets."[10] Examples of such particle markets included empty nesters, step-families, the baby boomlet, immigrants, the disabled, savers, the affluent, the elderly, and others. The restaurant industry was also one of the country's most regulated industries. Myriad regulations on such issues as hygiene, fire safety, and the consumption of alcoholic beverages governed daily operations.

Still another requirement for a successful restaurant was the maintenance of consistent *food quality.* Maintaining a level of consistent food quality was challenging. Any variability in food quality was typically viewed as deficient.

Founding Outback Steakhouse — From Down Under to Where?

In March 1987 three friends—Chris Sullivan, Bob Basham, and Tim Gannon—opened their first two Outback restaurants in Tampa, Florida. Each of the three had started early in their careers in the restaurant industry—Chris as a busboy, Bob as a dishwasher, and Tim as a chef's assistant. Between them they had more than sixty years of restaurant experience, most in the casual dining segment. The three met when they went to work for Steak & Ale, a Pillsbury subsidiary, shortly after they completed college in the early 1970s. Chris and Bob went to executive roles in the Bennigan's restaurant group, part of the Steak & Ale group. The two men met their mentor and role model in casual dining legend Norman Brinker. Brinker had headed Pillsbury's restaurant subsidiary. When Brinker left Pillsbury to form Brinker International, Chris and Bob followed him. Among Brinker International's casual dining chains was Chili's. Brinker helped the two men finance a chain of 17 Chili's restaurants in Florida and Georgia. Chris and Bob described their contribution as "sweat equity."[11] Brinker was considered a leading pioneer in the development of the causal dining industry.[12] Brinker International, the restaurant holding company that Brinker created, was widely considered an industry barometer for the casual dining segment.

Brinker International, the parent company, acquired Chris and Bob's interest in the Chili's franchise for $3 million in Brinker stock. With about $1.5 million each, Chris and Bob turned their attention to a long-standing dream—their own entrepreneurial venture. They considered several options, finally settling on the idea of a startup venture consisting of a small chain of casual dining restaurants. Each of the two men brought special skills to the table—Chris in his overall strategic sense and Bob in his strong skills in operations and real estate.

In early fall 1987 the two men asked Tim Gannon to join Outback as its chief chef. Tim had left Steak & Ale in 1978 to play a significant entrepreneurial role in several restaurant chains and single-establishment restaurants, primarily in the New Orleans area. His last venture was a restaurant with Pete Fountain at the New Orleans World's Fair. The venture at the World's Fair had experienced early success and then suddenly encountered severe financial difficulties, leaving Tim with virtually no financial resources. In fact, when Gannon accepted Chris and Bob's invitation to join them, he had to sell his one remaining prized possession, a saddle, in order to buy gas money to travel from New Orleans to Tampa.

Tim brought with him recipes drawn from 25 years of experience. His first tutelage had been under a French chef in Aspen, Colorado. Concerning his initial teacher, Tim said:

I was an Art History major (who) found his way to Colorado to Aspen to ski. My first job was as a cook. That job became exciting because the man I worked for was a chef from Marseilles who had a passion for great foods. I grew to love the business. . . . I have made the restaurant industry my whole life.

Bob Basham especially wanted a restaurant concept that focused on steaks. The three men recognized that in the United States in-home consumption of beef had declined over the years, primarily because of health concerns. However, they also noted that the upscale steak houses and the budget steak houses were extremely popular in spite of all the concerns about red meat. That observation came from their market research, which Bob Basham described as follows:

We visited restaurants to see what people were eating. We talked to other people in the industry. Basically we observed and read trade magazines. That is the kind of research I am talking about. We did not hire a marketing research crew to go out and do a research project. It was more hands-on research . . . . the experts said people will eat less red meat, but we saw them lining up to get in. We believed in human behavior, not market research.

The partners concluded that people were cutting in-home red meat consumption but were still very interested in going out to a restaurant for a good steak. They saw an untapped opportunity between high-priced and budget steakhouses to serve quality steaks at an affordable price.

Outback operated in the dinner house category of the casual dining segment where 75 percent of all such establishments were family-owned and operated. The top fifteen dinner house chains accounted for approximately $9 billion dollars in total sales.[13] Dinner house chains usually had higher sales volumes than fast-food chains. However, dinner houses typically cost more to build and operate.[14]

The initial investment for Outback came from the sale of the Chili's restaurant franchise. Both men were able to forgo taking cash salaries from Outback for the company's first two years. Funding for the early restaurants came from their own resources, relatives, and the sale of limited partnerships. During 1990 the founders turned to venture capitalists for about $2.5 million. Just as the venture capital deal was materializing, Bob Merritt was hired as CFO. Trained as an accountant, Merrit had extensive experience with the financial side of the restaurant business. Prior to joining Outback, Merritt served as the vice president of finance for JB's Restaurants. Merritt had IPO experience, and the founders later decided a public offering was warranted. The company went public in June

1991. The market had a general aversion toward restaurant stocks during the mid- and late 1980s. However, Outback's share offering, contrary to expectations, traded at premium. CFO Merritt recalled his efforts to borrow funds in 1990 even after the venture-capital infusion:

In November 1990, Outback was really taking off . . . . The most significant limitation was capital . . . . So, I shaved off my beard—because Tampa is a fairly conservative community-and went from bank to bank. I spent every day trying to borrow. I think we were asking for $1.5M so that we could finance that year's crop of equipment packages for the restaurants. We basically met with dead ends . . . . [It was] very frustrating . . . . So Chris and I started talking about where the market was. One strategy, I felt, was to sell a little bit of the company to finance maybe 18 months of growth, get a track record in the Street and come back with another offering with credibility. [So] we priced the transaction at about a 20 percent discount relative to the highest-flying restaurant stock we could find and, of course, the stock traded up from 15 to 22 on the first day. At that point we were trading at a premium for restaurant stocks.

Outback's continuing success made possible two additional stock offerings during the following eighteen months. All together, a total of $68 million was raised. By the end of 1994, the founders owned almost 24 percent of the company, which was valued at approximately $250 million.

Outback's Strategy and Structure — "No rules — just right"

The Theme — *"Cheerful, comfortable, enjoyable, and fun!"*

The three partners debated for some time about the appropriate theme and name for their restaurants. They wanted a casual theme but felt that the western theme was overused by budget steak houses. Ultimately, they focused on an Australian theme. None of the partners had ever been to Australia, but U.S. attention was focused there. Bob Basham explained:

In late 1987–88 when we started there was a lot of hype about Australia. We had just lost the Americas Cup not long before that. They were celebrating their bicentennial. The movie Crocodile Dundee had just come out. [So, there] was a lot of interest in Australia when we were looking for a theme . . . that was probably one of our hardest decisions . . . (we) wanted to stay away from a western theme . . . . [We] started talking about Australia [which] is perceived as very casual and we wanted to be a casual steakhouse. It is a good marketing niche tool and we continue to take advantage of it in our ads.

Bob's wife, Beth, ultimately wrote the name "Outback" with her lipstick on a mirror. As Tim Gannon put it, the name epitomized:
[what] we wanted to convey. We wanted to be a hearty good-fun atmosphere and [the name] represents our personalities too. The three of us live robust, fun lives.

The founders of Outback were convinced that any enduring concept must place a heavy emphasis upon fun, family, quality food, and community. Bob Basham explained:

I don't care what business you are in, if you aren't having fun, you shouldn't be in that business . . . . Chris, Tim, and I have a lot of fun doing what we are doing, and we want our people to have a lot of fun doing what they are doing. We try to set it up so they can do that.

Tim, whom the other two partners described as being the "hospitality" part of the team, elaborated on the entertainment aspect of the Outback theme:

We are in the business of entertainment and the way we entertain is through flavors. Service is a big component of that. We want our customers—someone who comes in at 7 P.M. and waits until 9 P.M. and leaves at 10:30 P.M.—to view us as their entertainment. We owe it to them!

Outback employees who waited on customers typically handled only three tables at a time, and this allowed closer customer attention.

Choosing the Menu — "Kookaburra Wings, Victoria's Filet, Chocolate Thunder Down Under"

The company gave Australian theme names to many of the menu items. For example, Buffalo chicken wings were called "Kookabura wings," a filet mignon was called "Victoria's Filet,"

and a rich chocolate sauce dessert was titled, "Chocolate Thunder Down Under." The menu also included a wide variety of beverages, including a full liquor service featuring Australian beer and wine. The menu for the trio's casual dining operation featured specially seasoned steaks and prime rib and also included chicken, ribs, fish, and pasta entrees. Tim explained the menu selections for Outback:

At Outback we don't look at other menus or trends . . . . [The] best things I learned in a lifetime I put in the menu.

The company's house specialties included its "'Aussie-Tizers' . . . and delectable desserts."[15] The company's signature trademark quickly became its best-selling "Aussie-Tizer," the "Bloomin' Onion." The idea for a large single-hearted onion cut to resemble a blooming flower, dipped in batter, and fried was originally developed by a New Orleans chef from a picture in a Japanese book. Tim added seasonings and enlarged it to "Outback size." The company expected to serve nine million "Bloomin' Onions" in 1995.

The menu, attention to quality from suppliers, and the emphasis on exceeding customer expectations all contributed to the high food quality. At about 40 percent of total costs, Outback's food costs were among the highest in the industry. "If we didn't have the highest food costs in the industry," explained Bob Basham, "we would be worried."

Outback's founders paid particular attention to the flavor profiles of the food. As Bob Merritt put it:

One of the important reasons for our success is that we took basic American meat and potatoes and enhanced the flavor profile so that it fit with the aging population . . . . Just look at what McDonald's and Burger King did in their market segment. They tried to add things to their menu that were more flavorful. McDonald's put the Big Mac on their menu because they found that as people aged, they wanted more flavor. McDonald's could not address that customer need with an old cheeseburger which tastes like cardboard . . . . That's why Tex Mex is such a great segment. That's why Italian is such a great segment because Italian food tends to have higher flavor profiles. It's not happenstance. It's a science. There's too much money at risk in this business not to know what's going on with customer taste preferences.

The founders knew that as people age, their taste buds also age. Thus, they recognized that their baby-boomer customers, those born in the 1946 to 1964 period, would demand more flavor in their food.

The 1995 menu remained essentially the same in character as originally envisioned in 1987. The price range of appetizers was about $2 to $6 with entrees ranging between $8 and $17. The average check per person was approximately $15 to $16.[16] The changing of menu items was done with care. For example, a new item planned for 1995 was the rack of lamb. As Tim Gannon explained, the menu was an issue to which all three founders turned their attention:

Where we all come together is on the menu. Bob comes to the plate thinking how the kitchen can put this out and how it can be stored. Chris will look at it from how the customer is going to view it. Is it of value? I come to it from a flavor point of view. Is it an exciting dish? We all add something to the final decision.

Tim and the staff at the company's original restaurant located on Henderson Avenue in Tampa, Florida, undertook most of the company's R&D. The founders approved any menu changes only after paying careful attention to development. For example, Tim and the Henderson staff had worked for a number of months on the rack of lamb entree. Tim explained:

We have been working with it [the rack of lamb entree] for some time on the operational side trying to get the cook times down. The flavors are there. Chris is excited although it [the rack] is not a mainstream product. It is an upscale product for us . . . . We are still fine-tuning the operational side to be sure it is in balance with other things we are doing. We are serving 800 dinners a night, and you can't have a menu item that throws the chemistry of the kitchen off.

Quality Fanatics — "We won't tolerate less than the best"

Outback executives and restaurant managers were staunchly committed to the principle that good food required outstanding ingredients. Tim explained the company's attention to the suppliers:

I have been to every onion grower from Oregon, Idaho, and all the way to Mexico looking for a continuous supply of single-hearted onions. I talk to the growers . . . . If it's a product you serve, you cannot rely on the words of a distributor to say, "This is what we have." I have to get into the fields and see what they have. If I am going to take 50 percent of the crop like that, I have to get into the fields to know, to see, how the crop is developed. So that took me into the fields of Idaho to see what makes onions get that big and what makes double hearts because they are hard for us to use. We do that with everything, the species of shrimp, which boats have the ice, what's the best safety standards. [I go] with the guys who purchase the cattle and learn to look for what they look for . . . . That's the only way you can produce great food.

Supplier relationships were long-standing. The company made beef purchases centrally for the entire Outback system. The company's original menu was designed by Tim Gannon with help from Warren LeRuth, one of New Orleans's premier chefs. LeRuth recommended Bruss, a Chicago-based meatpacking company, as a source of high-quality beef. Tim explained why Bruss was such a great partner as a supplier:

We couldn't even get samples [from the others]. We were on a low budget at the time. This company believed in us. They sent us samples after samples . . . . Their cutters were more like craftsmen; the

sense of pride that the Chicago butchers have about their product is really what we wanted in our restaurants. Bruss was at about $37 million at the time. Today, they are at $100 million, and we represent $75 to $80 million of that. We've been a great partner for them as they have been for us.

In 1994 Outback had two major suppliers of beef, but Bruss continued to supply over half of the Outback restaurants. About 60 percent of Outback's menu items were red meat entrees, and its best-selling steak alone accounted for about 25 percent of entrees sold. The attention to quality extended, however, to all suppliers. Vanilla, used only for the whipped cream in just one dessert item, was the "real thing" from the island of Madagascar. Olive oil was imported from Tuscany and wheels of parmesan cheese from Italy. Tim explained the company policy:

. . . if any supplier replaces our order with a cheap imitation, I will know about it and they will not supply us anymore . . . . I will not tolerate anything less than the best.

The attention to quality and detail was also evidenced at the individual restaurant level. For example, croutons were made daily at each restaurant with 17 different seasonings, including fresh garlic and butter, and cut by hand into irregular shapes so that customers would recognize they were handmade.

In addition to his oversight of supplier quality, Tim Gannon also focused on continual training of the restaurant staff throughout the Outback system. He held about ten meetings a year in various parts of the country with staff members from various regional restaurants. Typically, about 50 kitchen managers and other kitchen staff attended these meetings. There was a presentation from a special guest with half of the group in the front of the restaurant. In the meantime, the other half of the group worked on "the basics" in the kitchen. Then the two groups exchanged places. Tim felt these meetings were critical for generating new ideas, sometimes from very new kitchen staff employees. For example, one new employee had urged attention to the dessert sauces. Discussion of this issue ultimately resulted in a reformulation of the sauces so that they did not so easily crystallize as well as the installation of the warmers that held the sauces at a constant temperature. This innovation allowed the restaurants to serve desserts more quickly.

The restaurant general managers also emphasized food quality. This commitment was illustrated by Joe Cofer, manager of the Henderson Street restaurant in Tampa, when he said:

We watch the food as it comes out of the kitchen, touching every single plate to make sure every single plate is perfect—that's our commitment to this restaurant [i.e.,] to watch the food. We can take care of every single table by watching the food. If we have a problem at a table, we go to talk to them.

Designing a Restaurant — "Bob Basham's Memorial Kitchen"

Facility design was also a critical component in quality food preparation. Bob Basham especially paid attention to kitchen design, so much so that Chris and Tim termed Outback's kitchen design Bob's "Memorial Kitchen." Fully 45 percent of Outback's restaurant unit was generally dedicated to the kitchen. Analysts and other industry observers had pointed out that Outback could enlarge the dining area and reduce wait times for customers. However, Bob Basham explained the logic behind the company's restaurant design:

Restaurants get busy on a Friday night or a Saturday night when most people go out to eat. That's when you are trying to make the best impression on people. [But] physically, the kitchen cannot handle the demand. So if you have standards in your operation of a 12-minute cook time . . . . [it's] impossible to execute that way. We all decided we would not have it happening in our restaurant. So we underdesigned the front of the house and overdesigned the back of the house. That has worked very, very well for us. To this day we limit the number [of tables]. Even in our busiest restaurants where people tell us we could be twice as big and do twice the sales, we still discipline ourselves to build our restaurants one size.

The interior design was a "subtle decor featuring blond woods, large booths and tables [with] Australian memorabilia—boomerangs, surfboards, maps, and flags."[17] A typical Outback occupied over 6,000 square feet, featuring a dining room and an island bar. The restaurant area had 30 to 35 tables and could seat about 160 patrons. The bar had about six to nine tables with seating for about 35.

Location Is Everything? — "You're going to put a restaurant where? For dinner only?!"

The company's first restaurant was located on a site that had held several restaurants before Bob and Chris leased it. Early Outback restaurants were all located in strip shopping centers or were retrofits of existing freestanding restaurant sites. When the company first started, lease costs for retrofits were lower than the cost of constructing and owning a building. Bob Basham explained the rationale behind Outback's location strategy:

. . . We call it our A-market B-location . . . . we didn't have enough money to go to the corner of Main and Main. So we felt that if we went to a great market [that] had great demographics that we needed, and got in what we called a B-location, that typically most restaurant companies would think of as a B-location, we felt we could be successful there if we executed great, and that strategy continues today.

However, as the company expanded into other parts of the country, the cost structure shifted. In 1993 the company developed a prototype that was being constructed in most new locations. The company devoted significant effort to site evaluation efforts that focused on area demographics, target population density, household income levels, competition, and specific site characteristics such as visibility, accessibility, and traffic volume.

Conventional wisdom in the restaurant industry suggested that facilities should be utilized as long as possible during the day. However, Outback restaurants were open daily for seven hours from 4:30 to 11:30 P.M. This dinner-only approach had been highly successful. The dinner-only concept had led to the effective utilization of systems, staff, and management. By not offering lunch, Outback avoided restaurant sites in high-traffic, high-cost city centers. Furthermore, the dinner-only theme minimized the strain on staff. Tips were typically much higher for dinner than for lunch or breakfast service. Outback restaurants averaged 3,800 customers per week and were usually filled shortly after opening. In an industry where a sales-to-investment ratio of 1.2:1 was considered strong, Outback's restaurants generated $2.10 in sales for every $1 invested in the facility.

Operating Structure — "No organization charts here"

Management remained informal in 1995. Corporate headquarters were located on the second floor of an unpretentious office building near the Tampa airport. The headquarters offices were about two miles from the original store on Henderson Boulevard. Headquarters staff numbered approximately 80. Corporate existed as a service center. As Bob Merritt put it:

We exist here to service the restaurants . . . . There is nothing I can do from Tampa, Florida, to make sure the customer has a great experience in Kansas City, nothing except to put in management people who have great attitudes, who like to take care of people, who are highly motivated economically, and make sure they have hired the best and most highly motivated people, and trained them to get the job done. It is absolutely our point of differentiation. You can get at the food and all the other stuff, but in the end what makes this company work is its decentralized nature and our willingness, particularly Chris and Bob's willingness, to live with the mistakes of their subordinates and look at those mistakes as opportunities to teach, not opportunities to discipline. That is the pervasive element of our corporate culture that makes it work.

There was no human resources department at corporate. However, Trudy Cooper, vice president for training and development, had been involved in the hiring of associates at most new restaurants until 1994. In 1994 Cooper added two coordinators who helped with new restaurant openings. One of the coordinators supervised training in the front operations and the other supervised the kitchen. Each selected 15 other high-quality employees from restaurants throughout the system to work on a temporary, one to one basis with the new employees during an opening. The two coordinators and the special training staff all returned to their home restaurant assignments once an opening was completed.

Training at a new restaurant site took place over a two-week period. Outback absorbed all the costs related to an opening into the marketing/advertising budget. The restaurant staff had four practice nights. On the first night, a Friday, the guests were family members of the staff. On the second and third nights, Saturday and Sunday, the invited guests were community members, including construction workers, vendors, and other VIP guests. The fourth night, Monday, was charity night. Trudy Cooper described a new restaurant opening:

We have those people on site for about two weeks. We have classroom sessions, then a food show and a wine show. We do a mock night. We do two nights of role play. We do a night with the media followed by a charity function. All of the proceeds go to charity. It is $10 a person for heavy hors d'oeuvres and an open bar. We make quite a bit of money on that night for the charity chosen by the restaurant manager.

Local press representatives were invited to a special briefing session an hour in advance of the opening night. All the proceeds from opening night went to a charity of the restaurant manager's choice.

A typical Outback restaurant staff consisted of a general manager, one assistant manager, and a kitchen manager plus 50 to 70 hourly employees, many of whom worked part-time. Job candidates for the restaurant staff were required to pass an aptitude test that assessed basic skills such as making change at the till. Every applicant interviewed with two managers. A friendly and outgoing disposition was a critical job requirement. The company also used psychological profile tests to better understand an applicant's personality.

Outback placed a great degree of emphasis upon learning and personal growth throughout the company. Trudy Cooper called it "Our learn-teach-learn approach." Chris Sullivan further explained:

I was given the opportunity to make a lot of mistakes and learn, and we try to do that today. We try to give our people a lot of opportunity to make some mistakes, learn, and go on.

"Every worker an owner . . . "

The three founders keenly remembered their early desire to own their own restaurant. Consequently, Outback provided ownership opportunities at three levels in the organization: at the individual restaurant level; through multiple store arrangements (joint venture and franchise opportunities); and through the newly formed employee stock ownership plan.

Top management selected the joint venture partners and franchisees. As franchisee Hugh Connerty put it, "There is no middle management here. All franchisees report directly to the president." Franchisees and joint venture partners in

turn hired the general managers at each restaurant. All of the operating partners and general managers were required to complete a comprehensive 12-week training course that emphasized the company's operating strategy, procedures, and standards.

From the beginning, the founders wanted ownership opportunities for each restaurant general manager and formed the limited partner arrangement. Each restaurant general manager committed to a five-year contract and invested $25,000 for a 10 percent stake in the restaurant. Initially, the arrangement was in the form of a limited partnership. However, the company was in the process of converting all agreements to general partnerships backed with liability insurance.

Under the program, the restaurant general manager received a base salary of $45,000 plus 10 percent of the pre-rent "cash flow" from the restaurant. "Pre-rent" cash flow for Outback restaurants was calculated monthly and defined as earnings before taxes, interest, and depreciation.[18] Each manager's name appeared over the restaurant door with the designation, "Proprietor." An average Outback generated $3.2 million in sales and a pre-rent "cash flow" of $736,000. Average total compensation for managing partners exceeded $100,000, including an average $73,600 share of the restaurant profits. If the manager chose to leave the company at the end of a five-year period, Outback bought out the manager's ownership. If managers chose to stay with Outback, they could sign up for five additional years at

the same restaurant or invest another $25,000 in a new store. After the company went public in 1991, the company began to give restaurant managers non-qualified stock options at the time they became managing partners. The options vested at the end of five years. Each manager received about 4,000 shares of stock over the five-year period. Outback's attractive arrangements for restaurant general managers resulted in a 1994 management turnover of 5 percent compared to 30 percent to 40 percent industry-wide.

By early 1995, eleven stores had celebrated their five-year anniversaries (see Exhibit 3). Of the eleven managers, two had left the company. One later returned. Four had gone on to new stores in which they invested $25,000 with the same repeat deal. Five stayed with their same stores, renewing their contract with additional options that would vest at the end of the second five-year period. Joe Cofer, manager of the Henderson Street Outback in Tampa, indicated how his position as general manager of the restaurant affected his life:

I have been with the Outback for about 4 1/2 years now. I started out as a manager. Sixteen months ago I was offered a partnership in the Henderson store. I grew up in Tampa, right down the street, and have lived here nearly my whole life. So when they offered me this store, it was perfect . . . . If you walk in the restaurant and look at the name on the sign, some people I went to high school with say, "How in the heck did this happen?" . . . . The other organization [I worked for] had long hours when you were open from 11:30 in the morning until 1 or 2 in the evening. Those hours have a tendency to burn people out . . . . At Outback, from the [supplier] level all the way down to the dishwasher level we all work as a team. That is another difference between Outback and the organization I used to work for . . . . Here at Outback we don't have those rules and regulations . . . Chris always claims he plays a lot of golf in the daytime and has a lot of fun . . . . He will come up to you and ask, "Are you having fun?" [We say] "Oh, we're having a great time." He says, "Okay, that's the way you need to run this stuff."

Multiple-store ownership occurred through franchises, joint venture partnership arrangements, and sometimes a combination. The founders' original plan did not include franchises. However, in 1990 a friend who owned several restaurants in Kentucky asked to put Outback franchises in two of his restaurants that had not done very well. The founders reluctantly awarded the KY franchise. The two franchised restaurants quickly became successful. Under a franchise arrangement, the franchisees paid 3 percent of gross revenues to Outback.

After the IPO the company began to form joint venture partnerships with individuals who had strong operating credentials but not a lot of funds to invest. Under a joint venture arrangement a joint venture partner invested $50,000 and in return received a $50,000 base salary, plus 10 percent of the "cash flow" generated by the restaurants in his/her group

after the restaurant general managers were paid their 10 percent. Therefore, a joint venture partner who operated ten Outbacks generating $600,000 each would end up with $54,000 per unit or $540,000 total plus the $50,000 base. Since Outback's general managers were experienced restaurateurs, the joint venture partners focused primarily on area development, including site research for new locations and hiring and training new managers. The company instituted its employee stock ownership plan in 1993 for employees at the restaurant level. At the time the ESOP was established, all employees received stock proportional to their time in service. Each employee received a yearly statement. The stock ownership program required no investment from the employees and vested after five years.

Advertising and Promotion — "We have always established that Outback is quality product at a great value"

Vice president of marketing Nancy Schneid came to Outback in 1990. Before working for Outback, Schneid had been first a media buyer in a large advertising agency and then an advertising sales representative for Tampa's dominant radio station. She met Chris and Bob while she was at the radio station and they were running their Chili's franchise. Although Chili's advertising strategy did not usually include radio advertising, Chris and Bob chose to use a significant level of local radio advertising.

Nancy was well aware of Chris and Bob's success with Chili's. When they established Outback, she became an early investor in the form of a limited partnership. She explained how the radio station she worked with was able to help the three entrepreneurs with advertising:

When they first opened Outback they were struggling. Our radio station was expensive to advertise on . . . . So I made an opportunity for them to go on radio on a morning show that had a 35 percent share of the market and an afternoon show that had a 28 percent share of the market. That gave them the opportunity to tell the Tampa Bay community about the concept [which was] in a very B location on Henderson. Tim Gannon came at 5:00 A.M. and set up a cooking station downstairs. He cooked and ran food upstairs while Chris and Bob talked to the DJ. They basically owned the morning show.

Outback used very little print media. Print advertisements typically appeared only if a charity or sports event offered space as part of its package. Thus, Outback ads might appear in the American Cancer Magazine or a golf tournament program. Billboards were used to draw customers to specific restaurant locations. TV advertising began in 1991 after the local advertising agency, the West Group in Tampa, was selected. The company produced about three or four successful TV advertisements per year. Although not a company spokesman, well-known model Rachel Hunter had participated in several of the ads and had become identified with Outback.

Hunter's New Zealand origin was generally interpreted by audiences to be Australian.

Except for the development of the TV advertisements, advertising and marketing efforts were decentralized. As VP Schneid put it:

We are very much micro-managers when it comes to the spending of our media dollars . . . . We are very responsive to the needs of the community, for example, Big Sisters and Brothers . . . . [Our advertising, marketing, and community involvement efforts] help us build friends and an image of great food at a great price.

Community Involvement — "We have been rewarded . . . out of proportion to our needs, and we want to give some of that back"

Central to Outback's operating strategy was a high degree of visibility and involvement in the community. Outback sponsored the Outback Bowl that first aired on ESPN on New Year's afternoon 1996. In addition, the company was involved in a number of charity golf tournaments with a unique format involving food preparation and service at each hole. Community involvement involved not only top management but everyone at Outback. Each new store opening involved community participation and community service to charities. Other community involvement took various forms. The Tampa-based corporate staff included a full-time special events person with a staff that catered to charity as well as for-profit events in the Tampa area. For many charity events Outback provided the food while staff donated their time.

For example, a black-tie dinner for 400 was scheduled for May 1995 at Tampa's Lowry Park Zoo, a special interest of Outback's three top executives.

Every local restaurant managing partner was likely to have a Little League or other sports sponsorship. Basham explained:

We are really involved in the community . . . . I think you have to give back. We have been very, very fortunate, we have been rewarded . . . out of proportion to our needs, and we want to give some of that back to the community . . . . I think if more people did that we would have a lot less problems in this country than we have right now . . . . I have certainly been rewarded out of proportion to any contribution I feel I have made, and I just feel I should give something back. That goes throughout our company.

The Founders' Relationship — "The three of us kind of stay on each other, challenging each other, kid each other a lot, but more than anything support each other to make this thing work"

The three founders contributed in different ways to running the company. Each shared his perspective on his own as well the others' roles. Chris gave his view of the trio:

. . . Bob and I became corporate-type restaurant people, and sometimes that is more systems-oriented and not so much hospitality-oriented. Tim really brought that to our success. But more than that, he is easy to get along with. He absolutely gets done what needs to get done. He needs a little prodding. Bob and I need a little prodding. So the three of us kind of stay on each other, kid each other a lot, but more than anything support each other to make this thing work.

Bob explained the synergy among the three:

We have been together eight years. I think we have a balance between our strengths and our weaknesses. There are some things Chris does extremely well that I don't do well. There are things that Tim puts into the formula that Chris and I could not do as well as he does, and hopefully there are some things that I do well that they would need. I think just the three of us have synergies together that have really worked very positively for us. We kind of all feed off of each other . . . . Right now, each one of us has a different role in the company. I concentrate on operations, the people side of the business, the day-to-day going-on of the business.

I think Chris has a little more of the strategic overview of the company, keeps us going in the direction we need to be going. He is very good at seeing things long-term. Tim is our food guy. Tim makes sure that we can all have a lot of fun. He has a lot of fun in his work. So we have a balance there. We all contribute and it all works.

Tim gave his perspective on how he fit in:

. . . My challenge: How do I fit in? . . . Partnerships of three are always hard but it has worked very well. I now understand my role and have been treated well . . . . [There is] nothing in life greater than having a great partnership . . . . We meet all the time. I never make a menu decision without them, Chris has eyes for the guest and Bob has eyes for the employee . . . . A lot of organizations bust up at the top, not bottom! I only want to work with Outback.

Competition — "We have all we need of the greatest kind of flattery"

A number of competitors in casual dining's steak dinner house subsegment had begun to make their presence felt. The most formidable competition was the Wichita, Kansas-based Lone Star Steakhouse & Saloon. However, there was also a growing set of players with a formula involving rustic buildings and beef value items that began operations in early 1990 and 1991. These included Sizzler International's Buffalo Ranch, Shoney's Barbwire, S&A Restaurant Corp.'s Montana Steak Co., and O'Charley Logan's Roadhouse. In addition, a number of chains had added or upgraded steak menu items in reaction to Outback.

Chris Sullivan explained his view of competition and what Outback had to do:

Our competitors-there are a lot . . . [We] can't run way from it—it's a fact. I think a lot of companies get in trouble because they start worrying about what the competitor is doing and they react to that. We really ask our people and we talk about—just go out and execute and do what you do best. The customers will decide . . . If we continue to do what we have been doing, we feel very, very confident that we will continue to be successful regardless of the number of competitors out there because with our situation, our setup, and the proprietors we have in our restaurants, I don't think there is anybody who can compete with us.

Outback's Future Outlook

The company as a whole was optimistic about its future. Wall Street analysts were skeptical, however. Citing the numerous entrants into the industry, they argued that casual dining operators such as Outback were close to saturation and questioned whether the firm could withstand the intense competitive pressures characteristic of the industry. However, Outback's management was unperturbed by Wall Street concerns or by the increasing competition. Joe Cofer summarized the management attitude:

I've heard so many times, "I love coming to your restaurant because your staff is so upbeat, they are so happy." They are always great people to have work for you. People just love the people here . . . . I see us as a McDonald's of the future, but a step up. I don't think anybody can come close to our efficiency because it is so simplistic and everyone is so laid back about it from the owners on down. And we are having such fun, making so much money. No one wants to go anywhere. I will never work for another company as long as I live . . . . You have that feeling mixed with the great food. I don't think anyone is a threat . . . . You have a very good investment with the stock. The stock has split three times in the last three years . . . . This is just going to split more and more and more. I'm just going to hold on to it forever. Hopefully, it will be my retirement.

The company intended to drive its future growth through a four-pronged strategy: (1) continuous expansion within the United States with an additional 300 to 350 Outback concept stores, (2) the rollout of Carrabbas Italian franchise as its second system of restaurants, (3) development of additional restaurant themes, and (4) International franchising. Chris Sullivan explained:

. . . We can do 500 to 600 restaurants, and possibly more over the next five years . . . . Our Italian concept, Carrabbas, that is in its infancy stage right now . . . has the potential to have the same kind of growth pattern that we have had in Outback . . . . We will continue to focus on Outback and continue to build that because we have a lot of work left there. Develop Carrabbas and use that as our next growth vehicle and continue to look . . . for a third leg on that stool, and who knows what is going to be hot in a couple of years.

. . . The world is becoming one big market, and we want to be in place so we don't miss that opportunity. There are some problems, some challenges with it, but at this point there have been some casual restaurants chains that have gone [outside the United States] and their average unit sales are way, way above the sales level they enjoyed in the United States. So the potential is there . . . . We are real excited about the future internationally.

In the face of the dire predictions from industry observers and analysts, Outback CEO Chris Sullivan put his organization's plans quite simply: "We want to be the major player in the casual dining segment."[19]

Enron and Arthur Andersen: Beyond the Debacles

During the last decade of the 20th century, Enron Corp. became a major player in the energy sector of the economy and a growing force in other businesses, with total revenues across all businesses of US$101 billion in 2000. Even with the company's expansion into non-energy commodities, energy represented Enron's primary business venture. On November 9, 2001, the merger of Enron and Dynegy Corp. was announced. The merger soon unraveled as Enron's questionable accounting practices and financial dealings—in particular, highly irregular partnership arrangements—were discovered. Enron, with recorded revenues of approximately $140 billion during the first three quarters of 2001, experienced a catastrophic collapse in the market value of its stock.

The merger was called off. Enron sued Dynegy and Dynegy countersued Enron, with each accusing the other of wrongdoing. In early December 2001, Enron filed for bankruptcy. Just days before this filing, 500 of the company's employees were paid $55.7 million in bonuses. More than 4,000 Enron employees were fired at the time of the bankruptcy filing. (1) Moreover, numerous companies around the world suffered significant losses as a result of the Enron debacle.

The Demise of Arthur Andersen

In mid-December 2001, the U.S. Congress initiated hearings on the Enron debacle. Executives from Arthur Andersen, Enron's auditor, testified about possible illegal acts and violations of securities laws by Enron officials as well as about Andersen's role in the situation. In January 2002, the U.S. Justice Department initiated a criminal investigation into the debacle. This investigation uncovered evidence of destruction by Andersen employees of documents related to Enron's questionable activities. David Duncan, head of Andersen's audit team for Enron, was fired and later admitted to ordering the shredding of Enron-related documents shortly after learning of the Justice Department's investigation. Enron fired Andersen as its auditor. Subsequently, Andersen was charged with obstruction of justice, stood trial, and was found guilty. Numerous auditing clients severed ties with Arthur Andersen, and the accounting firm was virtually destroyed. (2) An appeal to the Fifth U.S. Court of Appeals was pending at the time of writing this case update.

The Bankruptcy Aftermath at Enron

Meanwhile, bizarre events related to Enron continued to unfold. A former Enron executive committed suicide, apparently in remorse over the Enron debacle. The *Powers Report,* prepared by a special committee of Enron's board of directors, blamed Enron executives as well as the auditors, lawyers, and board members for the improper partnerships. In testimony before Congress, key Enron executives either denied responsibility for what had happened or asserted Fifth Amendment privilege against self-incrimination. Jeffrey Skilling, former Enron CEO, testified that the company was in "great shape" when he left his position. He also asserted that he was the victim of "outrageous lies" and insisted that he was not responsible in any way for Enron's collapse. Kenneth Lay, Enron's former chairman, asserted his Fifth Amendment rights shortly after resigning from Enron's board of directors. (3)

Sherron Watkins, Enron's vice president of corporate development, was one of the few beacons of proper behavior in carrying out her responsibilities. Being aware of the questionable partnerships and the off-balance-sheet accounting, Watkins sensed the doom Enron was facing. She told her boss, Kenneth Lay, and a friend at Arthur Andersen, who then told Andersen's head Enron auditor, David Duncan. In testimony before Congress, Watkins said she believed that Lay was probably duped by Skilling and others. (4)

In the ensuing months, several Enron executives were charged with various criminal acts, including fraud, money laundering, and insider trading. Former Enron executive David Delainey, closely connected to former CEO Jeff Skilling, pled guilty to one count of insider trading and paid almost $8 million in fines. He also agreed to cooperate in the government's Enron investigations. (5) Lea Fastow, former assistant treasurer at Enron and the wife of Andrew Fastow, Enron's former chief financial officer, was charged with six criminal counts, including conspiracy to commit wire fraud, money laundering, and four counts of filing false tax returns. When a plea bargain agreement fell through, she pled not guilty to all counts. (6)

Ben Glisan, Enron's former treasurer, was charged with two dozen counts of money laundering, fraud, and conspiracy. He pled guilty to one count of conspiracy to commit fraud in exchange for the other charges being dropped. Glisan received a prison term, three years of post-prison supervision, and financial penalties of more than a $1 million. Glisan admitted that Enron was a "house of cards." Glisan was a close associate of Andrew Fastow, former Enron chief financial officer, who faced almost 100 counts of money laundering, fraud, and conspiracy. At the time of writing, Fastow maintained his innocence. (7)

As of late 2003, Enron was still struggling to work its way out of bankruptcy. Enron's creditors sought permission from a federal bankruptcy judge to sue more than three dozen former Enron executives, Arthur Andersen, and three law firms for negligence and failure to fulfill their duties as corporate officers. A final report by Enron's bankruptcy examiner in late November 2003 concluded that Kenneth Lay and Jeffrey Skilling had breached their fiduciary duties and might be liable for repaying millions of dollars to Enron. Lay and Skilling, of course, disputed the bankruptcy examiner's findings. (8)

Culture and Leadership: The Seeds of Enron's Demise

Enron's collapse did not happen overnight; it was long in the making, dating from the early 1990s. Along with the company's rapid growth came the development of a corporate culture and leadership that was obsessed with stock prices, bonuses, and exotic accounting practices.

Rich Kinder, Enron's chief operating officer (COO) from 1990 to 1996, was obsessed with stock prices and earning targets. He focused his attentions on operations and cash flow, and would "terrify people if they didn't meet their goals." (9) Then when Jeff Skilling took over from Kinder, there was still an obsession with stock prices but a drastic "flip-flop" in the method for maintaining Enron's favorable stock prices.

Skilling seemingly paid little attention to expenses or day-to-day operations, instead delegating those responsibilities. Skilling was concerned about expanding both revenues and profit margins. To accomplish this, Enron began an extensive program of buying, expanding, and launching businesses in both energy and non-energy domains. To help run these businesses, Skilling sought the best and brightest new hires, ones who would be "ruthless traders." Skilling wanted people who could prosper in a "go-go, high-achievement environment." Unfortunately, there was insufficient monitoring of these new hires to ensure that they learned the fundamentals of good management. (10)

Under Skilling, a very rigorous and threatening evaluation process was instituted for all Enron employees. Known as "rank and yank," Enron's employees annually ranked their fellow employees on a 1 (best) to 5 (worst) scale. Each of the company's divisions was arbitrarily forced to give the lowest ranking to one-fifth of its employees. These employees were then fired. Employees often downgraded their peers in order to enhance their own positions in the company. (11)

Enron's bonus program was another major contributor to the company's demise. "Those who closed major deals were paid up to 3 percent of the value of the entire deal, payable when it was struck, not when the project actually began earning money." (12) The bonus program encouraged the use of non-standard accounting practices and the inflation of deals on the company's books. Deal inflation within the company became sufficiently widespread that "more effort was put into hiding the consequences than owning up to the problem." (13) In fact, four partnerships were created solely for the purpose of hiding losses.

The company was very decentralized and de-emphasized teamwork—each division and business unit was kept separate from the other businesses. Consequently, very few people in the Enron organization knew much of what was going on in the company from a "big picture"

perspective. Basically, people heading their divisions and business units knew what was happening in their part of the company but not throughout the company. Fostering this decentralized operation, which also lacked sufficient operational and financial controls, was "a distracted, hands-off chairman, a compliant board of directors and an impotent staff of accountants, auditors and lawyers." (14)

Into the Future

The Enron and Arthur Andersen debacles have destroyed businesses and many people's lives—and most likely will continue to do so for some time in the future. The ethical failures of both Enron and Arthur Andersen have sent shock waves through the global business community, among employees of both small and large corporations, and among private citizens. After a two-year ride on a "roller coaster of volatility," the discovery of ethically bizarre decisions and actions seem all too frequent and commonplace. All of these events should leave us wondering: "What enduring lessons for humanity will these debacles end up providing?"

Questions for Integrative Thinking

1. Explain the collapse of Enron in terms of failures of the four functions of management—planning, organizing, leading, and controlling.
2. What managerial initiatives and actions might

have prevented Enron's collapse?
3. Why was Arthur Andersen affected so drastically by the Enron debacle? What should (or could) Andersen have done differently?
4. What key lessons regarding ethics and social responsibility have the Enron and Arthur Andersen debacles provided?

Research Questions for Keeping Current

New evidence in the Enron and Arthur Andersen debacles unfolds with great frequency. An excellent source of current as well as archived information about Enron as well as Arthur Andersen's relationship to Enron is the *Houston Chronicle*—http://www.chron.com/content/chronicle/special/01/enron/. Search its pages for information that keeps you abreast of this unfolding saga. The following questions are intended to provide some useful focus when conducting your search:

1. What is the current status of Enron Corp. with respect to its attempt to recover from bankruptcy?
2. What is the current legal status of key Enron executives who have been accused of involvement in Enron's misdeeds?
3. What is the current status of Arthur Andersen?
4. What useful lessons for businesses and businesspeople continue to emerge in the aftermath of the Enron and Arthur Andersen debacles?

eiling" affects the careers of
cupational settings. Analyze the

of diversity training programs.
nplish, and how? Are they work-

— "What's the

spect to the criteria for evalu-
ne textbook?

asure the social responsibil-
iew the scholarly research in
as and expectations.
the "status" of major organi
ibility performance. How
n as models of social respon-

mples of the "best" and the
uance or social responsibil-
an (a) international, (b) na-

earned?"

for minorities and
sity have been

os and Cons?"

can easily read or listen
e bottom line? Is global-

as having strong diver-
? What do they do dif-

e of different racial, eth-
s work together. What are
Review various definitions   s do managers and work-

- Get specific data on how the "glass
  women and minorities in various oc
  data and develop the implications.
- Take a critical look at the substance
  What do these programs try to accom
  ing or not, and how do we know?

PROJECT 2

Corporate Social Responsibility
Status?"

QUESTION

Where do businesses stand today with r
ating social responsibility discussed in th

Possible Research Directions

- Create a scale that could be used to me
  ity performance of an organization. Rev
  this area, but also include your own ide
- Use your scale to research and evaluate
  zations and local ones on social respons
  well are they doing? Would you use then
  sibility for others to follow, or not?
- Conduct research to identify current exa
  "worst" organizations in terms of perforr
  ity criteria. Pursue this investigation on
  tional, and/or (c) local scale.

PROJECT 3

Globalization — "What Are the Pr

QUESTION

"Globalization" is frequently in the news. Yo
to both advocates and opponents. What is th
ization good or bad, and for whom?

Possible Research Directions

- What does the term "globalization" mean?
  and find the common ground.

- Read and study the scholarly arguments about globalization. Summarize what the scholars say about the forces and consequences of globalization in the past, present, and future.
- Examine current events relating to globalization. Summarize the issues and arguments. What is the positive side of globalization? What are the negatives that some might call its "dark" side?
- Consider globalization from the perspective of your local community or one of its major employers. Is globalization a threat or an opportunity, and why?
- Take a position on globalization. State what you believe to be the best course for government and business leaders to take. Justify your position.

PROJECT 4

Affirmative Action Directions — "Where Do We Go from Here?"

QUESTION

Consultant R. Roosevelt Thomas argues that it is time to "move beyond affirmative action" and learn how to "manage diversity." There are a lot of issues that may be raised in this context—issues of equal employment opportunity, hiring quotas, reverse discrimination, and others. What is the status of affirmative action today?

Possible Research Directions

- Read articles by Thomas and others. Make sure you are clear on the term "affirmative action" and its legal underpinnings. Research the topic, identify the relevant laws, and make a history line to chart its development over time.
- Examine current debates on affirmative action. What are the issues? How are the "for" and "against" positions being argued?
- Identify legal cases where reverse discrimination has been charged. How have they been resolved and with what apparent human resource management implications?
- Look at actual organizational policies on affirmative action. Analyze them and identify the common ground. Prepare a policy development guideline for use by human resource managers.
- As you ponder these issues and controversies be sure to engage different perspectives. Talk to and read about people of different "majority" and "minority" groups. Find out how they view these things— and why.

PROJECT 5

Fringe Benefits — "How Can They Be Managed"

QUESTION

Employers complain that the rising cost of "fringe benefits" is a major concern. Is this concern legitimate? If so, how can fringe benefits be best managed?

Possible Research Directions

- Find out exactly what constitutes "fringe benefits" as part of the typical compensation package. Look in the literature and also talk to local employers. Find out what percentage of a typical salary is represented in fringe benefits.
- Find and interview two or three human resource managers in your community. Ask them to describe their fringe benefits programs and how they manage fringe benefits costs. What do they see happening in the future? What do they recommend? Talk to two or three workers from different employers in your community. Find out how things look to them and what they recommend.
- Pick a specific benefit such as health insurance. What are the facts? How are employers trying to manage the rising cost of health insurance? What are the implications for workers?
- Examine the union positions on fringe benefits. How is this issue reflected in major labor negotiations. What are the results of major recent negotiations?
- Look at fringe benefits from the perspective of temporary, part-time, or contingent workers. What do they get? What do they want? How are they affected by rising costs?

PROJECT 6

CEO Pay — "Is It Too High?"

QUESTION

What is happening in the area of executive compensation? Are CEOs paid too much? Are they paid for "performance," or are they paid for something else?

Possible Research Directions

- Check the latest reports on CEO pay. Get the facts and prepare a briefing report as if you were writing a short informative article for

Fortune magazine. The title of your article should be "Status Report: Where We Stand Today on CEO Pay."

- Address the pay-for-performance issue. Do corporate CEOs get paid for performance or for something else? What do the researchers say? What do the business periodicals say? Find some examples to explain and defend your answers to these questions.
- Take a position: Should a limit be set on CEO pay? If no, why not? If yes, what type of limit do we set? Who, if anyone, should set these limits—Congress, company boards of directors, or someone else?
- Examine the same issues in the university setting. Are university presidents paid too much?

PROJECT 7

Gender and Leadership — "Is There a Difference?"

QUESTION

Do men and women lead differently?

Possible Research Directions

- Review the discussion on gender and leadership in the textbook, Chapter 13. Find and read the articles cited in the endnotes. Then, update this literature by finding and reading the most recent scholarly findings and reports.
- Interview managers from organizations in your local community. Ask them the question. Ask them to give you specific examples to justify their answers. Look for patterns and differences. Do male managers and female managers answer the question similarly?
- Interview workers from organizations in your local community. Ask them the question. Ask them to give you specific examples to justify their answers. Look for patterns and differences. Do male workers and female workers answer the question similarly? Do the same for students pressing them to share insights and examples from their experiences in course study groups and student organizations.
- Summarize your findings. Describe the implications of your findings in terms of leadership development for both men and women.

PROJECT 8

Superstars on the Team — "What Do They Mean?"

QUESTION

Do we want a "superstar" on our team?

Possible Research Directions

- Everywhere you look—in entertainment, in sports, and in business—a lot of attention these days goes to the superstars. What is the record of teams and groups with superstars? Do they really outperform the rest?
- What is the real impact of a superstar's presence on a team or in the workplace? What do they add? What do they cost? Consider the potential costs of having a superstar on a team in the equation: Benefits − Costs = Value. What is the bottom line of having a superstar on the team?
- Interview the athletic coaches on your campus. Ask them the question. Compare and contrast their answers. Interview players from various teams. Do the same for them.
- Develop a set of guidelines for creating team effectiveness for a situation where a superstar is present. Be thorough and practical. Can you give advice good enough to ensure that a superstar always creates super performance for the team or work group or organization?

PROJECT 9

Management in Popular Culture—"Seeing Ourselves Through Our Pastimes"

QUESTION

What management insights are found in popular culture and reflected in our everyday living?

Possible Research Directions

- Listen to music. Pick out themes that reflect important management concepts and theories. Put them together in a multi-media report that presents your music choices and describes their messages about management and working today.
- Watch television. Look again for the management themes. In a report, describe what popular television programs have to say about management and working. Also consider TV advertisements. How do they use and present workplace themes to help communicate their messages?
- Read the comics, also looking for management themes. Compare and contrast management and working in two or three popular comic strips.
- Read a best-selling novel. Find examples of management and work themes in the novel. Report on what the author's characters and their experiences say about people at work.
- Watch a film or video. Again, find examples of management and work themes. In a report describe the message of the movie in respect to management and work today.

Note: These ideas are borrowed from the extensive work in this area by my colleague Dr. Robert (Lenie) Holbrook of Ohio University.

PROJECT 10

Service Learning in Management — "Learning from Volunteering"

QUESTION

What can you learn about management and leadership by working as a volunteer for a local community organization?

Possible Research Directions

- Explore service learning opportunities on your campus. Talk to your instructor about how to add a service learning component to your management course.
- List the nonprofit organizations in your community that might benefit from volunteers. Contact one or more of them and make inquiries as to how you might help them. Do it, and then report back on what you learned as a result of the experience that is relevant to management and leadership.
- Locate the primary schools in your community or region. Contact the school principals and ask how you might be able to help teachers working with first- through sixth-grade students. Do it, and then report back on what you learned with respect to personal management and leadership development.
- For either the nonprofit organization or the primary school, form a group of students who share similar interests in service learning. Volunteer as a group to help the organization and prepare a team report on what you learned.
- Take the initiative. Create service learning ideas of your own—to be pursued individually or as part of a team. While working as a volunteer always keep your eyes and ears open for learning opportunities. Continually ask—"What is happening here in respect to: leadership, morale, motivation, teamwork, conflict, interpersonal dynamics, organization culture and structures, and more?"